24

*People
in
Glass Houses*

People
in
Glass Houses

Growing up at Government House

Adelaide Lubbock

HAMISH HAMILTON
LONDON

First published in Australia 1977
by Thomas Nelson **Australia Pty Ltd**

First published in Great Britain 1978
by Hamish Hamilton Ltd
90 Great Russell Street London WCIB 3PT

Copyright © Adelaide Lubbock, 1977

British Library Cataloguing in Publication Data

Lubbock, Adelaide
   People in glass houses.
   1. Victoria, Australia — History
   I. Title
   994.04'1'0924   DU222
    ISBN 0 241 10059 3

Typeset by Savage & Co. Pty Ltd, Brisbane
Printed in Singapore by Times Printers Sdn. Bhd.

For my grandchildren in Australia and England

Contents

List of Illustrations

Between pages 84 and 85

Acknowledgements

My chief thanks go to my sisters, Pamela Cunynghame and Victoria Woods, for checking my memories of our childhood, adding recollections of their own, and confirming my interpretation of the characters who figure in my story. My sisters' critical yet kindly appraisal and advice has been immensely valuable in helping me to balance the narrative and choose from the wealth of material in my possession what to include and what to leave out. The decision to cut many a pearl of price from my mother's letters and photograph albums caused us much thoughtful deliberation. I hope the result may please the reader.

I owe a special debt of gratitude to Professor Geoffrey Blainey, AO, of the University of Melbourne, and to his wife Ann, for their advice, support and encouragement without which the manuscript of this book no doubt would still be languishing in a drawer of my desk. To them I express my warmest thanks.

I also gratefully acknowledge the constructive and helpful suggestions made to me by friends and relations in Australia, England and Canada. Those who kindly read the manuscript and gave me their comments include my cousin Juliet Daniel and Tom and Pamela Matthews in England; Marnie Bassett, Maie Casey, Helen Rutledge and Mollie Turner Shaw in Australia; my brother-in-law James Douglas Woods and Marion Walker in Canada.

Finally, my particular thanks are due to my friends of many a long years' standing, Sir Walter Bassett, KBE, MC, and Lady Bassett, Litt.D. Monash (Hon.), Dame Helen Blaxland of the New South Wales National

Trust, and Mr and Mrs Pierre Grandjean of Evandale, Tasmania, for welcoming me so warmly into their homes and providing me with hospitality while I was working on the final draft of the book. In conclusion I should like to pay tribute to Sue Ebury, the charming and expert editor of Thomas Nelson (Australia) Ltd, with whom I have had the happiest association in preparing this book for publication.

Foreword

When the new Governor of Victoria stepped ashore in February 1914 he probably hoped that his term of office would be so successful that, in the tradition of constitutional governors, it would not be long remembered. Rewarded with the post for his services to England rather than for any known services to Australia, and belonging to an English family more aristocratic than that of perhaps any previous State Governor, Sir Arthur Stanley sensed that he should tread softly in a land where politicians were becoming more radical and nationalist. Moreover, he came to office when the power of a Governor to dissolve an elected parliament or to ignore the advice of a chief minister was debated more vigorously than at any time until recent years; between 1908 and 1914 the governors of Queensland, Victoria, Tasmania and the Commonwealth were each involved in such controversies. Stanley was also entering a web of protocol because Melbourne was the seat of the Federal Governor-General as well as the State Governor. 'I wish we were there', said Lady Stanley of the Federal government house, 'instead of this nasty little villa'. Her nasty little villa happened to be a mansion in the suburb of Malvern.

Lady Stanley, young and vivacious, swayed between the joys of vice-regal life in Australia and the regret that it did not quite match the English pageantry which it imitated. Each week she posted home to her mother four sheets of paper containing news, gossip, and political and social comments which at times were so observant that if they had accidentally been made public, might have forced her husband to resign. Long after she ceased to walk on rolls of red carpet, she savoured the years spent in Australia. Once compelled, in old age, to wait briefly for some minor service, she announced in the voice of an empress, 'Shall I tell them who I am?' Now, thanks to this fascinating book, we know. In fact we now know more about her than about her husband who apparently carried out his duties as Governor with diligence and good humour, and then quietly faded from Australian memory, for he had faced no constitutional crisis, caused no scandal or sensation and made no enemies.

While the mother wrote racy letters from the centre of the stage, a small daughter was in the wings - wriggling, playing, but nearly always watching. Her childhood was studded with the waving of Union Jacks, the presenting of illuminated addresses, processions through streets and the marshalling of regiments of chairs on public platforms. As a child, Adelaide Stanley was tugged in opposite directions by the demands of her parents' position, by the competition of English upper-class and Australian middle-class values, and by the mixture of privilege and deprivation which children in glass-houses can't escape. This unusual environment helped perhaps to etch events and emotions on her mind.

Through the combination of her own memories, her mother's observations, and the fluent and visual prose of both women, readers can enter 'government house' at a time when it was probably no less influential than the outback as a focus of popular Australian attitudes and mythologies. It may well be that this warm-hearted book - written partly through the eyes of a child - tells more than the collected despatches of any Australian Governor about the essence of his office during the late-summer of the British Empire.

Geoffrey Blainey, 1977

Preface

My mother had many talents, as she herself would have been the first to admit. Foremost among these was the ability to write a good letter. Her style was so vivid and individual that the recipients, as they read her words, would seem to hear the very tone of her voice and laugh, would see the expression and gesture as she mimicked some comic or outrageous character, and visualise the scenes of city and bush life in Australia which she evoked with such keen wit and perception.

Nearly 300 of her letters to her family have been preserved, but the bulk of this correspondence is between her and her mother, Mrs Henry Evans Gordon (Marmee), written during World War I when my father was State Governor of Victoria, Australia. It is mainly from these letters that I have drawn the material for this book.

As the wife of the Governor, my mother kept a book of newspaper cuttings which is three times the size of my father's. In this enormous tome is recorded in detail all her doings during the five and three-quarter years my father held office. She also kept a snapshot album from 1914 to 1918, so from these sources I have been able to check references, verify dates and reconstruct the chronology of events of that period in the most painless possible way.

My mother and grandmother, in their correspondence, pursued their own individual line. They seldom *answered* one another's letters but each wrote of their daily life. My grandmother's are full of home chat and private family jokes. Her robust sense of fun and straightforwardness of character blow like a fresh gust of air through everything she wrote. My

1

mother's letters are concerned with the burden of her official position and the demands made on her privacy, comments on various personalities and anecdotes about her children. She also discusses the arts, politics and religion with animation and good sense; and the war from such a personal angle that one is sometimes astonished by her self-centredness. It is clear that she was intensely devoted to my grandmother and her letters are filled with the most effusive expressions of love. To the end of her long life she maintained a lively and sympathetic interest in the world around her, especially the young people. She saw many changes, from the pampered ease of her Edwardian heyday and the splendours of the vice-regal scene to life in a small flat with one maid. Yet she never mourned the loss of past glory although she retained, almost undiminished, her rather endearing partiality for being in the limelight. Indeed, she never quite relinquished her role of 'Governor's Lady' and would assume her vice-regal manner and expect the red carpet treatment if not accorded the deference which she considered to be her due. Long after both World Wars were over, when on a visit to her daughter Victoria and family in Canada, she was once kept waiting her turn in a queue. 'Shall I tell them who I am?' she said imperiously, and this remark became a family joke.

My father's correspondence hardly reflects his personality at all. Although highly articulate in conversation, his letters might be those of an intelligent schoolboy. They are matter-of-fact to a degree, and pedestrian in content. Unlike my mother, he rarely discusses people or speculates on situations or events, but fills his letters with factual accounts of his State duties and his leisure activities, with a dry comment now and again on the vagaries of his children. Surprisingly, he sometimes uses 'baby-talk' in his terms of endearment to my mother and addresses her alternatively as his 'Fairy Queen' or 'Titania'. Occasionally one catches a glimpse of pent-up emotion in the tone of his letters – particularly when he was left behind in Australia after the war had ended – and one senses an undercurrent of 'little-boy-lost'; a loneliness of heart which is the more touching for its very reserve of expression.

Finally, I have added my own recollections to my mother's description of her early married life and her vice-regal experiences. It will be observed that I did not see eye-to-eye with her on many subjects – notably parental control and obedience to my elders and betters. Consequently, as a child, my relationship with her was often stormy, but after I grew up and was no longer under her management, as it were, all disagreements were healed. As often happens, childhood memories are far sharper and more clear-cut than those of later years. Thus I have been able to recall with exactitude the thoughts, feelings and impressions of my early youth, and the events described in the following pages as though they had happened yesterday instead of nearly seventy years ago.

High Elms, 1977

Part I
1905–1913

1

Early Days at Alderley

On an early summer's afternoon in 1905 a young man was seeing a lady off on the 4.12 p.m. train from Victoria to Ightham, a small village in Kent. She was leaning out of the first-class carriage window smiling at him and talking with graceful animation whilst he gazed back at her, tongue-tied. The guard blew his whistle and she held out her hand to say good-bye. The young man grasped it and held on, breaking into a run as the train gathered speed. Finding his voice at last he shouted above the puffing of the steam-engine 'Miss Gordon, will you marry me?' But he didn't hear her answer as by this time the train was going too fast and he had to let go of her hand. Undeterred by this somewhat ludicrous situation, he took the next train down to Ightham and, presenting himself at the house of the lady's family, he renewed his proposal which in due course was accepted.

My parents, Arthur Lyulph Stanley and Margaret Evans Gordon, were both close on thirty years old when they became engaged. Their backgrounds and natures were dissimilar, yet throughout their married life I hardly ever heard them have the slightest disagreement, or even an argument. They were utterly devoted to one another.

My father, one of a large family of brothers and sisters, didn't care much for women's society. He preferred, on the whole, the company of the board room and club to that of the drawing-room. He was a man of firm liberal views; a free-thinker, logical and unbiased in his approach to any problem, he could also be withering in his criticism of those whom he considered either foolish or unprincipled. He was normally reserved in manner, but this outward austerity was leavened by a brisk sense of humour, and, on occasions, a schoolboy love of practical jokes.

The Stanleys were an ancient family belonging to a world of large country estates and grand London houses and their doings were often recorded in the society columns of the Press. The Gordons were not 'fashionable', but moved in an intellectual milieu, and their friends were artists, musicians and writers – both in England and on the Continent. My mother was one of four girls who were brought up in extremely sheltered circumstances, even for those Victorian times. No 'unsavoury' topics were ever allowed to be mentioned, no even faintly improper subject was ever discussed. Coarseness and vulgarity – 'loose talk' as she would have described it – were considered degrading to the mind and character and the 'facts of life' remained veiled in prudish mystery till long after my mother and her sisters were grown women.

Margaret was considered the gifted one of the family, having inherited the histrionic talent of her maternal forebears the Kembles and the charm and sensibility of her handsome Scottish father. But in spite of her attractive looks and engaging personality, she does not seem to have had even the shadow of a love affair before she met my father. I have wondered many times whether it was simply because she was too virginal and unworldly to attract any young man's interest; or whether she fended off unwanted attentions with ·that incomparable finesse and tact which she displayed throughout her long life in stage-managing not only her own relationship with others, but also the affairs of her family and friends who never turned to her in vain for sympathetic advice and understanding of their problems.

Arthur and Margaret were married from Prestons, my grandparents' country house, in Ightham's little fifteenth-century church on 29 August 1905. They spent much of their early married life at Alderley Park, the Stanleys' home in Cheshire, or at Penrhos, the Welsh estate. Thus my mother had the opportunity of getting to know her in-laws at close quarters.

Life with the Stanleys was the antithesis of the gentle, deeply affectionate family circle which formed my mother's background, with their love of art and music, and their delight in amateur theatricals. The Stanleys were down-to-earth, turbulent members of the minor aristocracy, holding radical views, highly literate, possessing remarkable memories, and· well informed on subjects which claimed their interest such as politics, economics, philosophy and religion. They had little appreciation or knowledge of music or the visual arts on the whole, and their taste in these matters was regarded as somewhat philistine by my mother. She observed them critically but always affectionately and, although their aggressive opinions and vociferous assertiveness sometimes bewildered her, their peculiarities were a never-failing source of amusement which she turned to good account in her letters to her own family.

Two years before my parents married, my grandfather, Lyulph Stanley, succeeded his brother Henry to the title and estates. Uncle Henry was so eccentric that he appeared quite mad to almost everybody, including his own family. As a young man he had joined the Diplomatic Service and had spent long mysterious absences in the Near-East. On succeeding to the title in 1869 he had returned to England dressed as a Turk and professing the Mohammedan religion. He was accompanied by a low-born lady of Spanish extraction named Fabia Santiago whom he had picked up in his travels and to whom he had been secretly married, according to his story, for seven years. Fabia was squat, fat, and swarthy, with a heavy black moustache. She never learnt to speak English properly but conversed in a mixture of Pidgin-French and Spanish. There was a great scandal over the marriage, especially as Uncle Henry himself seemed doubtful as to its validity. At any rate, later he went through forms of marriage in both Anglican and Roman Catholic churches, as well as the Mohammedan ceremony which presumably had been performed at the time of his marriage abroad.

He quarrelled bitterly with his family, in particular with his mother and brother Lyulph, and refused to speak to any of them. He shut himself up at Alderley where he translated Camoëns' *Lusiads* from the Portuguese, studied Arabic, and subscribed to the first British mosque at Woking. At Penrhos he repaired and redecorated in the Moorish style two little old stone churches on the island of Anglesey, no doubt scandalising his tenants who were all good Chapel folk. One parson, however, was so grateful for the restoration of his church (even though the altar was surrounded by heathen-blue tiles) that he put up a stone memorial arch with a slate plaque extolling Uncle Henry's generosity, and presented him with a beautiful silver-gilt Elizabethan cup which was found in the church when the 'improvements' were being carried out.

When Uncle Henry died it was discovered that Fabia had had a husband living when Henry married her, by whom she had had two sons. Thus, unknowingly, he had married a bigamist. Fortunately she and Uncle Henry were childless, so the title and estates passed to my grandfather who expunged Fabia's name from the peerage.

Uncle Henry was buried in a wood at Alderley – feet first, according to the Mohammedan custom, we were always told – as he was not eligible for entombment in the family vault in Alderley church, being an infidel. My father went to the funeral with my great-uncle Algernon Stanley who had become a Catholic priest in reaction against his brother Henry's refusal to give him the living at Alderley. This he had expected as his right, being the youngest son. During the ceremony my father heard Uncle Algernon mutter 'Lived like a dog – buried like a dog!' and when my father took off his hat to show respect as the body was lowered into the grave, Uncle Algernon growled 'Not your hat, you bloody fool, your boots!'

According to Bertrand Russell, my grandfather's nephew, Lyulph was the cleverest of the family. He was a Fellow of Balliol and a friend of the Master, the famous Doctor Jowett, although my grandfather, being an agnostic, did not agree with Jowett's religious views. He sat as Liberal member for Oldham, in Cheshire, from 1880 till 1885 when, unwilling to support Gladstone over Home Rule for Ireland, he lost his seat and never entered Parliament again. He was Vice-Chairman of the London School Board for a number of years where he led the 'Progressives' and fought unremittingly against the Anglican church in the interests, as he saw it, of elementary education. In his autobiography Russell says of my grandfather:

> There was little glory to be got, and his motives were, I think, entirely public spirit and pugnacity. In spite of his refusal to follow Gladstone on the Irish question, he remained a genuine Liberal. He was an ardent supporter of Free Trade and (what is really remarkable) he took the chair for me during the [First World] War when my pacifism made me unpopular and many of my relations fought shy of me. His knowledge was encyclopaedic and his wit brilliant though too caustic for success in politics.[*]

As one of his contemporaries put it more unkindly, 'Lyulph Stanley represents political garlic'.

To his grandchildren, or to me at any rate, he appeared both alarming and fascinating from his habit of testing one's general knowledge by firing questions at one and expecting an intelligent answer. These quizzes usually took place at meal times in front of the critical assembly of the whole family. 'Now tell me,' he would say, fixing one suddenly with his Jovian bright-blue eye, 'What do you know about The Marian Heresy?' – or some equally abstruse subject. As one floundered for a reply or admitted one's total lack of knowledge, his gaze would sharpen to a malicious twinkle and he would exclaim 'How ignorant you are!' and proceed to

[*] *Amberley Papers*, vol. 1.

enlighten his humiliated victim on the subject. Sometimes, however, by some marvellous chance one knew the answer to a question. Then he would be unstinting in his approbation and one's heart swelled with almost intolerable pride and elation.

My grandfather married one of the beautiful daughters of a Yorkshire ironmaster, Sir Lothian Bell. My father was their eldest son. At the time of his engagement there were two other sons living, Edward in the Colonial Service, Oliver in the Army, and four surviving daughters: Margaret, the eldest and the quietest of the family, was married to a sailor, Captain (afterwards Admiral) Sir William Goodenough; Sylvia, sharp-tongued and sharp-witted, engaged to Anthony Henley in the Scots Greys; twenty-year-old Blanche, a good-natured hoyden, and Venetia, the youngest, the beauty of the family.

In 1905 my father was adopted as prospective Liberal candidate for the Eddisbury Division of Cheshire to fight the coming election, and my mother, who was inclined to poke fun at the Stanley's political fervour, which she did not share, described one of the election meetings to Marmee.

> Arthur writes that the election will most likely take place on 17th or 19th [January] ... Cambell Bannerman* is coming down to speak for Arthur on Wednesday and I am looking forward to meeting the old Donkey and seeing how his personality strikes me.
>
> There was a political meeting here yesterday held by the Knutsford candidate – a mild, ineffective little man who made an address composed of the most flagrant platitudes. ... Lord Stanley was chairman and there was another old person who got up and talked for ¾ of an hour and was wound up to go on for another 3 when Lord Stanley suddenly gave him a huge tug by the coat from behind and told him to stop – which so surprised him that he did – at once. We all came to the meeting which was held in the Tenants' Hall [at Alderley] and Venetia brought all the dogs who kept interrupting the speeches by growling and going for one another and having to be smacked and quelled into order again.

My father was duly elected and he represented Eddisbury till the General Election in 1910, when he lost his seat.

I was born on 30 May 1906 at 26 St Leonard's Terrace, Chelsea, my parents' London house. My mother said I was very small, pink and smooth, with a thick mop of hair. They must have told her before she saw the baby that it had a disfiguring red birth-mark covering its right hand and extending up the arm to the shoulder. I never discovered what

* Liberal Prime Minister 1905–1908.

her reaction was although I once asked her, long after I was grown up, but she gave me an evasive answer. She never alluded to this birth-mark and my impression is that she dismissed it from her thoughts (as she did other unpleasant subjects) so firmly that she persuaded herself that it was of no importance. To me, however, my 'red arm' was a source of self-conscious misery when I became aware that I was different from others, and this, no doubt, complicated my outlook as a child.

In March 1907, my mother was again pregnant although she wrote to Marmee 'I don't believe there is another Bibs coming at all as I am as thin and flat as the pavement and only weigh 8 stone'. Sylvia Henley's first child, Rosalind, had just been born and the letter continues with a description of the christening in Alderley Church.

> It was a characteristic ceremony as all the dogs got loose after having been carefully shut up, and had to be hurrooshed back from the church with the usual yells and stone-throwing. Two strangers – tourists – were looking at the church when we arrived and were evidently petrified with astonishment at the levity of the christening party – especially when Venetia made a remark in a stentorian voice about 'drowning the young gorilla'. They also seemed to think it much out of order that Bibs [myself] should be installed in the middle of the aisle in her perambulator. She was asleep for most of the service but woke towards the end and started a long and loud conversation with Ellen [my nurse] whose attempts to try and quieten her 'silently' were most humorous.

It appears I was a model child for the first year of my life. The birth of my brother Edward in October 1907 was the signal for running up my true colours. I instantly became unmanageable, throwing tantrums and screaming fits long before I could talk, 'kicking and biting and scratching like a little wild animal' my mother said, and Nanny Ellen added, 'She's a regular Stanley for going blue in the face with rage'.

Edward was the most beautiful little boy. He had enormous, appealing dark-blue eyes under a thatch of dark hair. His mouth was tremulous and sweet, but this angelic appearance concealed the heart of a small demon. We fought like Kilkenny cats and I, being the bigger and braver of the two, always won our battles and was as often punished for my aggression.

My parents continued to be much at Alderley – my father busy with his constituency and my mother wrapped up in him and her babies. My grandmother was away a lot, leading a social life and bringing Venetia out 'into Society' – that small enclosed world of the Upper Classes which existed in those days. Although my mother never explicitly says so, she gives the impression that everyone was more at ease when my grand-mother was away.

On one of these occasions she describes my father in a riotous mood, very different from the impression of 'cleverness' and intellectual superiority which he and his family sometimes made on outsiders. 'Tibaldi [my father] amused himself last night by whitening his face all over with zinc ointment in my room, and then covering it with powder. You never saw such a sight! He then enveloped himself in black draperies and went to frighten Oliver in bed. It ended in a fearful scuffle and a passage fight.' I wonder whether today many men of my father's age would behave so childishly!

Although the Stanleys were given to quarrelling, they were clannish and extremely inquisitive about each other's affairs. Consequently, they spent much time visiting one another's houses. Visitors came and went at Alderley, and often there were house parties of twenty or more people.

Mr Asquith, the Prime Minister, and his second wife, Margot, came frequently, bringing with them his daughter Violet who was Venetia's crony. My mother didn't care for Violet and thought her conceited and off-hand in her manner.

Clementine Hozier also came, chaperoned by her redoutable grandmother, great-aunt Blanche Airlie, my grandfather's sister. Clementine was being courted at this time by Sydney Peel, whom my mother found delightful. 'I hope Clementine will finally make up her mind to have him,' she told Marmee, 'as she might go much farther and fare worse' (a judgement not borne out by subsequent events). 'Aunt Blanche's visit went off very well. She was suave and amiable but she *loathed* Violet Asquith and put on her greatest *Grande Dame* manner whenever she spoke to her or alluded to her ... She was also gravely contemptuous of old Sir Hugh Bell [my grandmother's brother who was 'in trade'] and showed it palpably whenever he spoke to her ...'

Venetia brought her gang of smart young friends and kept a menagerie of animals: a monkey, several dogs, a fox, a penguin, and, for a short time, a bear.

> Venetia has come home having bought up nearly the whole of Hamley's toy shop on her way through London. Amongst other things she has bought a toy monkey – an exact replica of the live one – which she brought into my room and terrified me with ... We are going to have rather fun tonight as the sham monkey is to be placed on the chimney-piece among Papa-in-law's favourite china. He will be in a great fuss and will roar to Venetia to remove her beastly monkey.

Fluto, the monkey, was a weird little beast, as unpredictable as a hobgoblin. It would lie in wait on the top of a book-case or curtain-pelmet and drop suddenly on the backs of unsuspecting passers-by below.

I remember Fluto very well as it lived to quite a ripe old age. It finally went into a decline and died from the result of eating its own tail.

The bear, whose name was Lancelot, caused a furore of alarm amongst the tenants and employees at Alderley. It used to amble about the grounds and bang on the doors of the various lodges, standing on its hind legs and terrifying the inmates; or it would lumber into the kitchen in search of food, playfully knocking down plates and dishes, and sending the cook and kitchen maids into hysterics. It would lead the dogs on to chase the deer in the Park, and once it chased Nanny Ellen who was walking in the garden with Edward and me on either side of her and Pamela in the pram. One of my earliest and most vivid recollections is of being dragged along by Ellen, uttering united screams of fright as we careered down the garden path pursued by the bear. We only just reached the house in time to escape its clutches. I don't suppose it meant any harm, but though it was only a cub it was as big as a Newfoundland dog and could easily have knocked us over with one swipe of its paw. After this adventure my grandfather ordered Venetia to get rid of Lancelot so she gave him to the London Zoo.

In the winter the Stanleys all hunted, but as soon as summer arrived their craze was to go on expeditions in the motor car. My grandparents still kept a victoria and a brougham but these were only used for workaday jobs such as meeting people at the station. The motor car was used purely for jaunting about, although my grandfather usually preferred to drive in the carriage, when he could look about him, call on tenants, and drive through the woods. 'I had a most characteristic drive yesterday with Papa-in-law,' said my mother, just before Pamela was born.

> First of all there were great arguments and fussings as to the arrangements for the afternoon. Most of the party were going on a motor expedish, and he said he would take me for a quiet drive in the victoria – so this was settled. Then it turned out that poor old Mudder-in-law wished to drive with me in the victoria, but she was told off for a dull walk with Caroline Grosvenor, and then he and I started. 'Now Margaret, I shall take you to see the Epileptic Home and you will enjoy seeing what has been done for those poor epileptics.' However for once I was firm and refused absolutely to go and see the epilepts as probably the baby would arrive a sort of Sophy Butler [the village idiot at Ightham] in consequence.

My mother, a *malade imaginaire* at the best of times, always went through great fears and tribulations when she was pregnant, believing in every old wives' tale ever invented and adding a few more theories of her own. She was always sending for the doctor to discuss her symptoms and prescribe for her imagined ailments. In those days doctors humoured their patients and she was told she was a very interesting case and advised to take tonics, or rest most of the day, or go abroad for a 'cure'. At this time she was convinced she was carrying twins and even when only one baby arrived she would always say that it was a most rare case as there had been *two* afterbirths! Pamela was credited with peculiar and mysterious attributes which my mother alluded to as 'fey' on account of her having been really a twin.

Pamela was born at Alderley in September 1909, none the worse for the jolting she had had in the drive with my grandfather. She was a placid baby with blue eyes like saucers and she gave no trouble to anyone. But Edward and I continued in our wicked ways, drawing closer into an alliance against the intruder. My mother said on her return to Alderley after taking a cure in Italy:

> I found the darling babies all very well, but a very bad report from Ellen of A's and E's conduct since I have been away. Adelaide smashed her doll's head to atoms on Edward's head which of course hurt him and made him yell. When I asked her why she did such a thing she replied, 'Well, you see I thought I *wasn't* doing it.' [she] made Arthur and me laugh yesterday. She was standing with her head on one side looking at Jock [our fox terrier] and we heard her say 'Oh Jock, what a beastly dog you are!' ... I heard piercing yells from the nursery the other day and asked Adelaide 'Why were you being naughty at tea?' 'Because I'm going to be *very* good tomorrow, you see.' Which was as good, I think, as any answer in *Alice in Wonderland*.

2

The Grown-ups

As the mists of babyhood clear, a memory emerges here and there, floating like an island in a still largely unremembered past. Myself, standing on the nursery table at Alderley, screaming frantically at the sound of the nursery maid's work-roughened fingers catching the satin ribbon of my new beaver bonnet, and not being able to explain how it set my teeth on edge. Being chased by a flock of hissing geese, bigger than myself, down the farm road at Penrhos, and being snatched up to safety in the arms of one of the farm hands. I can recall my terror of the dark and of going blind and, from the earliest age, of death. But happier recollections also stand out, such as the cosy comfort of being given a hip bath in front of the nursery fire, while nightgown, red flannel dressing-gown and bedroom slippers hung warming over the high brass fender; or the delicious smell of my mother's bedroom compounded of Violette de Parme Poudre de Riz, orris root sachets, bay rum, and methylated spirit from the burner upon which she heated her curling tongs. These hairdressing necessities were kept on a china tray with the following legend inscribed upon it:

> Now list to me, ye ladies fair,
> And when you wish to curl your hair,
> For the safety of your domicile,
> Pray place your lamp upon this tile.

My father as a disciplinarian was more effective than my mother whose authority I was prepared to flout – but he had certain advantages over

16

her. For instance, he was very good at magic. He could swallow objects such as crumpled bits of paper or little balls of my mother's embroidery wool and make them come out of his ears or his nose. There was a game called 'Crow-Hole' in which you were imprisoned between his knees till you pushed the right button on his waistcoat, calling 'Crow-Hole!' in order to be released. And then there was his gold repeater watch which he would take out of his waistcoat pocket and dangle on his watch-chain. If you blew hard enough on the watch it would fly open and emit a little tinkling fairy chime.

Both my parents seemed god-like beings to me – superior to any other member of the family, or indeed the human race – until my faith was shattered one winter's evening at Alderley. My father was standing as Liberal candidate in a by-election for Oldham in November 1911. I was sitting with Nanny Ellen eating bread-and-milk by the nursery fire while we waited to hear the results. Presently my father and mother appeared and announced that he had lost and the Tories had gained the seat. I had no idea what this meant but clearly, from the commiseration and exclamations of disappointment from Nanny Ellen, he had suffered a defeat in some encounter which deprived him of glory. The dreadful truth broke upon me that he was not infallible, after all, and my heart was filled with desolation. I burst into a storm of wailing and weeping and I can remember my mother taking me on her lap to comfort me, and the slippery feel of her sealskin jacket against my tear-wet cheeks. My misery and despair at my father's humiliation – as I felt it to be – were so poignant that even after all these years the recollection of that moment is still vivid.

Our house in London overlooked the Chelsea Royal Hospital Gardens, which we always called 'The Opposite Gardens'. Before the Coronation of George V the troops from Chelsea Barracks engaged in the ceremonies would muster for rehearsal in our street and we would watch the Red-coats drilling in the Gardens, and the horses munching the lilacs over the railings as they stamped and snorted and jingled their bits in a long line below our nursery window.

We watched the Coronation procession from a balcony somewhere on the route. I had a pale blue silk coat and a white ostrich feather in my bonnet, but this was small consolation for not having been taken to Edward VII's funeral, as the Henley cousins were, although younger than me, and dressed in black, to my deepest envy!

I don't remember the King and Queen in the Coronation procession, but only the Prince of Wales, Princess Mary and the other Royal children, riding in an open carriage. They were eating sweets. I also remember the Drum-Major in a resplendent uniform, mounted on a huge white horse, whirling his drum sticks and throwing them into the air and catching them again between drum rolls. After a bit, Edward pulled my hair and I punched him back and we rolled on the floor beneath the grown-ups' feet in mortal combat until we were removed from the balcony.

When I was small the streets of London were full of horse-drawn traffic. I think it was considered too dangerous by many people to drive a motor car about in such crowded thoroughfares, although the new red motor omnibuses were beginning to supersede the horse bus. There were hackney cabs for hire – four-wheeled growlers, and two-wheeled hansom cabs with the cabby perched up behind – and the well-to-do drove out in their carriages and pairs which were stabled in the mews at the back of their town houses. In cases of serious illness or a confinement ('Ladies in straw' Nanny Ellen used to call the latter) in a street or square, straw would be laid along the whole length to muffle the noise of the traffic. London smelt then of horse dung and straw instead of exhaust fumes, and no sound louder than the clip-clip of horses' hooves and the rumble of carriage wheels disturbed the air. The ear-splitting scream of jet aircraft overhead and the thunderous roar of the traffic, combined with the pollution from diesel and combustion engines as in London to-day, would surely have sent the elegant and leisurely society of sixty years ago into a nervous decline.

Edward and I were taken out for walks sitting opposite each other in a double pram by Nanny Ellen, followed by Maggie, the Welsh nursery maid, wheeling Pamela in another pram, and accompanied by Jock. We were always saluted by the Chelsea Pensioners and Edward would punctiliously return the salute. We would go into Hyde Park where we played with other children whilst the nannies hobnobbed and gossiped. On the way to the park we would sometimes see a German Brass Band playing in one of the squares. The players were dressed in blue uniforms with gold frogging and epaulettes and peaked caps, looking rather like the picture of Marshal Blücher at Waterloo in my history book. There were also Scottish sword dancers, organ grinders with monkeys and my favourite street show of all, Punch and Judy. At the cross roads we always gave a penny to the old crossing-sweeper. In the autumn the muffin man would come round in the misty blue twilight ringing his bell and carrying his muffins in a flat basket covered with a white cloth on his head. Then, as the lamp-lighter ambled down the street lighting the gas lamps with his stick, we would have hot-buttered muffins for tea after Maggie had drawn the curtains, made up the fire, and laid the cloth.

We began lessons much younger than children do to-day. Before I was three I was being taught to write by my mother by making lines of 'pothooks' and 'hangers' in a ruled exercise book. She also taught me to read out of a stubby little blue book entitled *Reading without Tears* in the fly-leaf of which is written 'Adelaide – May 1909', and which I still possess. I could read and write by the time I was five, but it took me much longer to be able to tell the time, or even to be able to count numbers. We learnt to speak French very early on as the Henleys had a French nurse and my cousins Rosalind and Kitty could hardly speak any English. As we were much together at Alderley we had to talk French in order to communicate with one another. Standing round my mother at the piano, we sang French, German and Italian nursery rhymes, as well as English ones out of two books illustrated by Walter Crane, called *The Babies' Opera* and *The Babies' Bouquet*. Both she and my father would read aloud to us in the evenings from Grimm's *Fairy Tales,* La Fontaine's *Fables,* and *Alice in Wonderland.* These were known as 'Penny Readings', no doubt derived from *The Penny Cyclopedia* and *The Penny Magazine* of an earlier generation. I started piano lessons when I was about five with a German Fräulein who would rap my knuckles with a ruler if I played a wrong note. We also had a nursery governess who came daily to teach us history, geography and arithmetic.

And then, of course, there was the dancing class. This was held once a week in the drawing-room of one of my mother's friends. I can remember the first time I was taken. All the little children were made to march around whilst the mothers and nannies sat around the room on gilt cane chairs. All of a sudden I was overcome with shyness and a sense of looking ridiculous. I began to howl with rage and embarrassment, unable, as usual, to explain why I was so upset. A lady took me on her knee and gave me a little silver model of a pheasant to play with. It was a pepper-pot in disguise and its head was the lid which you could pull off. Later on, I enjoyed the dancing class, as at Christmas time we gave a performance dressed up as fairies and princesses.

Lessons were nearly always agreeable to me, partly from a genuine wish to acquire knowledge, but also partly, I fear, from a desire to show off my knowledge in the family circle. My grandfather's love of general knowledge quizzes no doubt encouraged me in this rather unestimable aspiration.

On looking back, I suspect that my parent's methods of education were old fashioned, even for those days. Emphasis was placed on the study of the humanities whilst mathematics and scientific subjects were sketchily taught by incompetent governesses. Religious instruction was imparted almost entirely in the nursery, although my father sometimes would read

us the juicier stories out of the Old Testament. My mother preferred
the New Testament. She had a predilection for the Infant Jesus and the
Virgin Mary – Mother Love as depicted by the Italian masters – but she
instinctively turned away from the darker and more tragic aspects of
the life of Christ. Neither she nor my father accepted the dogmas of
the Christian Church although they subscribed to its principles. We were
never taught to say prayers, except by nannies and governesses scandalised
by our religious ignorance, nor were we made to go to church.

I never thought much about religion as a child, but I remember hope-
fully trying to believe in the stories I was told of God, benevolent and
bearded, presiding over the world from the sky above, angels with harps
flying around Him or sitting on clouds, whilst down below, in the depths
of the earth, the Devil lay in wait for sinners such as me, unless I repented
in time to be saved by God. When these tales were explained as allegories,
I was mystified, having a completely literal mind.

I wasn't so sure about Jesus being allegorical as he seemed to be an
altogether more credible character than God or the Devil. I was inclined
to accept him as a kind of super-magician on account of the miracles
he performed. These stories from the New Testament could very well
be true, I thought, as I had seen conjurors at children's parties perform
equally good miracles before my own eyes. But in any case, the stories
in the Bible were not nearly as interesting or readable as Grimm or Hans
Andersen's Fairy Tales.

When we went to Alderley or Penrhos the preparations for the move
would start days beforehand. Shiny black Saratoga trunks, leather port-
manteaux, canvas hold-alls, and wicker hampers blockaded the nursery
passage, and there was a delightful feeling of urgency and excitement
in the air. The night before we started, the prams would be packed with
the things which would not go into the rest of the luggage, and covered
over with hessian which was sewn up by Maggie with twine. A private
horse-bus was chartered to take us to the station and nannies, governesses
and children piled in with the luggage and were driven to Euston Station
in the early morning. At the other end we were met by the station fly
or the farm cart. We always travelled third class and the nannies took
a picnic basket with food and a little spirit lamp to brew up tea or
hot milk. They also took a chamber pot (which Nanny Ellen referred
to euphemistically as 'the article') for it was firmly believed you would
catch an unmentionable disease if you used any public lavatory. After
we had been fed and potted, we had our faces and hands cleaned with
a flannel upon which we were made to spit – a practice which I found

inexpressibly disgusting – and then we played games, or were made to lie down and rest. The journey to Alderley took about four hours, and to Penrhos, nearly six, which was pretty good going for those days of the steam engine.

Nearly all my early recollections of Alderley are winter ones. There was always a lot of snow and often the Mere was frozen over and everybody skated on it. We children were pushed about in chairs by the grown-ups with the dogs running barking after us.

Alderley was an enormous house with something like sixty bedrooms and many vast and cold reception rooms. It was built mainly of grey stone, its frigid neo-classical facade facing north over the rolling Deer Park to the Mere and the beautiful beechwoods planted in the eighteenth century by the Stanley of that day.

Our nurseries were on the second floor and we shared them with our numerous cousins and any visiting children, plus a regiment of nannies and nursery maids. Every evening we were taken down to the drawing-room between five and six o'clock, the girls dressed in white muslin threaded with pale blue or pink satin ribbons, red or bronze slippers, and coral beads or a locket round our necks. The boys were dressed in 'Kate Greenaway' suits or sailor suits. In the winter the passages and staircases were so cold that we were wrapped in Shetland shawls for the transit between the nursery and the drawing-room.

As we entered, a delicious waft of wood smoke came through the doors, mingled with the scent of Turkish cigarettes and hot-buttered toast. My grandmother, whom we called 'Muzzie', wearing a toque, pearl and diamond earrings, and several rows of pearls round her neck, would be seated at the tea table in front of a copper tea-kettle boiling over a spirit lamp flanked by a silver tea-caddy, teapot, milk jug and sugar basin on a silver tray. An array of china tea-cups and saucers patterned with green dragons surrounded the tea tray, and plates of sandwiches, scones and cake covered the table. Dogs would be all over the place – in front of the fire, lying on the chairs, or under the table. Occasionally they would be thrown a piece of plum cake or buttered toast, or given sugared tea in a china saucer.

When Boyles, the butler, and the footman had cleared away the tea tables we played games. There were special toys which were considered too good for the nursery, such as a miniature gilt chair which played Gounod's waltz from *Faust* when you sat on it, and a German musical box which tinkled out a folk tune whilst a little train ran wobbling across a bridge over a river, amongst snowy Alpine peaks, and in the foreground a goosegirl turned jerkily and raised her arms in time to the music. There was also a teddy-bear bigger than myself, and a picture book of animals which made the sound of each beast by pulling the appropriate string at the side. There were no dolls that I can remember.

My mother would play the piano and we would sing nursery rhymes with her. She taught me to do a little dance whilst I sang:

> One, two, three, look at me!
> Here I go – point my toe!

I discovered that this accomplishment went down very well with my grandfather and such was my success that it incited him to dance too, holding out his coat tails in a ludicrous way which sent everyone into fits of laughter.

At Christmas time the house was decorated with swags of holly, ivy, mistletoe, and yew, the aromatic scent of the greenery contending with the usual musty Alderley smell of damp, dogs and leather-bound books. The bell-ringers played carols in the hall, each man holding his little brass bell attached to a leather thong which he rang when the melody came to his particular note . . . And then there were the Mummers, who always performed in the Tenants' Hall.

The right to act in the Alderley Mummers belonged solely to the Barber family. Throughout the centuries they had handed down the text by word of mouth till the sense had become garbled in places. Nevertheless, the characters remained distinct and the story more or less intact, only varying in detail from other versions of this ancient folk-play, as performed in different parts of England.

The Mummers' Play was not the only theatrical entertainment we had at Christmas. My mother's acting talent was pressed into service and every year she produced a pantomime played by the Alderley School children and ourselves in front of an invited audience of tenants and neighbours.

I remember being an oyster in *Alice in Wonderland* and Edward and I acted in a French farcical sketch, *Le Saucisson de Lyon,* of which most of the audience cannot have understood a word; nevertheless, I remember the intoxicating sound of applause.

In 1912 there was a Grand Pantomime in four acts – *Aladdin* – which ran for two nights and to which the Press was invited. There were even printed programmes giving a list of the cast, the names of the costumiers (the various ladies' maids at Alderley) the musical director (the music master at the Alderley school) and the producers, my mother and Venetia.

According to a newspaper critic, in a two-column review, everyone performed their parts admirably, 'but', he continues,

... it is to Master Edward Stanley, one of the youngest performers, that we must award the palm. Master Edward, who is quite a little fellow, was by a fortunate inspiration, given the part of the Captain of the Imperial Guard. In this capacity he strutted majestically at the head of his men (all bigger than himself) and issued commands with all the ferocity of an Indian cavalry major. He was perfectly cool and composed and apparently knew not the meaning of shyness. He seemed to enjoy the performance exceedingly and was applauded until the roof echoed.... [He] created much amusement by pushing his head through the curtain and smiling amiably at the departing audience!

On Christmas Eve we hung up our stockings at the foot of my mother's bed, as we would never have been trusted to behave if we had been allowed to open them in our own beds. Besides, it amused my mother to see our reactions. Early on Christmas morning we were taken down to her bedroom and we precipitated ourselves on to the now bulging white stockings sprouting holly and a tinsel star tied with red ribbon at the top.

After breakfast the whole family and the guests assembled in the dining-room for the ceremony of 'Opening the Presents'. The grown-ups became as excited as the children and the aunts would impatiently snatch half-opened parcels from our fumbling fingers shrieking, 'Here, here, here, give it to me!' thus spoiling all the fun of discovering for ourselves what delightful object would emerge from the brown paper and tissue wrappings.

Then the church bells would ring out across the Park and the aunts and my grandmother and the lady guests would depart in a flurry to put on feather-trimmed hats and sealskin furs, leaving a Sargasso Sea of string, wrapping paper and cardboard boxes to be cleared away by the servants.

In the afternoon a tea party was given for the tenants' children. An immense Christmas Tree stood at one end of the Tenants' Hall surmounted by a spangled fairy doll and lighted with candles. Two footmen stood with wet sponges tied on the end of bamboo poles ready to snuff any guttering candles before they burnt down and set fire to the tree. The presents were piled on a table beside the tree and Muzzie, helped by my mother and the aunts, gave each boy and girl a parcel as they filed past, marshalled by Mrs Wallace, the housekeeper. My recollection is that there were at least a hundred children present.

The final thrill of the day was 'Snapdragon'. The lights were turned out and a dish of raisins in flaming brandy was brought in by Boyles, and everybody had to snatch a handful from the burning dish. Salt was then thrown on the flames which instantly turned a spectral green and made us all look like corpses. After dinner the grown-ups played 'Commerce', a card game only played on Christmas night, but we children had long since been put to bed, tearful and exhausted by the continued excitements of the day.

Such were our festivities at Alderley during Christmas. Perhaps it was all rather childish but there was something heart-warming in the reunion of such a large family, although the season seldom passed without some major row between one member of the tribe or another. Of course, Christmas seemed magical to us children and it was only when we grew older that we became aware of the quarrels and feuds which too often poisoned the atmosphere when the family was gathered together, either at Alderley or at Penrhos.

Now all is vanished into limbo. Most of the characters who conducted their lives so passionately are dead. Alderley was pulled down long ago and the property sold to Imperial Chemical Industries for a research station. Thus, after more than eight hundred years, the association of the Stanleys with Alderley came to an end.

Penhros, on Holyhead Island, had belonged to the Stanleys since the middle of the eighteenth century when it was brought into the family by Margaret Owen, a beautiful Welsh heiress and descendant of the original grantee, John-ap-Owen. She married Sir John Stanley of Alderley in 1763. No one knows when the original house was built and its history is lost in the shadowy and largely unrecorded past. The rambling grey stone mansion with its adjoining farm buildings enclosed by battlemented granite walls looked over a narrow strait to the green fields of Anglesey. Eastwards, the mountains of Snowdonia rose on the horizon beyond the Menai Straits. To the west and south, a belt of woods – gnarled sycamores and ancient beech trees – encircled the house and pleasure grounds, sheltering them from the frequent gales.

On this tree-protected side of the house was a terraced garden ornamented with classical stone urns and flower pots. Below this, a parterre of box hedges was laid out in a formal design, enclosing flower beds. Between these beds were paths arranged in geometrical patterns composed of black and glistening white stones. It was one gardener's full-time duty to keep these paths in order. Taking a line and templates cut out in the Estate smithy he would lay out the stones in the required patterns and roll them flat with a heavy iron roller.

Beyond the terrace and parterre stretched a broad lawn encircled by woods which were full of spring flowers – snowdrops, primroses, bluebells, and wild cyclamen. It was but a step from the garden through the woods to the sea with its little shell-strewn beaches curving between the rocky points where the oyster-catcher hides his eggs to this day, and the white sea birds walk upon the shining ribbed sand at low tide and the lonely cry of the curlew echoes over the water.

The front of the house faced north-west and was more exposed. Its plain Queen Anne style façade had been embellished at the beginning of the nineteenth century with castellated turrets and a 'gothick' porch. It looked out upon a circular sweep of grey gravel bounded by grass with a clump of wind-bitten trees shielding the house from the worst quarter of the weather. Beyond lay open grazing land sloping down to the sea. A drive ran down across the fields to a wooden front gate flanked by a pair of gothick lodges and a little castellated 'folly' stood on the edge of one of the fields overlooking the sea.

A short distance from the house was a large stone-walled garden with meticulously raked gravel paths flanked by herbaceous borders. Here were also formal rose gardens, hot-houses for grapes and peaches, and a row of bee hives. But to me the most entrancing spot was the 'fernery', a little Victorian hot-house for exotic plants with a miniature waterfall trickling into a rocky pool amidst overhanging ferns, and a smell of warm, damp greenery. Beyond this garden was the orchard, also walled, and beyond this yet another fruit and vegetable garden. The whole extent of the pleasure gardens and grounds was over eight acres and before World War I there were eighteen gardeners.

My grandparents looked upon Penrhos as a holiday house where only the minimum of comfort was necessary. Few concessions were made to the modern way of life. When I was a child there was no electric light or gas. There was no telephone until after World War I, no heating – apart from open fires – and only the most rudimentary plumbing and sanitation. All cooking was done on an enormous coal-fired range, and the rooms were lighted by oil lamps and candles. Many of the rooms had remained little altered since the day they were first furnished and consequently the house had a strong aura of bygone generations reaching back through the years to a remote and more primitive era.

Sometimes I used to be frightened of ghosts, particularly in the older part of the house where the servants were lodged. Here there was a warren of damp and eerie little rooms along dark passages and flights of crooked stairs connecting the different levels of the house where at night shapes and shadows would leap and crouch in the wavering candle-light.

Along these passages were hung dim likenesses of our Welsh forebears. In particular, there was a life-size portrait of an ancient crone laid out on a flower-strewn bier above which hovered two bucolic winged cherubs. This ancestress was known to us as 'the Dead Grandmother'. Under the picture stood a massive chest on top of which a nightlight was placed after dark. I had to pass this gruesome painting to get to my bedroom at the end of the passage, and as I ran the gauntlet the flickering nightlight made it seem as though the corpse was moving.

When I got to bed I would lie with beating heart and tingling scalp listening to the strange noises of the old house. I seemed to hear a footfall on a creaking stair, the rustle of somebody's gown or the tapping on a door – and sometimes the sound of heavy breathing and long-drawn sighs. These noises were said to be made by mice or rats in the wainscotting, and by owls in the ivy on the outside walls. And no doubt they were, but I was not entirely convinced by this explanation. I could sense the unseen presence of something or somebody, no matter what time of the day or night, and up to the last time I stayed at Penrhos, long after my marriage, I had the same feeling when I went to this region of the house.

Penrhos had a delicious smell of its own – a mixture of oil lamps, beeswax, new bread, old books and summer flowers combined with the fresh salt breath of the sea. This 'Penrhos smell' is perhaps the most nostalgic of all my memories.

The long summer days were mostly spent by us children on a sheltered beach known as the Bathing House Beach. On a little rocky promontory at one end was perched an ancient stone cottage, looking out to sea. This was the Bathing House. It consisted of two rooms, one above the other. In the top room there was a wooden table and some chairs, and an alcove in the roughly plastered wall stuck with cockle shells and spotted cowries from foreign seas. In the room below there was an antiquated and rusting kitchen range and a rotting wooden cupboard. Here were kept an assortment of prawning nets, buckets and spades, bass fishing baskets and other odds and ends. The fire in the range was never lighted within my memory, but long ago old family letters speak of picnics in the Bathing House when no doubt a dish of broiled Welsh mutton chops was cooked on that very stove.

When the nursery party arrived at the Bathing House the nannies would unpack a mass of impedimenta from the prams and the nursery maids would carry everything down the steps cut in the rocks to the beach. First, the rugs were spread, then water-proof bags were opened and bathing dresses, caps, rubber waders,* sand-shoes and towels were taken out. Then came buckets and spades, and the 'mending' which kept the nursery maids occupied when they had nothing else to do. Finally,

* Mackintosh bloomers with a bib.

the hampers with food and thermoses were stowed in the shade of the small trees which grew down to the beach. When all this was arranged we were dressed in our waders and allowed to paddle. When the tide came up we bathed in red and white striped bathing dresses and sand-shoes, with rubber bathing caps for the little girls. We were allowed to stay in for a quarter-of-an-hour as the water, being only a few inches deep, was warm and the shallowness made things absolutely safe.

I never liked building sand castles much. What I enjoyed best was look-ing for 'craggies', the tiny, rose-pink cowrie shells, delicately ribbed and sometimes faintly freckled. They were rather difficult to find. One could stare for minutes at a little heap of mixed shells and stones silted up against a ridge of seaweed or washed into the crevice of a rock, without seeing a single craggie. Suddenly, as if by magic, the scales would drop from one's eyes, and lo! a dozen craggies would all at once become visible like babies' fingertips amongst the periwinkles, top-shells, whelks and coloured pebbles.

At spring tides the sea would go out a very long way leaving various rocks exposed around which were deep pools where we fished for prawns. The grown-ups would stand knee-deep and we children up to our armpits as we dipped our nets under the seaweed-covered ledges of the rocks and drew them slowly up to the surface. There would usually be half-a-dozen large clicking prawns amongst the crabs and shells and broken bits of seaweed. Sometimes there might even be a small lobster if one was specially lucky. We put our catch in buckets filled with sea water and the prawns were always cooked and eaten for tea and breakfast with brown bread and butter. Prawning was the highlight of all Penrhos de-lights.

Muzzie would take us in the motor car to visit tenants on Anglesey. They were usually farmers living in bleak, haunted-looking grey houses surrounded by stone out-buildings of great antiquity. We would be wel-comed by the farmer's wife who curtsied to my grandmother and ushered us into the front parlour. The furniture was generally solid oak or elm, country-made, and often very old. A welsh dresser invariably stood against the wall, stacked with china, and on the walls hung life-sized daguerreotype portraits of old, bearded men with stiff collars and a button-hole, and women upholstered in ruched black satin with little caps on their heads and large lockets round their necks.

The table would be spread with a white tablecloth in preparation for tea, a gargantuan meal of new bread and home-made butter and jam, plum cake, and 'crampogs' – a delectable kind of Welsh pancake, paper-thin, piping hot, stacked in a muffineer and swimming with melted butter. The farmer's wife would nod and smile to us, talking in Welsh and plying us with food. I soon got to know the Welsh for 'darling', 'more cake', and 'good girl'

At times we would go for a picnic on Mill Island, a wild, romantic islet of lichen-covered granite rocks, bracken, gorse and heather, where a windmill called The Stanley Mill stood on the highest point of the island and ground the corn. But one of the outings we loved best was an expedition up the mountain to Twr Ellin, a castellated mock-medieval 'folly' built in 1868 by Uncle William for his wife. It stood upon the edge of a tremendous cliff on whose sheer face thousands of puffins nested. Far below lay the glittering expanse of the sea, peacock-blue on calm days, and stretching unruffled to the horizon except for the foaming track of the tidal rip which churned wickedly in little wrinkling waves past the South Stack rocks and lighthouse. Inland, a wide sweep of gorse and heather, interspersed with boulders, rolled away to the hump of the mountain's summit, silver-grey against the sky.

Ellin's Tower had been furnished by Uncle William with utilitarian Victorian pieces, solidly and depressingly hideous. By the time I remember it the penetrating sea fogs had already begun to rot everything inside, and there was a miasma of damp and decay that even the bright sunshine could not dispel. When the sea mist closed in, blotting the world out with its dense and swirling vapour, the North Stack fog signal station would start its banshee wailing. 'EEEE-*ONGK*! EEEE-*ONGK*!' it bellowed once a minute, like a cow that had lost its calf. We could hear its muffled and ghostly warning sounding through the night as far away as Penrhos; and the nannies would talk of shipwrecks and disasters at sea, which made my flesh creep.

And so the first time I went in a boat I was assailed by panic, although the occasion was designed to be a super treat. Some powerful influence[*] had arranged an excursion in the Trinity House launch to the Skerries Lighthouse, and Rosalind Henley and I accompanied the grown-ups.

We boarded the launch at Holyhead Harbour, and were installed on deck, well cocooned in rugs against the wind and rough seas. We set off towards the Skerries, some eight miles out to sea. Soon the spray began to fly as the launch bounced over the choppy water. I screamed in an agony of terror, certain that the next crump of the keel on a white-capped wave would send us to the bottom. I remember the grown-ups taunting me with cowardice. There was nothing for it but to endure, and indeed, finding that we were all still alive on reaching the Lighthouse,

* Possibly Winston Churchill, who was an Elder Brother of Trinity House and married to my father's cousin Clementine Hozier.

the extremity of my fear died down. But the horror of drowning had such a violent effect on my mind that I have only the haziest recollection of the rest of the trip.

Penrhos had a magical quality which even the least imaginative could sense. From my earliest days it cast a spell over my heart and still binds me with its memories. Now Penrhos has gone for ever, destroyed like Alderley in the aftermath of two world wars.

Today the house is a ruin buried beneath a thicket of sapling trees grown to maturity. The gardens and lawns have vanished without trace under an impenetrable undergrowth of tangled weeds and brambles. The woods have long since been cut down and the storm winds blow unchecked over the wilderness which was once our home.

Next to my parents, the grown-up person I loved best was my maternal grandmother, Marmee.

She was still beautiful in old age, with fine aquiline features and sad, deep-set eyes. She had an almost Rabelaisian sense of humour and, like my mother, was a brilliant mimic with an unerring eye for the ludicrous or pompous in character and situation. She was an excellent musician and linguist, a talented amateur painter with a gift for caricature and a writer of short stories and verse which, though they are rather too sentimental in flavour for modern taste, nevertheless have a certain literary competence and period charm. Unlike my mother, she was a completely straightforward character, often surprisingly forceful in her opinions and judgements, and incapable of putting on an act or succumbing to self-pity. She was shy and reserved in the company of people she did not know well and sometimes would appear uncommunicative and aloof. But she had a deeply compassionate understanding of human nature and the gift of unlocking the heart of a child. She became the loved and loving companion and confidante of her headstrong and furiously self-willed little granddaughter.

After my grandfather died in 1910 she withdrew from the world and lived at Prestons with her two unmarried daughters, Clatten and Poppety, (such were their nicknames), finding solace in gardening, painting, music and books. I remember her in a big cotton sunbonnet and galoshes, a trowel or fork in one hand and a wooden trug in the other, weeding, planting, staking and pruning in her lovely flower garden with its sweeping view over the Kentish Weald. In the evenings she would play the piano or read to me or tell me stories, or teach me to play patience. She always wore a lace cap indoors and a black or lavender-grey silk dress with a lace fichu: and she chain-smoked, keeping the cigarette in her mouth and dropping the ash down the folds of the lace and silk.

I thought of Prestons as a haven from the hurly-burly of life at Alderley or Penhros. It was a Victorian country house, gabled and tiled, of little architectural merit, but with a serene atmosphere. The interior was quite un-English, the panelled rooms being hung with Flemish tapestries and furnished with rather florid Italian pieces, carved, gilded and inlaid. Great china bowls filled with pot-pourri made every year by my grandmother scented the whole house. I remember nothing of nursery life or servants at Prestons – only my grandmother's presence and my love of being with her.

In 1912 we moved to another London house as St Leonard's Terrace was considered too small – although it had at least eight bedrooms. Number 49 Montague Square was a handsome late-Georgian town house with an L-shaped drawing-room and a dining-room large enough for dinner parties of sixteen people. Five or six courses were always served, sent up from the kitchen in a little lift worked by a pulley.

The rambling basement had stone-flagged floors and a dank musty smell. Apart from the kitchen, scullery and larder, there was a pantry where the glass and china were kept, and a butler's pantry where the silver was polished, the port decanted, and where my father's suits were brushed. There was a wine cellar with bins up to the ceiling, and a housekeeper's store cupboard. In front, looking out on the basement area through heavily barred windows, was the servants' hall, and at the back there was a cubby-hole with a skylight which served as a manservant's bedroom. As we had parlour-maids, this room was used as a box-room. There were coachmen's quarters and stabling in the mews behind, but I think these must have been let off separately as we didn't have a motor car or a carriage.

My parents' bedroom and dressing-room and the nurseries were pleasant and light, looking out on the tops of the plane trees in the square, but the maids' rooms in the attic were comfortless and bitterly cold in the winter. Only the head servants had rooms to themselves; the under servants doubled up two and sometimes four to a room. The servants had no running water on their floor and had to share the nursery bathroom, lavatory and sink. They always washed after lunch when they had finished their work and when no one else needed the bathroom. All the same, it must have been a scramble for six or seven servants to get washed and dressed between three and four o'clock and ready in their black afternoon uniform and starched white caps and aprons to start their next round of duty, answering the bells, making up the fires, taking hot water-cans to the bedrooms, cooking and serving the dinner, turning down the beds and putting in the hot water bottles and finally, clearing up for the next day.

I was promoted to a room of my own at Montague Square, not as a sop to my comfort but because I disturbed Edward and Pamela in the night-nursery and prevented them from going to sleep. At first I was not allowed a nightlight in my bedroom and I grew hysterical at being shut in the dark, but eventually my door was left open a crack as a concession to my fears.

I had formed the habit of escaping from the frustrations of real life into a realm of fantasy. At night, when the comforting shaft of light shone through the bedroom door, I was no longer an unruly little girl but a princess or a fairy, with two unblemished white arms, long golden tresses crowned with jewels, and beautiful as the dawn. Or I was a heroine like Grace Darling or Charlotte Corday - or even an angel with a 'shining countenance'. For this last role I devised a realistic get-up by draping myself with the sheet off my bed and smearing my face with vaseline. But this flight of fancy was not appreciated by the nurse or nursery-maid who found me out of bed late at night. I was ashamed of my secret imaginings and would have died rather than reveal them to any grown-up.

Both Edward and I were nail-biters. Our fingers were smeared with tincture of Barbados bitter aloes, a stinking dark-brown substance which stained our nails indelibly and tasted like deadly poison. This was supposed to put us off but it had little effect on Edward. It cured me eventually, not so much on account of its terrible taste and smell but because I was revolted by the sight of my fingers.

Nannies and nursery governesses, French and English, succeeded each other rapidly. Some were weak and ineffective, some were severe and even cruel, but one and all were defeated by Edward's wilful naughtiness and my rebellious temper. I came to look upon myself as incorrigibly wicked and I developed a kind of despairing resistance to discipline. I conducted a guerilla war against authority, crusading for the ideals of my private world which seemed so much more acceptable than the established order. In this I was aided and abetted by Edward when it suited his interests, but Pamela was never naughty and was always being held up as an example. She became the object of my irritation and I wreaked vengeance on her by pinching and slapping her whenever I could.

It must have been some time during the winter of 1912-1913 that I read a newspaper report of a lady who went to Selfridges and bought a fur coat which had been imported from some Eastern country. After a while she noticed queer, dead-white patches on her skin and eventually it was discovered that she had contracted leprosy from the fur coat. She was incarcerated in a leper colony where she was doomed to spend the rest of her life. Selfridges was very near Montague Square and was our chief shopping centre, but now it was shunned and we did not so much as walk down Oxford Street in its direction. I had always had a peculiar dread of leprosy ever since my father had read aloud to us *The Black Arrow*. Consequently, I went through agonies imagining I had caught the disease and would wake up screaming from nightmares that I had been sent to a leper colony and would never see my family again.

Part II
1914–1918

3

Away to Australia

Towards the end of 1913, my father was appointed State Governor of Victoria. Before World War I weakened the might of the British Empire, Governors of the Dominions were much grander personages than they are today. Even a State Governor was accorded a degree of importance unheard of nowadays, but which then was considered due to a representative of the Sovereign of the great British Empire.

And so, in order to uphold the customary vice-regal state, my parents left England accompanied by a large retinue of servants and attended by two *Aides-de-Camp*. Our suite consisted of a nurse, nursery maid and a German governess who had been with the Prime Minister's children and was highly recommended by Margot Asquith; my mother's lady's maid and my father's valet; a butler, a chef and a woman under-cook; a housekeeper and head housemaid – and Shandy, our puppy. The rest of the vice-regal office staff and the household were to be recruited in Australia.

The servants, with Shandy and the luggage, embarked on the *Osterley* at Tilbury while my parents, the ADCs, ourselves and attendant nurses and governesses went overland and joined the ship at Toulon five days later.

After we arrived in Australia I wrote an account of the voyage. I dictated it to my mother every evening when we came down to the drawing-room after tea, and I would not allow her to make any suggestions as to form or content, but insisted that it must be written my way and not hers. She did tactfully amend grammar and construction, and

remarked how 'Stanleyish' I was in my direct approach to my subject
and forthright style. It took me a long time and often would be laid
aside for months, but encouraged by my mother it was eventually finished
and typed by 'Sparkums', the Government House typist, in her spare time.
I have it before me now, illustrated by me and entitled with admirable
simplicity, 'The Book'. I plunged directly into my story with the announcement by my father that we were all off to Australia shortly.

> For a moment we were so surprised we couldn't say anything, and then we
> began to scream and jump about till Dar said 'Enough'. I felt frightened
> at the thought of going in a ship, but we were all very excited. The day
> to start came, and we departed from Victoria Station on a foggy, freezing-cold
> morning late in January 1914. The long saloon carriage was full of people
> kissing us goodbye but Edward said afterwards that he would have preferred
> to shake hands. They hurried off the train just before it pulled slowly out,
> leaving the crowds behind, and Mammie stood at the window for a long
> time. I saw her lift her veil and take out her handkerchief to wipe away
> her tears. Zellie, our governess, made me sit beside her while she told dreadfully
> dull stories, and I remember seeing the long lines of hop poles as we passed
> through Kent, and Pamela saying, 'Are we at Australia yet?'

When we disembarked from the steamer at Calais, we went straight
to the train for Toulon.

As our French nurse had been unwilling to come with us to far Australia, my mother had engaged a new English nanny and we had been
rather apprehensive about just how far we could go with her. But we
were not in awe of her for long, for by the time the three of us were
being put to bed on the train, she was reduced to threats of giving me
a whipping 'all bare' if I did not stop making jokes and laughing and
teasing the others. And Edward, once he was installed in the top bunk,
began to fiddle with an oblong white box labelled *Défense de toucher*
forcing poor Nanny to roar agitated warnings at him. I remember a
great bustle and confusion at Toulon, and Zellie harassing poor Captain
Gale about her old black bag which could not be found. We detested
this bag, because it was chiefly filled with our lesson books and her knitting. Finally, the whole vice-regal party was successfully marshalled on
board the *Osterley* and we sailed away at sunset.

My mother had written to Marmee from Paris in a daze of misery
at parting with her family; the fact that she was prepared for the wrench
of leaving England and that all the goodbyes were now behind her was
no consolation, and she talked resignedly about facing 'the inevitable ...
with courage and determination to do one's best'. But three days later
she was more cheerful.

Our first day of the sea voyage has gone by in glorious weather and calm, still sea. .... We are royally installed in the most luxurious cabins and everybody is most obliging and civil ... Edward has developed a passion for Captain Gale who takes him all over the ship to show and explain things to him. He talks about 'Gale and I' in a boastful way which I have to squash.

Zellie had her first attempt at teaching Adelaide this morning. It was not very successful, but I daresay it was rather distracting with so many new things going on ... [She] is finding Adelaide rather a hard nut to crack and her grey hairs will soon be brought to the grave, I should think.... [The children] have already found out that she cannot move very fast and delight in nimble gambades round ropes and corners which she finds difficult to negotiate ... [Zellie] is a terrific eater and has all sorts of odd meals. The Aides are much amused by her as whenever they come across her she is eating something.... I am liking my nurse very much and the children like her immensely too, which is all to the good ...

Nanny Kate Rigling was a short, compact little woman with an upright carriage and a comfortable lap and bosom. She had a kindly expression and a firmly persuasive manner. She spoke in a quiet and cultivated voice and her turn of phrase was almost invariably correct, yet occasionally she would produce malapropisms which were treasured by my mother and quoted with affectionate amusement by the whole family. My mother's words in her letter were prophetic. All, indeed, was 'to the good'. During the forty-odd years Kate Rigling remained with us, 'Old Nan', as she became known to future generations, was utterly and selflessly devoted to us all, and we, in turn, from my mother to her youngest grandchild, loved her as a close and cherished member of the family.

The *Osterley* called briefly at Naples, then Europe was left behind as we steamed for Port Said and the Suez Canal.

We arrived at Port Said early in the morning [says 'The Book']. All the passengers had to land while the ship coaled. We went on deck full of excitement at seeing a new place. There was a deafening noise going on. Two great black rafts were drawn up alongside crowded with the dirtiest beings I ever saw, and piled with sacks of coal. These creatures were shrieking, singing, laughing and squabbling in a great babblement while they shovelled coal in crashing waterfalls into the ship – so that the noise was dizzying. Everything was black, and we had been forbidden to go near anything for we all had light clean clothes on. A launch came to take us ashore. A black native carried Pamela down the gangway, to her disgust and dismay, and she drew her head back as far as she could while the native grinned broadly at her – Mammie told her to thank him for carrying her, which she did, and then said 'but I'm very glad it is over'. When we got back to the ship we found some conjurors on board. We watched one of them as he turned shillings into

tiny yellow chickens, and pulled threepenny-bits out of their tails. He even
made a chicken appear suddenly on Dar's nose and run down it exclaiming,
'Cock, what is this you do!' We all screamed and laughed until we nearly
fell overboard.

Toulon, Naples, Port Said, the Suez Canal – each had been more exciting than the last, but Colombo, in my opinion, was the best of all. We
children rode in rickshaws, gazed at the shops, and disgraced ourselves
by laughing loudly at the waiters in the Galleface Hotel, who wore floating white dresses and rolled their long hair in a chignon that was fastened
with a huge tortoiseshell comb.

From my mother's point of view, the voyage was proving a good
deal less idyllic.

I am quite sick of the 'beautiful sea-voyage' and long to be on land again.
It has been very hot now for the last week and the nights especially are
very trying, tho' we have electric fans and punkahs and every sort of modern
contrivance to make things cool.

The children, so far, are well though they all look rather ragged out by
the heat. Adelaide, after giving everyone a hell of a time for the first week,
has settled down more now, and lessons are pursued with Zellie in less starfish-
like attitudes than at first. But the Nannie is rather puzzled by her. I took
them in some soda-water to drink the other night and as I went out of
the cabin I heard Adelaide say 'Ah! you see Nannie? God heard Edward's
whining and He answered him at once!' Nannie's reply was the flattest 'Yes
dear, but he won't always.' . . .

Pamela picks up the most undesirable acquaintances. The first part of the
voyage she never could be separated from a little Indian dentist. He went
ashore at Colombo and sent them all the most wonderful toys on board.
She is now very devoted to three very low-looking Irish priests who are travelling together, and who call her 'Pummeela'. Poor Nannie says 'They do seem
such children for picking up with anyone!'

At last, on Sunday 22 February, we arrived at Port Melbourne. Crowds
of people were waiting in the heat of that brilliant summer's day to
see us land, and there were flags and decorations everywhere to welcome
us. I wore my best white muslin dress and was allowed to carry the
pink silk parasol which Muzzie had given me. My father was in his
Governor's uniform, the plumes waving from his cocked· hat, and my
mother wore a lovely lace and chiffon dress. They left the *Osterley* before
us in a launch and were taken on board the warship, *Melbourne*, where
they stayed until everything was ready for their ceremonial drive through
the streets. We children sat for hours in our car on the pier in the boiling
sun, waiting for the procession to begin, and by the time we arrived

at Stonnington, the State Government House, we were all so hot and hungry that none of us noticed or cared what it looked like. But lemonade and biscuits revived us sufficiently to explore the garden, where we were greatly pleased to find the three little plots that had belonged to the Fuller children.* We immediately claimed these for our own.

Later, the garden filled with schoolchildren, all dressed in white. From one of the upper balconies, we watched the schoolmasters pushing them into some sort of order until it became apparent that they formed the word 'Welcome', and then at last we saw the Escort galloping up the drive, followed by the open car with our parents inside. The schoolchildren burst into 'God Save the King' and we were called down for the introductions and official photographs. But this novelty soon palled; we had to be caught again and again to be photographed, because we had invented a game of rolling down the grass bank. Nanny was not pleased about this latter exploit. I had 'greened' (grass-stained) my drawers, and Edward's clothes were in a like state.

The newspapers and magazines were full of reports of the new Governor's arrival with photographs galore which I scanned avidly for pictures of myself. The Press was most complimentary to both my parents, emphasising the 'daintiness' and elegance of my mother and the youthful good looks of my father. It is true that the *Bulletin* in its usual brash and fleering style remarked that the new State Excellency's name appeared to be 'Lymph' and at the Swearing-in – 'or whatever it is' – there would certainly be a crush as even a well-worn cocked hat could draw a crowd. But the article ended with an ode of praise, the concluding verses of which were as follows:

> As poor Australians born, we know
> We may not scale the dizzy heights
> Where pure Imperial Governors grow!
> But still our weak aspiring flights
> Unto that sweet perfection lift
> Us from the dregs above the drift.
> And that is all the Govern-*nor*
> By Heaven is created for.
>
> From out the wastes of nothingness
> He's wrested like a splended pearl
> Snatched from the depths. Then Journals stress
> His gifts: his hair's entrancing curl,

* The previous Governor's children.

The perfect turn of calf and lip,
His glorious works of Statesmanship;
With what hard days and sleepless nights
He saved his country in sham fights.*

Her Ladyship – consider her.
Her splendid style, her winning grace,
The tact that's never known to err,
The subtle glory of her face.
A fit and lovely mate is she
For that most perfect Excellency:
Reviewing which we hardly can
Believe there's been a fall of man.

As there was no Federal capital city till Canberra was opened in 1927, Melbourne was, up to that date, the seat of the Governor-General and Federal Parliament. The massive and grandiose State Government House of Victoria, built in the affluent days following the Gold Rush of the fifties, was taken over as Federal Government House and the State Governor was relegated to Stonnington, a large house in Malvern, a suburb of Melbourne. My mother was mortified at living on the outskirts of the city and railed against the ugliness and inconvenience of the temporary State Government House in all her letters home.

---

* Presumably this is a reference to the Boer War in which my father fought.

4

'My Beloved Marmee'

The English mail went out once a week before the war broke out and a fat letter of four sheets of quarto paper cost a penny to mail overseas, which was no more than the local postage charge.

My mother wrote to Marmee and family by every post. In all her correspondence she never lost sight of the fact that the recipient of her letters was an audience to be played to, and she exerted herself to entertain her readers.

She was particularly close to her sister-in-law Venetia Stanley, and she sent her amusing and sometimes rather malicious accounts of vice-regal doings, always choosing the topics which would interest her most and jokes which would appeal to her sense of humour.

Venetia was planning to visit Australia in the near future and Muzzie had generously offered to pay for Marmee's passage out at the same time. My mother's spirits were partially buoyed up by these expectations and they helped her to withstand the waves of home-sickness that assailed her, but she was determined to return to England on a visit as soon as she could arrange it. Luckily she could not foresee the terrible events which would separate us all for five long years from country and family, or that English life as we knew it was gone forever.

My mother would sit letter-writing hour after hour in her little boudoir at a Louis XVI-style desk, her quill pen squeaking across the thick writing paper embossed with the Royal Crown as she covered page after page in her clear and pretty handwriting. By the first mail home she wrote to Venetia:

Our arrival and reception went off brilliantly, and George and Mary might well envy us the easy grace with which we played our parts! It really was very thrilling to be the point of the procession and I *longed* for you to be there to see the fun. Dear old Art looked the most beloved bullfinch in his tight uniform and cocked hat – and saluted, and listened, and replied to snoring Mayoral addresses with becoming dignity and cordiality, and the general opinion is that he has made a very good impression. Even the virulent *Bulletin* was quite friendly in its banter, so I hope we have made a good start.

Victor Hood* is rather like what I expected, and keeps us all in order and up to our duties. He is rather like Crippen to look at, only I don't think he has quite so much character! I am laying myself out to become good friends with him – I hope it won't end in Hyocene and bits of me under the kitchen floor. Our Aides are wearing well on the whole, especially Capt. Gale ... who is always ready to make the best of everything, and though he isn't a bit clever he has the art of making his company congenial. ...

We made our first appearance in public yesterday at the Races and I wore an exquisite 'Somatoff'† which was most highly commended by the Press, and a Gertie Millarish little bonnet with bunches of grapes over the ears which also called forth great approval. I got it at 'Zyrot' almost the day before I left and hid it from Art for fear he should think it rather actressy. ...

This house is worse than any circle in the Inferno and no art or skill can redeem it. Every wall and ceiling is decorated in weak cocoa-colour relieved by sky-blue and heavy gold. The drawing-room is a horrid little poke-hole with appalling pieces of heavily carved furniture and glass cupboards lined with green and copper-coloured plush. There are dreadful things called 'chiffoniers' with looking-glass backs and as heavy as Stonehenge to move; but I am being very firm about scrapping them all in spite of a good deal of opposition. I am now engaged in making love to the Prime Minister (a more formidable and less congenial undertaking than with our own dear P.M.) to try and wheedle some new carpets and chintzes etc., out of the Government. ... Give the P.M. a big love from me when you see him and tell him I will write him a letter later on and tell him the state of things out here.

She also wrote a characteristic letter to her father-in-law, recounting anecdotes which she felt would tickle his fancy, and flattering him in her usual graceful way.

Edward hobnobbed with all the sailors and was on terms of greatest intimacy with them. He also made many 'lady friends' and caused much amusement by asking one of them if she had any children. When she replied she had two he said 'Oh! And are you *married*?' He caused consternation one day by climbing one of the posts on the deck and, clinging to it in an ungainly fashion, he proclaimed in a loud voice 'Now I am Jesus on the Cross!'

* Hon. Victor Nelson Hood, Private Secretary.
† Fashionable *couturière* of the day.

I think Arthur has made a favourable impression, and I am sure it has made a great difference to him the fact of your having been out here so recently and having made yourself so popular. Everyone speaks of you with admiration and affection and that makes a bond at once between us and them. . . .

Yesterday was Cup Day at the races. I was lucky and won £2 having backed a horse for 10/-. I rather enjoy the races but I think it is dull work if you don't bet a little. I cannot persuade Arthur to – he cannot find any fun in it. It makes the race much more breathless to me if I stand to win or lose by it. It is rather fun arriving like Royalties and having God Save the King played when we arrive.

I made my first public appearance and speech last Monday, and nearly died of nervousness. Arthur helped me to prepare quite a neat little speech. But when I got up I was absolutely light-headed and didn't the least know what I had said until I saw it reported the next day in the newspapers. Poor Capt. Gale was as nervous as I was, but he said it sounded as though I was quite accustomed to public speaking and everyone was satisfied. . . .

I have a little game of making Capt. Gale laugh when we ought to be looking most solemn. We get little fun out of Victor Hood who is steeped in officialdom. . . .

Last night we went to a dinner at Government House – seventy people – and there was a dance afterwards which I quite enjoyed, especially as Sir Ian Hamilton made himself agreeable to me – also the little Governor-General* thawed and became quite frisky, I *wish* we were there instead of this nasty little villa . . . and I would entertain so gloriously in the big house, and it could be made rather lovely. . . .

Stonnington was far from being the 'nasty little villa' my mother called it. It was a large and imposing mansion built in 1890 for around £19,000 by a German carriage maker named Wagner, who made his fortune in the famous Cobb & Co. coaches during the Australian gold rush. After his death the property was leased to the Government of Victoria as the residence of the State Governor and it remained so for over thirty years. Subsequently it became a girls' school, a Red Cross Convalescent Home, Administrative Offices for the Health Department, and from 1953 it has been the State College of Victoria, Toorak. The education authorities are currently spending large sums on new buildings and improvements, but the old mansion still stands, much as I remember it.

Then, as now, you entered the grounds through large, cast-iron gates flanked by high railings. On the right stood a lodge, and on the left, a sentry-box manned by a policeman. The red gravel drive wound between English shrubs interspersed with palm trees round a large lawn till it finally reached the house. The pillared and arched verandahs and

* Lord Denman

stucco façade were painted mud colour and surmounted by a livid slate roof with a central mansard tower from the top of which flew the Union Jack. One entered into an oak-panelled 'baronial' hall with a huge open fireplace surrounded by a massive double-decker chimneypiece elaborately carved in the Italian Renaissance style with tritons and mermaids, curli- cues and garlands. There was also a good deal of stained glass and cop- pered floral decoration in the domed ceiling high above, as I remember. On the left of the hall were my mother's boudoir and my father's study. The boudoir, I used to think, was the most beautiful room I had ever seen. The walls were covered with ornate wall-paper and the 'rococo' ceilings and doors were painted with frescoes of Boucher-type cherubs with congested bottoms and cheeks, flying with garlands of roses amongst pink clouds against a cerulean sky. There were French windows leading out onto the verandah and looking over the garden.

My father's study was a room I dreaded to enter, for it was here I was sent, when all other control had failed, for a final and awesome *lit-de-justice,* and many a spanking was administered here in retribution for my misdeeds. My father, however, was always very fair. He would begin by stating the case against me and asking what I had to say for myself. I always had plenty, but my arguments were usally demolished and ended by me being put across his knee. One day I discovered a splendid way of curtailing this unpleasant experience. I started to pee, probably out of agitation, and was smartly put down and told to leave the room. Thereafter, my father was likely to devise other punishments, such as the cancelling of some treat, which I minded worse than being spanked.

On the right of the hall was a large and gloomy dining-room, again heavily carved and panelled in oak, and at the end was the drawing-room which always seemed to me to be deliciously cool and filled with the scent of flowers. It opened onto the verandah and looked out over terraced lawns and flower beds to the distant Dandenong Ranges. My mother kept to the custom of having the children down to the drawing-room every evening between five and six o'clock. After we had lived in Mel- bourne some time, we had to pause outside the drawing-room door to arrange our mouths in order not to talk Australian. We became quite bi-lingual in the end.

The Staff Offices led off the hall and here the Hon. Victor Nelson Hood reigned over his minions. 'Hoodiwinks', as we called him behind his back, was a figure much dreaded by all who came under his sway. He loathed children, and spent his time snooping on us and prowling about spying on the ADCs, typists and the servants. His interest, apart from this activity, was attending official functions and observing the most rigid protocol; his only apparent recreation was taking scenic photographs with a wide-angle lens camera on a tripod. The door of his office was always open so that he could see what was going on and we never went past it without a shiver of apprehension.

On the first floor a wide landing ran round the four sides of the hall forming a gallery with wooden balusters through which we and the servants used to peek at the grown-ups going ceremoniously arm-in-arm in to dinner on State occasions. On this floor there were the nurseries, the spare rooms and my parents' bedroom suite; and down a dark passage beyond a green baize door were the servants' rooms, our school-room, and the back stairs leading to the kitchen, laundry, butler's pantry and store-rooms. In a recess along the dark passage was an inlaid box shaped like a small coffin containing a metal cylinder with lots of little spikes sticking out of it; this was a musical box, no doubt once belonging to Mr Wagner. We were never allowed to touch it but once Edward and I found the key and wound it up. Immediately it began to tinkle out waltz tunes and operatic medleys and to our dismay we found we couldn't stop it. It played on and on in its ghostly way till Nanny heard and came upon us like an avenging angel.

Our best friends were the police constables Arnetty and Gardiner, Comrie, the orderly and dispatch rider, and for a time, Daddy Yates, the lodge keeper – but later we fell out with Daddy Yates. He was a gross, ginger-haired Irishman with a blistered red face, little pigs' eyes and a hoarse whisky voice. He was full of blarney and false good humour and we soon found out that he was not to be trusted. Mrs Yates was fat, pale and blowsy and was always 'poorly' which was probably caused by too frequent nipping at the grog. She had an H.M.V. phonograph with a frilly trumpet which played Harry Lauder records. Dyer the head gardener was a specially hated enemy, as was Martin the butler. Dyer would sneak up on us when we were playing in the garden and threaten us with muttered Irish curses, but Martin could be avoided for we could always hear his very squeaky boots and thus escape.

Nanny used to take us for walks down to Kooyong, where the Davis Cup Tennis Courts now stand, but in those days only the honey-scented wattle grew. Sometimes we went on to Gardiner's Creek, where we used to picnic and paddle in the creek and listen to the kookaburras laughing.

When we went shopping or to church, we walked the other way which wasn't so much fun, except that at the corner of Glenferrie Road there was a sweet shop which sold *Old Gold* chocolate, 'boiled lollies' and 'Sherbet suckers', as well as 'Bullseyes' and 'Aniseed Balls'.

Once a week we would take the electric tram down the Glenferrie Road to Hawthorn. Clang-clang it went over the Kooyong level crossing, up and down the hill where in summer mirage lakes lay in the dips of the switchback road. On we went, past the 'cutting', its earth face covered with the fleshy fingers and magenta stars of 'pigface', till we reached the corner where Scotch Preparatory School stood, its red-brick walls and slate-roofed towers surrounded by a few sickly pine trees. Here we got off and walked down Callantina Road to The Briars where Miss Mona McBurney the music mistress lived.

The Briars was an old-fashioned, dark little bungalow with two pink Cecil Brunner rose bushes in front. Miss McBurney would pick posies of this sweet-smelling little rose to give us when we came for our lessons. The house had a verandah with brown painted cast-iron 'lace' along the edge. Jasmine and honeysuckle grew all over it, luxuriant in the Australian sun.

There was Turkey-carpet patterned linoleum along the entrance passage, a dining-room and a parlour on either side of the front door, and at the back was brother McBurney's 'den', the kitchen and the bedrooms.

The dining-room was a sanctum of olive-green plush hangings and black horsehair-covered chairs; a crombobulous chiffonier and dining table bulged in the small room, and a plant in an Art-Nouveau pot stood on the windowsill. The windows were veiled in thick, yellowish lace curtains and the blinds were pulled decorously down half-way. It was always pitch-dark.

The parlour, where we had our lessons, was a small room filled with fascinating objects – a glass prism paper-weight, a musical box with a dancer and a hussar who revolved around the top, a plush photograph album, and a lovely box with a coloured picture of Cologne Cathedral let in on top, filled with beads and trinkets with which we were allowed to play. There were crochet-lace antimacassars on the chairs, fringes and bobbles everywhere, and some romantic but rather wishy-washy watercolours of Italy hanging on the walls. The mantelpiece was draped in dusty brown plush and had white alabaster figures of classical ladies under glass domes on either side of a black marble clock. The upright piano stood across one corner of the room with pleated silk let in behind its fretwork front, and on top stood a silver-point etching of Paderewski. I always used to think he was a woman with a moustache.

On special occasions Miss McBurney, her brother and her sister, Miss

Annie, would invite us to afternoon tea. Then the dining-room table was spread with a white cloth and laid with a flowered teaset, and three-tiered cakestands and silver filigree baskets piled with sugar cakes, biscuits, sandwiches and scones. We always had raspberry vinegar, a speciality of Miss Annie's, to drink with this feast.

Afterwards we had to play and sing our pieces, and Mr McBurney would give us 'The Yeoman's Wedding Day' and other stirring and vigorous songs. We used to get the giggles at this because he was a wizened mosquito of a man with a drooping moustache and a bobbling Adam's Apple, and his quavering tenor voice was ludicrously unsuited to the rendering of such rumbustious ballads.

Miss McBurney was a little stick of a woman with no chin, her scraggy neck and perfectly flat bosom enclosed in a boned net collar and 'front'. Her thin mousy hair was done up on top of her head with wisps escaping from the comb at the back. She always wore the same clothes year in, year out, perhaps being too poor to afford new ones. Her kind smile and understanding affection lighted many a dark day in my childhood and her capacity for arousing interest opened the doors of my mind to many a new musical delight.

We went once a week to Miss Jennie Brenan's Dancing Academy, held in a gaunt wooden hall off Toorak Road. Miss Brenan was a tall, graceful creature with a cloud of dark hair, lovely eyes, long legs like a race horse and elegant ankles. Her sister, Miss Eileen, was plump and fair and played the piano, and also taught 'Ballroom Dancing'.

Here I was first taught ballet dancing which I took up with such enthusiasm that I probably damaged my big toe joints permanently as a result. The girls were also taught 'Skirt Dancing', a sort of Isadora Duncan routine with scarves and (imaginary) swirling skirts, which I loved. ('Miss Brenan said she would ask me to dance the skirt dance all alone', I announced proudly.) Scottish and Irish reels and jigs were danced with the little boys, and these Edward liked best, although he hated the dancing class in general and was very naughty and insubordinate the whole time. We neither of us could bear ballroom dancing and Miss Brenan soon discovered that it didn't answer at all for us to partner one another as it invariably ended in scuffles and fisticuffs. In later life I have often met elderly Australians who attended Miss Brenan's dancing class at the same time and recollected with awe the unseemly behaviour of the Governor's children!

During the first few weeks after our arrival, Government House was crawling with journalists and reporters. My mother had them all eating out of her hand in no time and was not entirely displeased by the compliments paid to her, such as the following interview by the effusive and sickeningly coy lady-reporter from one of Melbourne's most prominent dailies:

'I am going to Italianise the drawing-room,' Lady Stanley remarked, laughing, and with exquisite tact brought her visitor into the charming home life of Government House.... 'We will talk out here,' she says, and leads the way to a cool shaded portico. 'No, we must have some cushions before settling down to talk.' There is no ringing for an attendant to bring the cushions. Lady Stanley just trips away and is back in a second, making a comfortable settee of the cane chaise-lounge [sic]. Then she snuggles in among the cushions, a winsome, appealing little figure in a pink cotton gown and a muslin sunbonnet, and begins to ask questions....

Lady Stanley has followed the arts rather than the excitements of the chase. Before her marriage she achieved some distinction as an amateur actress.... She is an accomplished musician and has something of the art of the professional in her landscape and figure painting.

Apparently unembarrassed by its gushing tone, my mother cut this article out and sent it to Marmee:

I am sending you some splendid specimens of newspaper interviews. The idea of 'Italianising' this monstrous drawing-room, I need hardly say, never entered my head. My big Venetian glass was being unpacked when the reporter arrived and I happened to mention it was Venetian and that I liked Italian things – you can see what good copy has been made of it!

In an attempt to make the interior of Stonnington 'habitable', my mother applied to the Government for a large sum of money. She also wished to have the drawing-room fireplace removed – 'it really makes me laugh to think of anyone putting up such a monstrous thing' – and for good measure threw in a request for a Bechstein grand piano, approaching the relevant minister in her most wheedling manner. Apparently he succumbed to her wiles as she got the piano and managed to get rid of most of the offending furniture, but the government officials adamantly refused to tear down the drawing-room chimneypiece although she said she had the best carpenter on her side, and there it remained until recently when modernisation of the heating arrangements at the College caused its removal.

She then decided to take the garden in hand and replace some of its worst 'suburban villa' features, such as bedding-out, with wide herbaceous borders and a profusion of roses, lilies, lavender and other sweet-smelling English flowers. But Dyer, the head gardener, was unco-operative, and for some time we gazed out on his scarlet geraniums.

A few weeks later she was discussing her official duties with Marmee:

> We are getting into the swing of life out here. It certainly is a busy one
> and makes me realise what the 'Home Life of our dear Sovereigns' must
> be – poor things. Day after day we have opening ceremonies and hospitals
> and institutions to inspect – I am kept at it even harder than Arthur. . . . I
> *cannot* understand how anyone gets to like it.
>   Mr Hood, of whom you remember we were feeling a little doubtful, is
> . . . a fussy old fellow . . . and gets beside himself with rage if anything goes
> wrong on State occasions. . . . Capt. Gale the other day didn't realise we had
> returned to the State Box at the Races and didn't take his hat off as we
> entered. Mr Hood dealt him a violent blow which nearly felled him to the
> ground. . . .
>   Did I tell you that at our last dinner party one of the Australian ladies
> arrived 'tipsy'!! I should have laughed if it hadn't made me so nervous. She
> kept sprawling over the table at dinner and saying 'Will your Excellency
> excushe a glove off?' I kept reassuring her she might take her gloves off tho'
> I had a horrid nervousness that she might begin to take off more! She was
> suppressed after dinner finally by Mr Hood.

Clearly, my mother was already beginning to find vice-regal life not
only tiring but tedious in the demands it made on her time. She took
to worrying about her health which was often her way of opting out
of disagreeable or unhappy moments, and pages in her letters are filled
with details of her symptoms and complaints of overwork. Characteristically, however, she managed to derive some amusement from the more
bizarre or comic episodes of her tour of duties.

> We have been to an exhausting function this afternoon tho' it had its repaying
> moments. It was a sort of exhibition and among other things there was a
> swimming performance given by a monstrous white slug of a girl* who per-
> formed ghastly feats under water such as eating a banana, which nearly made
> me sick – especially as the water was filthy and filled with horrible fishes and
> sham rocks and the sort of vermicelli that fishes eat. . . . She was also asked
> questions by a man to which she wrote most vulgar replies on a slate and
> she kept making great blandishments at Arthur who regarded her with a
> fixed and frosty stare which rather damped her ardour.
>   I received an alarming visit from the Archbishop's wife and twelve Church
> ladies the other day. Each one gave a short resumé of her particular branch
> of 'Church Work', and at intervals the Archbishopess swayed towards me
> and said in a threatening manner 'We look to *you*, Lady Stanley, to uphold
> the Sanctity of Marriage in this Land!' I murmured that I was sure she was
> far better able to do this than I – which is quite likely! . . .

* Annette Kellerman, who did her 'Turn' at the Aquarium annexed to the Exhibition Buildings.

Harry Lauder was touring Australia and his first night provided a welcome contrast to the Church 'smuggeries'. My mother longed to invite him to Government House, but Mr Hood was so scandalised at this suggestion that she had to withdraw in confusion. Ellen Terry was also about to visit Australia and my mother wondered whether Mr Hood would regard her in the same light as Harry Lauder, and object to her being asked to lunch. 'I should think Harry Lauder is probably much the most respectable of the two,' she remarked, 'but I shall show her some civility all the same.'

Naturally, my mother turned with relief towards any official duty which involved drama and the stage. There was a movement on foot to build a Shakespeare Repertory Theatre and she was put on the Executive Committee of this project. At first she was delighted but soon she was disillusioned by the total lack of talent and training. She advocated founding a Drama School before spending some £30,000 on a repertory theatre when there were no trained actors as yet. This proposal was unpopular and she regretfully concluded that little interest was taken in the arts or anything except racing.

At Easter my parents paid a visit to Bendigo, one of the best known of the Australian goldfields. The mines were still working during World War I but soon afterwards they cut out. My mother wrote:

> We travelled up in our splendid private car on the train and didn't get back till nearly midnight. . . . I came away with some specimens of gold which were presented to me but they are not worth turning into large sums of money, I fear. I want Arthur to take some shares in a new mine just opening there, but he will not be advised or influenced by my spirit of gambling – perhaps it would be coming rather near to another Marconi Scandal* if he was to dabble in gold mines.

The nuggets of gold brought back from Bendigo were much coveted by Edward and me. They used to stand on my mother's table in the boudoir – lumps of glistening white quartz veined with gold and exuding little gold nobbles here and there. We didn't believe that tale about the specimens being valueless and in the course of time the gold nobbles disappeared, surreptitiously picked off by us when the opportunity arose.

---

* In 1912 the Attorney-General Sir Rufus Isaacs, and the Chancellor of the Exchequer Lloyd George, bought shares of the American Marconi Company at a rate below that available to the public. Shortly after this transaction by Isaacs and Lloyd George the British Marconi Company received a contract to build a chain of radio stations throughout the Empire. In consequence, all Marconi shares boomed and soon rumours of corruption in high places began to spread. Lloyd George brought a libel action against a French newspaper and a Select House of Commons Committee was set up to investigate the scandal. As a result all charges of corruption were dropped.

At this time I began to see through my mother's extremely skilful act of presenting herself to the world in the image she had chosen. She rarely failed to have everyone at her feet in admiration – such was her sympathetic charm, and graceful manner when appearing in the rôle of the Governor's lady. I realise now how hard it was for her to submit to the discipline of official life, as she had had no training in any sort of job, and at first the only thing that carried her through was her ability to 'play act' successfully. I had never observed her outside the family circle and to my amazement she was not what she seemed to be.

But this constant effort of playing a part in public told on her nerves and in private she worked herself up into a state of emotional tension and irritation. She vented her feelings on me in particular, I suppose, because she sensed I wasn't taken in by her graciousness in public. I felt that she was not genuine and in my disillusionment I was bitterly unhappy and showed it.

The truth is that I had been thoroughly unsettled by the adventure of the voyage out, our changed circumstances and the impact of Australia on my impressionable mind. I instantly fell in love with the country, its sunlight and brilliant sky and the immense bush on the doorstep of the city. I longed passionately to be grown up and to ride away into the Outback, away from all constraint and dull childish ploys. What was the use of a short ride round the paddocks of Government House, supervised by Provis the groom? What was the use of the wretched old Zellie as a companion when what I wanted was the romantic figure of a Fairy Prince riding beside me under the Southern Cross? I told no one of these dreams but sometimes I would lure Zellie out for a walk after dark and gaze up at the shining stars and imagine I was free.

I was getting on worse and worse with Zellie and had developed a hatred for her. Even my father had come to be irritated and disgusted by her habits. I remember one day at lunch she squashed a large blowfly on the white tablecloth with her knife and he said to the footman, 'Remove the mess Mademoiselle has made!'. It was decided that Zellie would have to go.

Matters improved somewhat between my mother and myself as I gradually got used to our new lifestyle. She remarked that, for the moment, I was proving more amenable, but she doubted that this improvement would last. Zellie 'would not do' but she shirked the disagreeable task of giving her notice. 'I haven't mentioned it ... but I don't suppose she will be heart-broken ... the only annoying thing will be to have to pay her passage back...' On the other hand, she was delighted that Miss McBurney was a decided success with all of us. '[Adelaide] loves singing and is very quick at it ... Edward and Pamela stand hand-in-hand at the blackboard both trying so hard.'

Pamela, being the youngest, was her favourite at this time and she delighted in her odd little ways.

> She has taken to making speeches and goes away quite by herself with a sheet of paper which she holds well out in front of her, and talks away with varied voices and intonations, evidently representing more than one character ... but she will never allow anyone to be near enough to hear what she says ... the other day when on a visit to Federal Government House, she was found putting the Governor-General to bed on a sofa and covering him up with the hearth-rug. They were alone in one of the big rooms and I believe he was quite confused at being thus discovered – but it was a nice trait in him and made us forgive him his tiresome ways. Poor little man, he looks wretchedly ill and depressed. . . .

The State Governor had the use of a country house in the Macedon hills near Melbourne. It was known as Government Cottage but was large enough to accommodate a sizeable family and the usual retinue of servants. My parents went there on a visit of inspection just after Easter.

> It is very uninteresting really – great stretches of flat, burnt-up grasslands with the inevitable gum-trees the only feature of the landscape. Now and then the country gets a little more interesting and hilly and here and there one gets more vegetation, but it has no charm for me at all. I believe it is prettier in other parts [of Victoria] – Gippsland for instance, which is South-East of Melbourne, has some charming scenery.
>
> Macedon itself is quite pretty. It is high up in the hills, 3,000 feet above the sea, and there are good trees all round – fine firs, and some copper beeches and chestnuts – and a very pleasant garden full of flowers – roses, stocks, carnations and all the nice English things. The verbenas grow like weeds there.
>
> The house is just a little cottage with small accommodation and quite dull inside with pitch-pine walls varnished over, but nevertheless it has charm and I look forward to the time when we can go and cast off our official manners and smart clothes and lead a natural and lazy life – but it will not be till December which seems a mighty way off.

It took my mother some time not to seek English 'prettiness' in the Australian landscape but eventually she came to appreciate the spell of the country's strange and haggard beauty, the jewel-like quality of the light, the grandeur of the soaring eucalyptus forests and the immensity of the horizons. She had changed her opinion when later in the year she visited Black Spur in the ranges north of Melbourne.

We lunched at a little primitive sort of Inn kept by an old German* – (excellent purée of chestnut soup, delicious bread and cream, and a dessert of the most succulent pears you have ever tasted, and little grapes which tasted like passionfruit which were growing in profusion all over the house). After lunch we started for a walk and had our first sight of Primeval Forest. In places you had to bend quite low, the growth was so thick and you cannot imagine what the ferns are like – some of them grow like beautiful vases, in three tiers.... We saw many curious plants ... masses of Sassafras grow there and the bushmen make a kind of tea of it as they have great faith in it as a tonic.... What enhanced the attractiveness of the scenery to me was the absence of any human dwelling or any sign of human life. It was all silence and space and I felt quite moved by it.

During April, my mother found that she was pregnant, but nevertheless she had to fulfil her vice-regal engagements instead of lying on the sofa as she had done during her previous pregnancies. In spite of her condition, she made a three-day trip to install a Bush Nurse in the small township of Welshpool near the southern coast of the State, and wrote on her return:

... a most successful visit, tho' it was most strenuous. I have returned with a delightful kangaroo, presented to me by a villainous though attractive assassin of a man with whom I made great friends ... The children are of course enchanted with it and I am hoping that it will not rip their stomachs open in an excess of playfulness.†

The Bush Nursing Association was an organisation in which my mother took a great interest, not only because of their work but also because it gave her an opportunity of making trips into the country when she went to inspect their posts or install a new nurse.

Before the Flying Doctor brought the Outback within reach of medical care, the Bush Nurses provided a much needed link with civilisation in some of the more inaccessible districts of Australia. They were highly trained, resourceful women who pioneered the way for the present-day health service, and my mother was deeply impressed by their skill and fortitude.

---

* No doubt Lindt's Hermitage near Narbethong. Lindt was a distinguished traveller and an expert photographer. A treasure trove of his old photographic plates was found in his dark room at the Hermitage and they are now in the La Trobe Library. After Lindt died, The Hermitage carried on as a boarding house, and then was used as a Youth Hostel. It is now abandoned and in disrepair.
†The poor little joey sickened and died after a few weeks of captivity. We were not allowed to play with it.

In the middle of May the Denmans departed and the new Governor-General, Sir Ronald Munro-Ferguson, and his wife Lady Helen arrived in Melbourne.

Ten days after my father had made his official bow and my mother her duty call, a visiting French airman named Guillaux flew high above Melbourne in his 50 h.p. Blériot monoplane and descended in the grounds of Federal Government House, where the Governor-General and Lady Helen, together with my parents, were waiting to receive him. A large white sheet had been put out as a guide to land.

He was a tiny man, no taller than my mother, with a cool and imperturbable manner. 'He performed his feat of twice looping the loop with as much assurance as another man would take his dinner,' said the Melbourne *Argus*.

> The machine dipped and rose, withal so gracefully that the speed seemed very moderate. Descending to about 800 feet above the ground, Guillaux turned completely over and the first 'looping the loop' seen in Melbourne had been performed. ... The feat drew a long 'Oh!' from the onlookers below, and Guillaux waved from his perch high in the air. Again he came down, turned over, and made a perpendicular dive, apparently straight at the Government House party gathered on the lawn. So unexpected was the dash that those present scattered in various directions, but when about 30 feet from the ground Guillaud rose abruptly, flew up and up and, with a final wave, was soon out of sight.

We children were not invited to witness this thrilling display but my mother made the most of it in her description of the experience to us. I daresay that Guillaux may have felt a soupçon of malicious pleasure in making the solemn bigwigs skip in all directions in alarm, but my mother's account frightened me so much that I developed an unreasoning obsession against flying which has remained with me to this day.

My eighth birthday was on 30 May and my mother gave a children's party. I had a new dress made of white embroidered Swiss muslin with a blue silk sash. I knew none of the children but it didn't matter much as we had a cinema showing our arrival in Melbourne. This amused us greatly, although I was secretly disappointed that there were no shots of us children.

My mother defied protocol and Mr Hood by inviting some guests who were not on the official list, but she said she didn't care a 'dambolino for Society' and saw no reason to pander to the snobbery of the 'Toorak Push' as the smart set of Melbourne was called.

> The one bright spot this week was Adelaide's birthday party ... I went a great bust and had a cinematograph show for them after tea which was enjoyed

hugely. They put on some films of our arrival and of one or two of our functions and it was *most* ridiculous seeing ourselves as others see us. In one Arthur was making a speech and his movements and odd stiff gestures and his gabbling mouth with no sound coming out simply made us weak with laughter. . . . The children became quite hysterical except Pamela who asked in a hushed voice if 'Dar was saying his prayers?' Adelaide got 30 presents which quite staggered her. She behaved admirably all day, the only contretemps being that she set her head on fire in her excitement to blow out the candles on her cake. A large piece of hair was burnt, but that was all, tho' it gave her a fright and 'quite blanched her nerves' as she expressed it afterwards. . . .

Madame Melba the famous prima-donna was shortly due to arrive back in Australia. Her reputation in her homeland was a lurid one, chiefly owing to the poison-pen of John Norton, a journalist who owned a scurrilous magazine called *Truth*. My mother was looking forward to the prospect of meeting Melba in order to judge her character for herself and, also, on account of her interest in the theatre and music. To prepare herself for this future encounter with the *diva,* and perhaps with the idea of impressing her with her vocal talent, she decided to take lessons in operatic singing from a fat tenor named Walter Kirby who had once partnered Melba in her recitals in Australia and New Zealand. He was the butt of our contempt and derision. Edward and I used to imitate his singing by a series of gurks (which we called 'Baws') and we would mince about, rolling our eyes and copying his exaggerated gestures till we were reduced to fits of uncontrollable giggles; my mother, however, enjoyed her lessons although she, too, laughed at Walter Kirby.

The man who is teaching me is a preposterously ridiculous creature who illustrates his breathing exercises by violently rapid and appalling distensions of an uncannily mobile tum. As a matter-of-fact, he is a very good teacher and sings well himself, but is one of those fat 'Patapoufs' who can never make their way. I am beginning to study some airs and duets from *Roméo et Juliette,* and it will be rather fun doing some operatic music. Melba is arriving at the end of this month. . . .

Arthur had a large official dinner party last night in honour of the King's birthday. All the men from Federal Government House came and I went and dined with Lady Helen. She is in a terrible stew about their spending too much, I can see, and is bewildered and staggered by the cost of living out here. She had a man to hang their pictures, about 18 in all, and the bill came to £19. . . .

The children have taken a turn for the better after giving us weeks of hell. Arthur was called upon the other day to administer justice to Edward who licked his plate and squeezed a fistful of butter into Pamela's head. . . . He has spanked Edward once or twice . . . Adelaide as well.

And now household vexations added to her woes. The antiquated plumbing of Stonnington was collapsing, and there was 'Servant Trouble'.

> We are living the simple life this week as the plumbers who have been working in the house ever since we came here now say that we shall never be able to have hot water in the pipes unless they demolish the kitchen range and boiler and several other things. So we are dependent on one little gas stove that stinks with all its might in its protest against the heavy work put upon it.
>
> We have had rather a drama! Two nights ago we heard a tremendous noise of bumping and thumping in the back premises. Arthur went to investigate and found our little pearl of price – the chef – blind drunk! It was a dreadful shock as he is a very good cook and so obliging and kind to everyone, and very economical – in fact has all the virtues.

My mother never had any idea of what went on in 'the back premises', as she called them. Clay, the chef, had a violent temper and none of the other servants could abide him. He used to chase us with a carving knife if ever we went into the kitchen. He was eventually sacked and the woman under-cook took charge.

Mrs Drabble, or Drabbety (as we called her) was our ally and friend. She was from Derbyshire, a bony, gangling creature, with the sort of desperate and comic appearance of a character out of Edward Lear's *Book of Nonsense*. She would give us tit-bits from the dining-room table if we waited at the bottom of the back stairs and managed to evade the baleful eye of Martin, the butler.

On 23 June my father opened his first State Parliament. Only two slight mishaps marred the ceremony. The first was that my father inadvertently missed out a whole page of his Address and had to be tapped on the shoulder and shown his error by the ever-watchful Hood. The second was that my mother's knickers fell off at the Banquet just as the President of the Legislative Council was bringing up various people to be introduced.

> I stood for hours rooted to the spot [said she] and at last summoned up courage to take a bold leap out of them – which I did so successfully that people only had time to realise I was picking up *something* which I hastily whispered to the lady next to me was my petticoat – at which she was sufficiently horrified.

She stowed the knickers away in a large muff she was carrying – if it had been summer time her predicament would have been truly embarrassing!

July began badly with my mother having a miscarriage, no doubt brought on by unaccustomed hard work and her efforts to keep pace with her duties. Nanny was recruited to her bedside which was the signal for Edward and me to 'play up'. Zellie was flouted with impunity and poor little Jukes, my mother's maid, who was put in charge of the nursery, was persecuted by us both. After we had been put to bed, we invented a game to plague Jukie called 'Step on Nanny's Pedestal' which involved pirouetting on the marble top of the po-cupboard beside Nanny's bed and pushing one another off. Another game was to sit in the coal-scuttle and throw lumps of coal at each other which so distressed Jukie that she couldn't remember the right word and begged Edward to get out of the 'coal-bottle', which made us hysterical with laughter.

My mother lay in bed for four weeks with a lace cap on her head, speaking in a feeble whisper and drinking slops out of a tea-pot shaped feeding cup administered by two hospital nurses, while two doctors were in attendance.

After a month she was carried downstairs in a chair which unfortunately broke half-way down and she had a tumble which set her back another week or two.

Her letters to Marmee during this time are written in pencil, so weakly scrawled that they are nearly illegible. My mother was, in fact, progressing quite satisfactorily, according to her doctors, and Marmee does not seem to have been unduly alarmed. At the end of a letter full of family news and Ightham gossip she merely begs her 'darling little Mag' not to overdo it 'for the sake of Arthur and the children. Now put that in your little pipe and smoke it!'

While my mother had been languishing, my father had seized the opportunity of getting rid of Zellie. No doubt he was by now aware of the menacing international situation in Europe and found it expedient to remove a potential enemy alien from his staff as speedily as possible.

On 29 July my mother wrote to Venetia:

Arthur has sacked Zellie while I have been ill and outraged her because he did it directly after breakfast which she thought a most unfitting time. I am quite *sure* he chose that moment because he couldn't bear the way she eats her poached egg! ... [She] leaves in about three weeks time ... the ostensible reason for her going is that she has admitted that she cannot cope with Adelaide, who has suddenly taken a good phase and is no trouble for the moment. Sending her to school will be my last resource as I can bear her demonian ways better than I could put up with an Australian accent and little schoolgirl missish manners which I know she would be infected with. ... I shall have to try for a set of Daily Drudges. ...

Your last letters have been specially welcome and given me some pleasant distraction during the four weary weeks in bed. . . . How much I am looking forward to your coming out here darling, I cannot say. It makes me tremble for fear *something* may prevent it . . . We are wondering what the outcome of the Conference on the Irish Question with the King will be. It is getting so boring now and one longs for it to be settled.

Hitherto, beyond vague presentiments of 'something' unpleasant, my mother seems to have been completely oblivious of the dark war clouds now rapidly gathering. Neither can any inkling of approaching danger be found in the Australian Press. Towards the end of July *Table-Talk* published an issue of forty-two pages of sport, racing news, fashion and a social and theatrical gossip column. There were a few book reviews and some reports on local politics but no hint whatever of the looming catastrophe. Today, it is strange to read of the parochial small-talk and provincial daily round which filled the columns of the newspapers within a week of the outbreak of war. It is perhaps even more extraordinary that my mother, prone as she was to gloomy forebodings, should have been totally unaware of the deadly peril confronting the world, and should have dismissed the Irish Question as 'boring' and of no more significance than the buzzing of a mosquito.

5

War!

The bombshell of war burst on 4 August. My father was away on a
tour of inspection of the country districts, and my mother was staying
in Sydney at Yaralla,* with the Governor-General and Lady Helen. On
3 August she wrote a bewildered, heart-rending letter to Marmee:

> When this letter will reach you I don't know. It is almost incredible that
> since writing last week the whole world should be plunged into the anxieties
> and horrors of imminent war. Out here, we are so cut off from news except
> of the very barest, the strain of wondering and speculating what is happening
> and what is going to happen fills one with unbearable longing to be at home.
> Reports and rumours keep coming through the cable services, none of which
> are absolutely reliable, and we have not had the official cable from the Colonial
> Office yet that we are actually engaged in war. The terrible possibilities of
> what may happen one dare not think of....
>
> I am staying with the Gov. General so I get any news there is to be had
> as he is kept informed by Head-Quarters. The Australian Fleet is working
> against time, coaling and taking on ammunition and stores. They are off
> in a few hours, presumably to cruise about the Pacific, but of course nobody
> knows what their orders are....
>
> It is *agonising* not to know about one's own family, and it is very uncertain
> when letters can reach us. The P & O, the Orient and the Cape Lines have
> all stopped but we hope that perhaps our letters may get across America....
> I suppose that Sylvia, Blanche and Margaret will all be left husbandless. One
> can hardly realise the great and terrible reality of war is upon us at last and

* Yaralla, Concord, NSW, belonged to Dame Eedith Walker who leased it to the State Government.
It is now a convalescent hospital.

started by a wretched little country like Servia – though I suppose the ramifications go much deeper than the murder of the Arch-Duke and it has only acted as a spark. How will it end?? is the one thing that goes hammering on in one's head. Will it be short and sharp, or will it go on for months? I have little doubt, however, that by the time you get this the scales will have turned one way or the other.

Five days later she sent a letter off with a friend:

Brenda Blackwood is starting off this morning with Lord Freddie [Blackwood], Capt. Gale and a few others ... and I am sending this by her.... We are all doubting whether they will get home, or *when* they will, as the boats are all hung up at the various ports. They were going by America but those routes are cancelled and the P & O boat has only obtained special permission from home by cable to sail as she carries the mails. I only hope they won't have horrible adventures but I feel nervous about them, rather. We are living in a nightmare, and indeed everyone must be, but here it is so difficult to realise it all – and it is heart-rending to be so far away ... *Pray God* that we come out of it all right! I haven't seen my dear Tibaldi since war was declared. He made such a fine speech at the Town Hall and raised the people to 'the pitch of enthusiasm' ...

Indeed, according to the newspaper reports, my father's impassioned address roused his audience to frenzied cheering and many were in tears.

My mother hoped that, like the Blackwoods, she, too, would be able to get back to England in spite of the war, and she wrote to her mother-in-law:

My heart is simply *bursting* to be at home and when I went down to see the Blackwoods off and saw them slowly moving out of sight I don't think I ever had such a feeling of desolate misery in my life. I don't suppose for one moment that the war will be over as soon as people think ... and your visit, alas! alas! will be indefinitely postponed. I always had a horrid feeling of something preventing it – but how *little* did one dream what the cause would be....

The feeling out here is very patriotic. All the Labour people have declared their loyalty and are ready to send men and money if necessary. There is an idea of the Japanese fleet coming to protect us – which will be rather an irony after all the outcry here about White Man Australia ...

On 5 August *Table Talk* made its first mention of the War. The topic rated two paragraphs and the theme was 'What can the Kaiser do to *Us?*' But the following week there was speculation that if the war went on long enough there would be no continental buyers coming to Australia for the wool sales. There was a page of pictures of soldiers in uniform and debs draped archly in Australian flags entitled 'The Call to Arms – Australia Prepares!' and a short paragraph wondering whether it was 'seemly or in good taste to pursue the social round now the Empire is at war'. But on balance, frivolity gained the upper hand.

The war made a deep impression upon me. My first thought was to write to the Kaiser and point out to him how wicked it was to fight and kill people and I was sure he would be bound to see reason and call the whole thing off. But I also remember praying that it would go on long enough for me to take part in it and feeling appalled by secret guilt at such thoughts. Pamela and I were given Red Cross uniforms and we played at being V.A.Ds – 'Hot Cross Nurses', Pamela called them, but I laughed her to scorn and was heard saying 'Oh Pamela you *are*! You mean Red Hot Nurses!'

I took up knitting with enthusiasm but had to learn the British way as Zellie had taught me the German method which was considered unpatriotic. I started on a muffler of thick khaki wool striped with pale blue, and graduated to socks, but never managed to 'turn the heel' without help till the end of the war.

The ball-room at Federal Government House was turned into a Red Cross Depôt where 'comforts' were collected and dispatched to the troops. Here we took our offerings and sometimes I was allowed to help in the sorting and tying up which gave me a gratifying sense of taking part in the war.

Recruiting was going on with enthusiasm and men were pouring in to the centres in Melbourne from the country and being trained in the huge Army camp at Broadmeadows. My mother and father went out to inspect them, taking Edward with them. I believed that Edward really might get called up to the Colours and go to the war and I was beside myself with envy and rage. 'Edward is off his head with excitement at being taken [to the Camp]', my mother wrote on 19 August.

Poor little boy – he really thought he was going to the war with Captain Gale and Nannie found that he had packed a cardboard box with his Busby that Furney [Muzzie's maid] made him, and a mug for his drink and some old biscuits and bits of bread. There were bitter tears when he found he was to be left behind. . . .

Poor old Zellie sailed yesterday. We had the utmost difficulty in preventing her resolutely sitting here and refusing to budge. We sent her round by the Cape as there is no chance of ships being delayed that way. . . . All the servants were beginning to be restive and wouldn't have stood her much longer.

The fact was that they all thought she was a spy and McKenzie, our housekeeper, told dark stories of how she found Zellie creeping about in the hall in the middle of the night outside my father's study.

I was, of course, exultant at Zellie's defeat and departure. Edward and I were certain that she had been plotting to kill us and bring the Germans to the gates of Government House and take us all prisoners of war. I considered it a major contribution to the war effort that my insubordination had caused the enemy within our gates to have been unmasked and deported out of the country.

Lady Helen Munro-Ferguson had inaugurated the Victorian branch of the Red Cross under her patronage. This was to be a source of veiled friction between Lady Helen and my mother who, although she handled the matter with her usual artful diplomacy, made it increasingly clear in her letters that she thought Lady Helen was poaching on the preserves of the State Governor's Lady. Although my parents saw a great deal of the 'Mun-Fugs', as she called the Governor-General and Lady Helen, relations remained cordial between them, but it was borne in on my mother daily how difficult the position of the State Governors might become if they insisted on their 'rights' – and even more so in the case of their wives. Of course, it was partly my mother's fault that Lady Helen over-rode her authority; she genuinely was bored with public life and always put her family first. Lady Helen, on the other hand, had no children and was an ambitious woman bent on achieving personal power. She brooked no rivals and, taking advantage of my mother's pliant nature, she unblushingly usurped her prerogatives.

A blood row soon blew up between Lady Helen and the Lady Mayoress of Melbourne who had organised her own 'Comforts Fund'. She was furious with Lady Helen for setting up a rival society. My mother intervened and did her tactful best to defuse the situation. After a 'shattering interview' with the Lady Mayoress she eventually persuaded her to join with the Victorian Red Cross Committee and work with her. 'But', she added, 'there is a very natural feeling that they [the Victorians] want their things to go to their own men and it is impossible to make them understand that if things are ear-marked for special regiments or individuals the chances are that they will never get them.'

No sooner had war been declared than Mr Hood left for England to offer his services to the War Office. They were rejected and he returned in the New Year to resume his duties as Private Secretary. Captain Wilson, the second ADC, sailed with Mr Hood to join up, so my father was left with no staff. 'However,' said my mother, 'a very kind, capable man – the Chief Inspector of Lunatic Asylums – has come forward to offer me his services as Secretary for the Red Cross. I daresay he will be able to treat me for Anaemia of the Cerebellum at the same time . . .'

My mother's letters home now were filled almost exclusively with war news and speculation as to the outcome. There was dismay at the growing casualty lists, and the mails were erratic.

> The scarcity of reliable news keeps one in a state of anxious restlessness that no amount of occupation can dispel . . . I can't help feeling a dread fear of the German troops proving more efficient [than the Allies] when one thinks of all their thorough-going preparation and their scientific cleverness and how all their genius has been expended on the training and equipment of their troops. I try not to be pessimistic but it is difficult to keep the dread out of one's heart . . .
>
> I have a horrible feeling of 'skrim-shanking', being out of it all here . . . tho' perhaps there are some things that are more difficult to bear with a cheerful spirit at this distance than at home on the spot . . . I would have given Arthur without a murmur with the rest – you will hardly believe it but I (cowardly *me*) am sorry that Arthur cannot go and have his whack at the enemy – I know he minds, too. At other times I can't help feeling a pang of thankfulness, but all the same, I can't bear to think that I am not called upon to bear as full a share of sacrifice as others.

One wonders what Marmee's reaction was to this somewhat egocentric view and apparent eagerness on my mother's part to offer up her husband on the altar of her patriotism. In her defence it may be said that at this time people grew quite hysterical with 'war-fever' and many women resorted to the cruel action of publicly giving any man of military age 'the white feather' as a badge of their cowardice, no matter what the reason might have been for him not wearing uniform. No one had, as yet, the faintest idea of the full horror of modern warfare, and the unutterable suffering and grief it was to bring on the world.

Sir Oliver Lodge had been visiting Australia with other members of the British Association and he dined at Government House before his return to England. He regaled my mother with accounts of his psychic experiences. 'I could only wonder', she commented, 'that a man with so great a mind and intelligence should be influenced by what appeared to me to be the most flimsy and ludicrous fraud . . . If he had not been so perfectly serious I should have felt inclined to be flippant.'

Mr Hood now being safely out of the way, Ellen Terry was invited to lunch. 'She looks old, old, *old*,' said my mother, 'but tho' she is such a wreck there is something eternally young about her . . . It is most pathetic to see her stranded out here, and, of course, since the war all her engagements have been cancelled ...'

I can remember Ellen Terry sitting in the garden with my mother, her face all covered with powder and rouge, and dressed in flowing garments. Pamela recited a poem to her and Ellen Terry praised her accent. My mother was much gratified.

Madame Melba often came to the house. She and my mother became great friends, although I don't think my father cared for her too much. He was bored by her aggressive prima-donna airs. We loved her as she was kind to us and gave us wonderful grown-up presents. To this day I have a smooth white Copenhagen china cat, curled up asleep, which she gave me.

She was a stocky woman of middle height, rather coarse-complexioned, with an imposing singer's bust. With men she was inclined to be tomboyishly flirtatious, and she had an arch habit of pirouetting round on her heel when she wished to be specially fascinating and which I believe used to embarrass my father. She had a jolly sense of humour and an impulsive and basically generous nature. I think she was more often loyal to her friends than they were to her. Her speaking voice as I remember it was rather strident and gave no hint of the pure and flute-like quality of her singing.

Sometimes she came and practised her roles in the drawing-room at Government House, and we were allowed to listen. I made up my mind to become an opera singer when I was grown up – an ambition I eventually achieved. I was spellbound by the effortless ease of her singing – she just opened her mouth and the miraculous sounds came pouring out. But what we liked best was when she lost her temper with Mr Carruthers, the accompanist. She would scream abuse at the wretched, squirming creature in between roulades and trills, and sometimes even box his ears. She used to walk about the room gesticulating and acting as she sang, and we would gleefully watch the accompanist flinch as she approached the piano during these peregrinations.

The first opera I ever heard was *Rigoletto*, with Madame Melba as Gilda. I sat entranced, watching her sing and act, especially when it came to the bits we had heard her rehearse. The highlight of the performance for me was at the end of the last act, when Sparafucile comes in with Gilda's body in a sack after he has just murdered her. Madame Melba was too heavy for him to hump on his back, so he dragged her bumping in the sack right across the middle of the stage and deposited her at Rigoletto's feet. I thought this was the best part of the whole opera, but I wondered whether she boxed Sparafucile's ears afterwards, as she had done the accompanist's!

Summer came with scorching north winds and Edward and I went riding before breakfast with Provis, the groom. Sometimes we rode away across the paddocks as far as Caulfield race course where we would gallop madly round the track, regardless of Provis's imprecations. 'Adelaide ... of course, loves managing the pony', said my mother, 'but at one time she got very reluctant to go out ... she said Provis was so very dull and that she preferred to be among people who talked more interestingly!'

Zellie had been replaced as governess by a 'dear little Frenchwoman' whom my mother 'hit upon' and she came for an hour each day. Our only other lessons were our music classes with Miss McBurney three times a week and I am afraid we ran riot over her.

Pamela parried any attempt to scold her or make her learn her lessons by sudden accesses of affection which effectively disarmed my mother's authority. 'She is such a darling ... I have never seen a child with such an irresistible faculty of attracting everyone to her,' she said. Edward, of course, was 'terrifically military' and the garden resounded with his shouts of drill commands and savage yells as he killed thousands of Germans.

Edward and I were always looking for German spies – a game which led to much trouble. We used to hold long conclaves in a little dark cupboard known as the 'Bullycrub Room', a derogatory name Daddy Yates invented for Edward and me and which took our fancy. We hatched many a brave deed here, such as getting up in the middle of the night to dig trenches in the garden to entrap any marauding Germans and making booby-traps for old Dyer. But these Commando tactics were always discovered and punished. We were sorry that the grown-ups (especially my father, being the Governor and therefore particularly vulnerable) should be so blindly ignorant of the dangers by which they were encompassed, unaware of our power to save them from destruction.

Another of our haunts was a stone courtyard at the back of the laundry where the soap-suds came rushing out of the drain pipes into a cess-pit when Minnie the laundress was washing. We called this unsavoury hideout 'Dryniby-Plice' and hatched further mischief within its gloomy walls.

On one occasion we got up on the roof and set the flag at half-mast. It was part of a deep-laid scheme to confuse the enemy, but it only resulted in a flood of telephone calls to the harassed Private Secretary's office demanding to know what catastrophe had occurred, and a spanking for us.

Another time Edward dressed up in my father's plumed cocked hat and I in some of my mother's motoring veils and a pair of her shoes and we paraded up and down the road outside the entrance to Government House. Daddy Yates and Arnetty, the fat police constable on guard, chased us and didn't we just cop it! Afterwards we heard that it had been reported by passers-by that a Japanese Admiral and his wife had been calling on the Governor – which was a consolation to us and helped us to bear up against universal disapproval.

There was also trouble in the schoolroom. The new French governess was small, black-eyed and elegantly turned out. She would come tripping into the schoolroom on very high heels and wafting scent about her. She proved perfectly useless as a teacher and disciplinarian. Edward and I used to play 'shipwrecks' during her lessons. This consisted of turning the table upside down, rocking it furiously to and fro and rowing with the fire-irons. Madame Dugdale would twitter at us: '*Voyons, mes enfants! Soyez donc sages. Remettez-vous gentiment à table.*' To which we paid no attention whatever. She soon gave up and was succeeded by an Italian lady called Signorina Dapostoli, who taught us French and Italian. It was thought unpatriotic to learn German, so Zellie's efforts in that direction were thankfully forgotten. But the Signorina's stamina was no better than Mme Dugdale's. She would burst into tears at the least provocation and she, too, was routed. I don't remember being taught any English subjects at this time but I have a hazy recollection of learning long division in French!

The Christmas holidays were approaching and it had been found impossible to engage a governess to continue our education at Macedon. Therefore my mother decided to give us lessons herself while we were in the country. My father undertook to teach us arithmetic, it seems, but I don't remember him giving us any lessons. Probably he was too busy with his duties, and in any case, I think he was temperamentally unsuited to teaching children. Already Edward and I spoke and read French as easily as English and were beginning to write it pretty well. 'Beloved Pamela doesn't pine after education,' said my mother. 'She is so full of imagination and so happy in her own little world that I shall leave her undisturbed for the present.'

Mount Macedon is the highest peak of a range of hills some forty miles north-west of Melbourne. Government Cottage lay on its southern slope – a gabled, two-storeyed, mock-Tudor house backed by the steep forested hill-side and surrounded on its other three sides by a large and romantic garden shaded by beautiful English trees. Here German spies and Red Hot Nurses were forgotten and we lived another life of fantasy.

We were met at Woodend Railway Station by the creaky old buggy driven by 'Spickly-Eye', thus nicknamed by us because of his squinting, twinkling eyes. He could do magic and was in league with Nanny who was, in reality, a kind of benevolent witch, unpredictable in her ways. Her witch-name was 'Didabon-Leftleg-Mosquito-Stanley' and at night she would fly out of the window and join 'Spickly-Eye' on the top of Mount Macedon to weave spells.

'Spickly-Eye' had been a gold digger in his youth and used to tell us exciting stories of his adventures. He could remember Ned Kelly well, he said, and called him 'a bonzer bloke'. We used to play at being bush-rangers and we cut ourselves armour out of cardboard and bailed up the servants and the gardeners. There was an old lady who lived some-where near Macedon who also remembered Ned Kelly. Her name was Jones and when we were taken to visit her she would tell us how he came to her mother's house when she was a child and she would sit on his knee while he gave her boiled lollies out of his pocket.*

Edward and I had an enthralling game at this time called 'Morning-light Woods' in which two characters named 'Tappy' (Edward) and 'Meddle' (me) had many strange adventures, including gold-digging and exploring. We lived in the branches of a deodar tree in the garden. Some-times Pamela was allowed to join in as a character named 'The Paltry Fiend', but she generally got things wrong, calling herself 'Poultry Fiend', and there were cries of 'Oh Pamela you *are!*'

Edward still expected to be called up in the near future and would write 'man-to-man' notes to the various Commanders giving them re-ports on the war situation. He wrote the following epistle to Lord Kitche-ner, after the sinking of the German battleship *Emden* by the Australian battleship H.M.A.S. *Sydney* off the Cocos Islands, enjoining my mother in a covering letter to forward it immediately.

'To Feald-Marshal Lord Kichener, Minister of War, England.
Dear Lord K.
    We have Red Cross Pracktise this morning. Battle Pracktese today. We are fixing up raccings [racings] for the Soldiers. I herd a note that the *Emeden* has been wrecked at Coacas.'

And here follows a series of Morse Code signs, unfortunately undecipher-able by me!

We seldom played with other children as my mother didn't like us mixing with the offspring of the 'Push', many of whom had country

* Could this have been the daughter of Mrs Catherine Jones, the luckless landlady of the Glenrowan Hotel?

houses at Macedon. Jean Manasseh, the sloe-eyed, black-haired daughter of the Syrian who kept the general store, sometimes joined in our games and there was a cocky-farmer's family who lived on a property about a day's ride away. Later on, Lord and Lady Freddie Blackwood's children, Basil and Veronica, who were living with their uncle and aunt, the Munro-Fergusons, were allowed to come and stay. Basil and Edward were inseparable but Veronica was a funny elf of a child, younger than any of us, who didn't fit in, and was described by my mother as being 'A *not* very attractive child. Very *farouche* and very plain but, poor little thing, she has become touchingly fond of Arthur and at a party they went to the other day was found wandering about wanting to "show her present to Dar!" Lady Helen is not fond of her and spoils the boy.'

O'Brien, the head gardener, was as charming as old Dyer in Melbourne was cranky. He lived at the lodge by the front gates and we used to go to tea with Mrs O'Brien and her daughter Dulcie who had long brown corkscrew curls and velvet eyes. Their tame sulphur-crested cockatoo used to shriek at us and bob up and down on his perch, eyeing us wickedly sideways. Once he bit me when I poked my finger into his cage. Although I howled loud and long with fright and pain, I got little sympathy as I had been forbidden by Nanny to do this. Mrs O'Brien let us do exactly as we pleased, which Nanny disapproved of.

My mother gave us lessons in her sitting-room and very enjoyable they were compared with the ineffectual, dreary hours spent in the schoolroom with incompetent governesses. She had a remarkable gift for teaching small children and it is to her I owe my subsequent interest in the subjects she taught me, particularly history, and English and French literature. Every evening my father read aloud to us. We would be given pencils and paper to draw on to prevent us fidgeting, which neither he nor my mother could bear.

I remember being terrified of Blind Pew and Billy Bones in *Treasure Island* and refusing hysterically to go upstairs to bed for fear they would be lying in wait for me on the landing. *Huckleberry Finn* was a great favourite and so was *Ivanhoe*. The *Jungle Books* rather bored me, I regret to say, and Dickens I positively disliked (apart from *David Copperfield* and *The Tale of Two Cities*) as the stories were not full enough of adventure and the people in them were all low-class. What a little snob I was!

Sometimes my father read Shakespeare to us. We soon discovered when he was expurgating the text as he would mutter 'Ah – er – um, um' and afterwards Edward and I would rush to the book and read the 'rude' bits. 'Arthur is not at all dexterous at seeing what is coming,' my mother told Marmee, 'and dashes along through the unsuitabilities in fine style. I see the wretches A. and E. bursting at each other when they have an inkling that he is careering over dangerous ground.'

As the year drew to its close the war news got grimmer and more alarming. My mother wrote to Marmee at the beginning of November.

> I have just come back from a special performance of a Show of War Pictures given for the Gov. Gen. and ourselves. My heart turned sick at the war pictures taken at Termonde and Louvain – the utter desolation and destruction and brutality of it all! Oh my little Marmee, what a nightmare it all is! One seems to have lost one's bearings altogether and the world seems to have gone mad! . . .

Every time my mother made an expedition into the country she felt that at last she had visited the real 'outback'. In fact, although the places she visited were primitive enough in those days, she never penetrated beyond the settled districts of Victoria and New South Wales. She never rode a horse, camped in the open, or was without a chauffeur-driven motor car and attendant ADC. Just before Christmas she and my father went by train on a visit to a little bush township in Gippsland called Gunyah, where my mother was to install another Bush Nursing post. They arrived in the evening at the town of Morwell, some ninety miles east of Melbourne, now the centre of the Yallourn coal and gas industry.

> We were received at the station by the Shire President who started 'God Save' in a high falsetto which was joined in by an invisible crowd as the station was pitch-dark. It was a lovely summer's night but there was no moon so it was difficult to realise who one was being introduced to – for directly 'God Save' was ended, names of the Councillors and prominent people of the district were called out and a blind fumbling to shake the right people by the hand ensued.
>
> At last we were allowed to leave the station and were escorted to a wooden hall close to where a concert was given and which lasted till nearly 12 o'clock . . . Arthur and I were beginning to get *sodden* with the atmosphere, the aching incandescent gas lights, and length of the programme, and we exchanged glances of infinite relief when once more (for the third time that evening) the National Anthem was given out – but the end was not yet! To our horror a feast had been prepared in an adjoining room and we had to sit down to a solid meal and what is written down in the Programme at these functions as 'Tea or Lunch and *Informal Chat*' which I think is delightful. At last we got back to our car and slept on board it in Morwell station. This is a junction and the noise throughout the night effectually abandoned all hope of

sleep – especially as a train of starving stock was drawn up alongside of us and made the night hideous with their 'Informal Chat'.

Early next morning we arrived at a place called Boolarra where the inhabitants and school children were drawn up on the platform to receive us. The children are always more rivetted by my clothes and eye glasses* than by poor Tibaldi's speeches – but the adults *revel* in his addresses, and he is wonderful in the freshness and novelty he manages to put into each one. Sometimes he makes 7 or 8 in the day.

After this ceremony the vice-regal party drove in a fleet of cars to Gunyah. On the way they stopped at a hamlet consisting of about a dozen small houses, a school and about fifteen children. 'They had never seen a motor before and were wildly excited at the sight of six of them,' said my mother.

The last part of the road to Gunyah was terrifically bad and we were shot up and down and from side to side till we were sore. At last we arrived and found a little crowd awaiting us outside the wooden room that serves for a church and meetings and dancing and everything ... The Bush Nurses received us and looked incongruous figures in that wild setting in the neat spic-and-spanness of their uniforms.

After lunch we were taken to see one of the largest gum trees chopped down. It is wonderful to see the skill with which the bushmen do it. They drive stakes in at intervals up which they climb, and they stand on one of them and chop, sometimes at a height of 70 feet as the trunk is much thinner and easier to cut at that height ... Some of the bushmen had worked all the previous day to cut the jungle so as to make it possible for me to go through it. We went down, down into the loveliest dark, cool greenness, out of the glare of the upper world. It felt as though one's ordinary life and existence had stopped altogether. I couldn't believe that any of you really existed or that the war was going on or that anything mattered. The intense silence ... gave me a hypnotised feeling that I was dreaming ... It was a new sensation to be standing on spongy, thick wet moss in this dry country – but it was a very disagreeable experience to find that it was active with leeches ... This rather spoilt my pleasure for the rest of the time, as I kept on thinking I felt them up my legs, and I lost all modesty in investigating ... Then we took to our motors to get back to the station at Boolarra where we again slept. We had to have many handshakings and goodbyes. The Shire President made a speech of course, in which he said 'Your Excellencies have behaved yourselves splendid all through the day and we haven't found you a bit of trouble to entertain – for you seemed to enjoy everything downright 'earty' – which was gratifying as well as amusing.

* My mother was very short-sighted but did not like wearing spectacles. Instead she had a tortoiseshell 'lorgnette' suspended by a gold chain round her neck which she would raise and peer through when she wanted to see anything clearly.

At last we regained our saloon at Morwell Junction and there found telegrams announcing the capture of the three German cruisers* ... all fatigue dispersed at the glorious news – Arthur waving the telegram and shouting 'Good news!' and the people came flocking back to hear. A. jumped up on a car and read the cables and everyone went mad for joy ... It was a splendid finish to the day and I don't believe the people will ever forget it!

About Christmas time it became very hot, even up at Macedon, and I was allowed to sleep out on the verandah. There were all sorts of strange night sounds – the bullfrogs croaking in the dam, a distant dog barking, the call of the mopoke, like some hoarse, nocturnal cuckoo down by the creek, and the scampering of the possums on the galvanised-iron roof. I used to put a piece of fruit out to lure the possums down and if I lay perfectly still, sometimes one would scramble down the verandah post and take the fruit, not a yard from my nose, making a little churring noise.

On Christmas Day, as is usual in Australia in spite of the heat, we had turkey and plum-pudding, mince-pies and Christmas cake. There was a Christmas Tree and more beautiful presents than we had ever had before. I was given a Brownie No. 3 camera (which I kept till I married) and was presented by my father with a fat fox terrier puppy which I christened 'Dingo-Pawp' 'whose conduct in the house' my mother remarked 'was of the loosest description'. It made messes everywhere, to Pamela's concern. 'I'm glad', she announced gravely, 'that I don't have to "sit down" as often as Pawp.'

My mother's efforts at teaching us were proving too much for her and she took to setting us little tasks before breakfast which, of course, we never did. 'I fear they will forget their French,' she sighed when she asked us to repeat our homework. When it came to Pamela's turn, she got very red and said: 'I *dint* learn the Alphrebet but Edward *did* teach me to kill bluebottles with a pencil.' On the other hand, we took enthusiastically to singing Italian folk songs. Edward loved learning the words and was much quicker at remembering them than I was, although I considered that my accent was more authentic. I used to sing 'Funiculi-Funiculà' as a duet with my mother who believed I showed promise as a singer. 'Her voice is so pure and clear and she sings with *intense* feeling and understanding.' Poor Pamela was so overcome by the quality of my *pianissimo* that she would dissolve into tears – 'so that we can only

---

* Battle of the Falkland Islands December 1914 in which five German Battleships were eventually sunk or captured. 'Thus came to an end the German Cruiser warfare in the outer seas.' W. S. Churchill, *World Crisis 1911–1918*.

sing very robust music when she is there,' my mother concluded with
amusement.

In the New Year Madame Melba came to stay at Macedon. She would
sing to my mother's accompaniment and that crystal voice echoed through
the house as we stood still and listened. I did my best to imitate her
as I thought I shouldn't wait till I was as old as Madame Melba before
being able to sing as well; and away I'd go, singing *Rigoletto*, *Bohème*,
and *Figaro*, so as not to waste time in starting my career as a *prima
donna*.

6

'Borning Babies'

Early in January 1915, Mr Hood returned from England, more sour than ever. Captain Gale was wounded and lost an arm. I was sorry about this as we all liked Captain Gale, but I was glad he was invalided out of the army, and no longer in danger of being killed. The casualty lists mounted from day to day and many women were beginning to wear deep mourning and long black veils. I, too, wished to be veiled in black so I persuaded Nanny to let me buy some yards of black 'book muslin' at Mr Manasseh's store, and I would dress up secretly and play at being a 'war widow'. Nobody was allowed to join in this private fancy and when we got back to Melbourne I used to shut myself in the Bullycrub Room and lock the door against Edward and Pamela, although this was strictly forbidden.

I began to worry that by the time I was grown up there would be no more men left to marry and I tried in a devious way to find out what my chances were from Nanny and my mother.

> Adelaide is in a very fussed state of mind just now about her future marrying arrangements. She asked, 'Will all the people who will want to choose me sit in a ring with me in the middle dressed as a Bride? And if I don't like the Bridegroom who chooses me can I get away from him?' Nanny then tries to what she calls 'diffuse' her mind and suggests the most blatantly impossible things such as 'if we hurry now, Adelaide, we may be in time to see a snake have his supper'.

My mother replied to my questions with a sharp rejoinder that if I continued to be so naughty nobody would want to marry me. This added

73

to my anxieties as I feared that on top of the man shortage, I would never find a bridegroom willing to overlook my deplorable character and blemished right arm. Since coming to Australia we had inevitably been more in the public eye than in England, and not only the children at the dancing class but many grown-ups had commented on my birth-mark. 'What have you done to your arm – have you burnt it?' was the usual question, which always caused me the most miserable embarrass-ment.

Nanny was going on a holiday after Christmas and one of the nurses who had looked after my mother during her miscarriage was engaged as a temporary. Almost as soon as Nurse Tebbutt arrived there was a drama. One day, during the rest hour after lunch, Pamela started scream-ing in a panic saying that she had swallowed a button. I joined in the screams, shrieking that Pamela was dying, and my mother came running, alarmed at the pandemonium, but she later recounted the incident to Marmee in her usual humorous manner.

> Pamela is none the worse, so I suppose the button has pursued the normal course. Edward, with characteristic calm, lay and listened to the commotion without moving and when it was all over he called Grace to ask her what had caused it. When he heard what it was he remarked 'Then she will die shortly'.
>
> Adelaide was very unhappy about her dog Dingo a few days ago as he was ill, and the question naturally arose as to whether, if he died, he would go to heaven. Edward said in a matter-of-fact tone 'Well, I expect God would whack him harder than Drabbety does if he eats *his* boots'. Adelaide became hysterical with laughter but Pamela was shocked and said reproachfully 'Oh Edward, you *know* God doesn't wear boots – only slippers or galoshes'!

I now began to be haunted by a recurring nightmare, brought on by hearing rumours of an island near the docks in Melbourne which was used as a leper colony, mostly for Chinese seamen, it was said.* There were stories that the poor creatures could be seen from passing ships, mopping and mowing on the landing-stage, their faces snow-white and eaten horribly away and waving their fingerless hands. In my dream I would see the bedroom door opening slowly, slowly, and round it would come a gruesome faceless, armless leper swathed in white bandages. Silently this figure would approach my bed as I lay rigid with terror,

---

* Coode Island, by the junction of the Maribyrnong and Yarra rivers, and adjacent to the Victoria Docks. A quarantine station was set up in 1900 for the isolation of plague and other 'exotic' diseases. It was only once used when 15 cases of plague were admitted in 1905. No cases of leprosy were ever recorded. It was kept on a care and maintenance basis and eventually shut down when all cases of notifiable diseases were transferred to the Fairfield Hospital.

and would stretch out a glistening stump and *touch* me. So vivid was this dream that I could not believe it was an hallucination. The recollection of the lady who bought the fur coat at Selfridges still froze me with horror and I kept examining my body in an agony of apprehension for the fatal patch of leprous skin to appear.

In my childhood there were still a number of Chinese left in Australia, the remnants of the Chinese invasion of the gold-fields in the previous century. These old men ran laundries or had market gardens in the purlieus of Melbourne. They could be seen, often dressed in Chinese style, hawking their produce in little covered pony-carts round the streets. One such old mummy of a Chinaman called Ho-Lee used to drive his cart about near Stonnington, and whenever I saw him I would run away shrieking hysterically, for fear he should come near enough to transmit the dreaded leprosy to me.

The Governor-General and Lady Helen came to stay with us at Macedon and a garden-party was given in their honour. I enjoyed myself very much and was encouraged to show off by the Governor-General, provoking my mother's comment that 'anything in the form of a party upsets Adelaide's equilibrium'. She then observed tolerantly to Marmee:

... but really [the children] provided a certain amount of amusement as the Gov. Gen. and Lady H. were the only other peep-show ... Their visit went off very well. I always find her easy and pleasant but he is a tedious man ... She really runs the Governor-Generalship and practically writes all his speeches and advises him on political matters. He is always coming in with most secret cables and documents to ask her advice about them, which makes the punctilious Hood jump and jig with indignation, and with much spluttering he alludes to it as 'PPPetticoat Government'. He has the greatest contempt, I think, for all women and not least, myself. By some ill-fated chance I have invariably mislaid the letters I have put by for him to answer and he waits, silent and glaring, while I feverishly hunt among the dreadful mush of letters and accumulation of papers till I can bear it no longer and say that I will send them to him later. Sometimes I put off doing so and he comes in about 10 minutes and the hunt and excuses begin all over again. I do *hate* the life – or at least the part of it that involves order and methodical ways.

Lady Madden, the Victorian Chief Justice's wife, now returned to Australia after a year in England. My mother had been warned that she was unco-operative in official matters, especially with State Governors and their wives. Therefore, she used all her wiles to charm the dragon and in this aim she was successful at first. Later on, Lady Madden was to cross swords not only with my parents but with Lady Helen herself, although my mother eventually managed to repair the damage and she

remained on good terms with this redoubtable lady during the term of
my father's office.

One of my greatest treats was to be taken shopping for clothes with
my mother, and I longed to be old enough to wear 'tea gowns' and
negligées and other glamorous confections which my mother had made
by her dressmaker. On these shopping expeditions we always had an ADC
in attendance and the shop-walkers would bow deferentially as my
mother placed orders for lengths of ninon, crêpe-de-chine, charmeuse and
voile. She never carried money. For the winter Pamela and I were dressed
in serge or else corduroy velveteen with brown woollen stockings and
button boots. Underneath we wore combinations, and 'liberty bodices' to
which were attached cotton drawers with woollen bloomers on top. We
were all made to wear a horrible garment called a 'Jaeger body-belt',
a porridge-grey knitted thing round our middles which was supposed
to ward off dangerous un-English diseases such as cholera and dysen-
tery.

My mother was appalled at the cost of things in Australia. 'The price
of things makes one reel!' she wrote to Marmee. 'I wanted some blue
serge to make [the children] everyday schoolroom dresses, and the only
prices were 16/6 and 12/6 a yard! I would have none of it and at last
found some corduroy velveteen at 6/11 with which they will be clothed
for the winter.'

Well do I remember those hideous dresses! They were sludge-coloured
and decorated with purple piping and ribbon and cut-steel buttons. They
went on winter after winter, even when we had out-grown them.

> I had one or two very ordinary hats sent up on appro'. Things that would
> have cost 2 guins or perhaps 3 at home, but marked at 8½ to 13½ guins
> here. I have now ferreted out a place where one can get shapes made, and
> Jukes and I have made 2 quite imposing hats, one of which was described
> in the papers as 'Lady Stanley in one of the expensively simple hats etc' ...
> The duty is terrific on clothes – for instance, if you have a gown sent out
> valued at £14, you have to pay £7 duty ... It is an expensive country to
> live in but in some ways it has its advantages. For instance, the people who
> are not well off enough to pay high prices all learn to make their own clothes,
> and to cook and do their housework. Nearly every girl in Australia can cook
> and run a house and dressmake ...

She wrote at the same time to her sister Poppety asking her for hair
ribbons for herself – 'They are the only means of keeping my head
together' – as it was impossible to get a thing in the Melbourne shops.
'Nattier-blue' is her favourite colour. 'It seems frivolous', she says, 'to

be asking for such things as ribbons these days, but one must go clothed.'

In April the postage went up to 2d and the mails to and from England were becoming more and more uncertain, often being sent via the United States by what was known as 'the 'Frisco boat'. Nevertheless, people were still able to travel backwards and forwards from Australia to England without too much difficulty. My mother was ever hopeful of getting home to her beloved Marmee, to whom she wrote:

> I am as wise as the serpent, and never let fall a hint or suspicion that we may not stay our full term. I see no uncertain signs that Tibaldi will not stay beyond three years – *but do not breathe this*. I have a hope of running home for a holiday next Winter – I mean *your* winter – but things are too uncertain now to make any definite plans.

The war was not the only reason for the uncertainty of my mother's plans. She was pregnant again and expecting the baby sometime in October. She may have been wishfully thinking of a trip to England after the baby was born but what she would have done about it and the rest of her children in her absence, not to speak of her duties to my father as the Governor's wife, does not seem to have entered into her calculations. She did not mention her pregnancy in her letters till the very last moment.

Although my mother was not conspicuously successful in coping with either Edward or me, it did not prevent her from frequently criticising Australian children for being badly brought-up to Marmee:

> Adelaide had her birthday party on Saturday. I can hardly believe she is nine years old. She is much smaller than most Australian children, who are *immense* in size, but she is much more advanced in mind. It is lamentable what a lack of manners and good bringing-up there is in children out here and I keep our children, as far as I can without appearing stand-offish, from associating much with others. There is a horrible tendency to encourage children in vulgar ideas of flirting with each other and saying a certain boy is quite in love with a certain little girl. This goes on at the dancing class, I have discovered – so it is now a rule that in the intervals A. E. and P. are to sit sternly by Nannie and not be allowed to go off and have nonsense talked to them by idiot mothers and others. I am glad to say they are untouched by any of this vulgarity, but Adelaide is quite conscious of the admiration her dancing causes among some of the little boys and she said naively the other day 'I always dance my best when Trevor Clarke is watching me.' The said Trevor Clarke is a stout, apple-cheeked youth of 13 who, Nannie says, never takes his eyes off Adelaide the whole lesson.

Had she but known it, my thoughts were much more 'vulgar' than she supposed. Certainly I was quite glad to impress Trevor Clarke and show off before the whole class, but I turned up my nose at him for being far too young. My sights were fixed on handsome young officers or romantic wounded 'heroes' lately returned from the Dardanelles, who now replaced the fairy princes of not so long ago.

Just at this time, however, I was making shift with the Governor-General who was a delightful beau, and very fond of all of us children, having none of his own. '[He] has sent her a charming little pendant,' said my mother, 'for which she thanked him in a letter saying "I shall wear it till my death" – to which he replied by a declaration that he will love her till death, which pleased her mightily.'

I have kept this token of love – a little heart-shaped locket – and his *billet-doux* to this day. 'I shall keep your charming letter and love you till I die. If I had not been such a stiff-jointed old man I should have been at your birthday party – may you have many of them and may I often come to them as your affectionate G.G.'

The Japanese Fleet visited Australia in June and the Admiral paid a visit to Government House. They were invited to play tennis and evidently thought the point of the game was to hit the ball as hard and as far as they could. Edward and I were stationed outside the wire-netting boundary of the court to retrieve the balls sent whizzing into the surrounding flower beds and shrubbery. The Japs gambolled about all over the court, chattering and squeaking to each other and bowing low at intervals to my father and mother. Edward and I were doubled up with suppressed giggles at their antics. My mother thought them 'little dears' and their efforts to make conversation in English she found irresistably comic.

> The two I hit upon to talk to spoke quite enough English for us to chipper away merrily. The poor little Admiral, however, to whom Arthur had to talk, could hardly speak a word and their conversation was like a sort of game of Puff-and-Dart – the Admiral making breathless attempts to utter something comprehensible and Tibaldi darting in shots at what he guessed he was driving at.

The war news from Europe continued to be shatteringly bad. Gassed soldiers began to swell the already huge casualty lists and fill the base hospitals. The Australians suffered terrible losses in the fiasco of the Dardanelles which dragged on till the final débâcle at the end of the year. 'As far as one can make out, no headway seems to be made at all,' groaned my mother.

It is so amusing (and sometimes irritating) to see how Australians do not realise that there are *any* troops fighting but their own. I am quite certain that if we ever accomplish getting through the Dardanelles it will be firmly believed and handed down in Australian history that it was the brave Australian troops and nobody else that did it!

War charities proliferated and as my mother got more involved in money-raising activities, so her difficulties with Lady Helen waxed more acute.

Lady Helen was an unpopular figure with many of the leading figures in Melbourne as well as with the other State Governors and their wives owing to her frigid and supercilious manner and ambition for power. The Press was particularly unfriendly towards her.

My mother felt a certain sly satisfaction at the way some of the newspapers ridiculed Lady Helen, contrasting her Excellency's dowdy appearance with the much admired chic of the State Governor's lady, although she deplored the vulgar and familiar tone of the articles. At some fund-raising function the *Bulletin* reported:

Lady Stanley is out like some beautifully dressed little blood-hound in quest of funds for our wounded soldiers ... [She] wore the duckiest little bonnet with her hair bunched out behind in a chignon. The bonnet had blue strings tied under her dear little chin, and her dress was shadowy blue chiffon and pink carnations.

Lady Helen wore blue satin which dripped away from a lot of cool transparency in the upper parts. She had three regal feathers in a tiny hat and, for a change, no red – not so much as a touch of red flannelette. We dress experts were as surprised as though she had appeared in a ruching of hessian overlaid with schnapper-coloured sugee.

Naturally, such disadvantageous comparisons cannot have pleased Lady Helen nor helped to mitigate her jealousy of my mother. This antagonism simmered underneath the surface for some time, in spite of my mother's tactful withdrawal from any avoidable confrontation, but it eventually boiled over into what she described as 'nearly, if not quite, a pull-hair fight' between them.

It had been suggested by various prominent Melbourne businessmen that a special Victorian Red Cross Appeal by the State Governor's wife would bring in a big response. Accordingly, my mother told Lady Helen of this scheme before launching it, but she was snubbed and told it was not necessary. Finally, Lady Helen was cajoled into agreeing on the condition that all money collected by my mother's appeal should be paid over to the Central Council of the Australian Red Cross over which Lady Helen presided, and allocated by her. 'We told her exactly what we meant to do and how ... and showed her all our communications to the Press,' said my mother. 'Well! The report of our first meeting in the papers, for some unknown reason, caused her to explode into the most howling rage ... and we received the *most* horrible letter from her which came as a bolt from the blue ... she was furious at the papers putting in as a heading "Lady Stanley's Appeal" ... [and] charged us both with disloyalty to her ... We were really *astounded.*' My father wrote a 'snorter' to Lady Helen refuting her allegations in cold but civil terms, and my mother expressed her astonishment and distress. Eventually the row was patched up 'but it gives me a terrible sense of insecurity' my mother concluded 'for her outburst revealed an attitude of suspicion and jealousy that must have been brewing for some time ... We have heard since that she has not liked to hear people saying that if only *I* made an appeal ... the money would come in ... She cannot realise the feeling that exists in the States for their *own* Governor and wife ... The results, so far, are splendid. In ten days I have been sent £53,000 ...'

Melba, too, was assisting my mother with her fund raising. She gave a 'Special Patriotic Concert in Aid of Lady Stanley's Red Cross Fund', assisted by her friend John Lemmoné, the flautist. A few days before the concert she stayed at Government House and in between rehearsals in the drawing-room she sang for us to dance to. 'I wish you could have seen Adelaide and Edward in their little fancy dresses', my mother said to Marmee, 'practising their minuet with Melba singing the air from *Don Giovanni* for them at the top of her voice'.

My mother had agreed to let us go to a children's Fancy Dress Ball in aid of the Victorian Red Cross organised by a committee of rich Melbourne ladies. She was reluctant to spend much money on our get-up, so after some deliberation and counting of the cost, it was decided that it would be nice and cheap to send us dressed as classical Greek figures. Pamela and I were draped in white ninon as 'Peace' and 'Plenty' respectively, and Edward was accoutred as 'War' - a suitably topical allegory, my mother thought, representing hope for the future and patriotic ardour for the present just and mighty cause.

We were wildly excited about the Ball, especially as it was to take place in the evening between seven and ten o'clock. I was worried, however, that the Greek draperies I had to wear as 'Plenty' would reveal my birthmark, and every night I prayed for a miracle that it would disappear before the night. I also feared that I might die before the great event. But when the time came I was too excited to mind very much about these matters. We created quite a furore at the ball, my mother said. 'I couldn't help a thrill of maternal pride running through me when I saw what a beautiful group they made, and heard the exclamations of admiration among the crowds who didn't know they belonged to me...' My mother took Pamela home early, leaving Nanny to chaperone Edward and me.

'A. led her a real dance [she continued] and managed to dodge her till nearly 11 o'clock. She was determined to squeeze every drop out of such an unlooked-for chance. The crush and crowd was terrific but apparently she took care of herself and danced and amused herself with a circle of admiring 'genkas' [gentlemen] till poor old Nannie at last ran her to earth. I don't think she will ever number among the 'Blots' at dances. Nannie, commenting on Adelaide's rather precocious behaviour at the ball, summed up with this delightful phrase 'She is not a flirtorious or flaunty child, but where there's a lot of gentlemen you can never tell where it will end'.

Alas, in spite of my success with the 'genkas' the evening ended in tears for me. At the close of the ball prizes were presented. Edward and Pamela both got First Prizes – I got nothing. I cried bitterly with mortification, and to console me my mother gave me a book by Mrs Ewing called *The Ruby Ring* which I still have. But I cannot re-read it without recalling the pangs of rejection I suffered on that occasion.

After the ball I fell ill with a bad cold and was put in the best spare room so as not to infect the others. This room had a tremendous carved chimney-piece inlaid with plate-glass panels. This whole edifice was set in a recessed, arched alcove with a plaster goddess-head forming the keystone of the arch. This I admired very much, as well as the stained-glass windows depicting exotic birds and fishes. There were carved door lintels and elaborate brass door handles and finger plates. A beautiful parquet floor completed the sumptuousness of the apartment. I lay back in an ornate brass double bedstead awaiting 'Romance', much to my mother's amusement.

'Adelaide is revelling at being kept in bed. I went in and found her dressed as a Bride with a tulle veil and decked about with flowers and scraps of finery – with each of the four brass bedposts also tied up in tulle as 'the four Bridesmaids watching over the Bride'. I couldn't help asking where the Bridegroom was, to which she replied, 'Oh, he will come to bed later and unveil me and then the Bridesmaids will retire'.

Meanwhile, at home there was a shaking of heads going on in London and County drawing-rooms over Venetia Stanley's unconventional behaviour. Her liaison with Mr Asquith, the Prime Minister, was an open secret and everybody was gossiping about it. Muzzie was deeply distressed by the situation but she had no influence over Venetia – indeed, she was rather afraid of her daughter. She was subjected to scenes from Margot Asquith who railed at her for not putting a stop to Venetia's affair with her husband. Muzzie wrote anxiously to my mother for advice and my mother replied:

> I feel distressed that you should have had such an upsetting episode with Margot and it is difficult to know how to take such violent outbursts which I fear *are* caused by jealousy of the P.M. and also largely by wounded vanity and humiliation at not being able to retain the position and influence she once had. She will *never* know any peace of mind, I am sure, until . . . perhaps, our V. is married.
>
> I don't think it is possible for you to do anything as regards V.'s friendship for the P.M., even if it causes you anxiety. The only thing which could do any good would be that V. should realise that her friendship for the P.M. was the source of annoyance and unhappiness to Margot – when I believe her generosity and large nature would induce her to avoid giving Margot pain and distress by being less intimate and seeing less of the P.M. – though it would no doubt be very difficult now to break off what is, after all, a very delightful friendship . . . As for the dear old P.M. you will never get him to see things from your point of view, I am certain. And there is always rather a fear of putting oneself in the wrong by any suggestions (however delicately thrown out) that you don't quite approve of his friendship for her . . . I always feel that V. is very safe, which is the main thing, as it is her cleverness and intellectual side that is involved much more than her affections, though no doubt she is very fond of the P.M. – But you don't think there are any signs of her being too fond of him, do you?

My mother was probably right in feeling that Venetia was 'safe' in that she was not in love with Asquith but enjoyed her power over him. The family seems to have continued to turn a blind eye on the affair, until Venetia suddenly announced her engagement to Edwin Montagu, a prominent Liberal politician and a Jew.* My grandfather was outraged and refused to have anything to do with either of them; Muzzie was bewildered and dismayed and wrote long, incoherent letters to my parents – 'all contradicting each other gloriously', my mother told Marmee. 'I think her main feeling is one rather of relief that V. is settled at least and that she will not be harassed by her vagaries any more.'

Venetia confided to her sister Sylvia Henley that her relationship with the Prime Minister was becoming too difficult to control. Therefore, she

---

* Parliamentary Private Secretary to Rt. Hon. H. H. Asquith, 1906–1908. Under Secretary of State for India 1910–15. Financial Secretary to Treasury 1915–16. Minister of Munitions 1916. Secretary of State for India 1917–22. Died November 1924.

had decided to extricate herself from the entanglement by accepting Edwin Montagu's proposal and making what she called a *mariage de raison.*

Asquith seems to have been very much in love with Venetia and was deeply distressed at losing her. The blow was struck at one of the darkest moments of his career. Churchill, Head of the Admiralty, and Lord Fisher, First Sea Lord,were at loggerheads; Kitchener was being rigid and intransigent; there was a grave shortage of munitions; and the Russian retreat was jeopardising the whole of the Allies' war strategy.

Sylvia went to Downing Street after Venetia had told her of her intention. She found Asquith quite bowled over by his misfortunes. 'Jacky Fisher has gone off, we don't know where!' he exlaimed. 'We shall have to have a coalition – and what's this thing I hear about Venetia marrying the Assyrian?'*

The whole family censured Venetia for her ruthlessness, and for 'turning Jewish for the sake of £8,000 a year!' Her cold-blooded acceptance of 'the Assyrian' (as they termed Edwin Montagu) for his money, shocked them all, including my mother, who shuddered at the alliance.

> He is such a repugging creature, and how she brought herself to accept him I cannot think. I had a very unhappy letter from the P.M. . . . I cannot help feeling very sorry and regretting that she had acted unworthily – as according to my ideas she has. I don't mind her having rejected Christianity as she never professed to be a Christian, but I do regret her having assumed the profession of a faith that she equally doesn't believe in, and this for the sake of money. *That* is the ugly thing. Arthur is also very sorry over it, but has not taken the line that ferocious old P.-in-law has, who will neither see her at present (tho' he says he will by-and-by), nor give her a present or any money for a trousseau. Venetia's future has always been rather a problem, and if she is going to be really happy and settled one must shut one's eyes and swallow the ugliness of her marriage – (and the bridegroom!).

When the next batch of English periodicals arrived I, as usual, read them through surreptitiously. They were full of Venetia's engagement and photographs. The story was so obviously scandalous, even to my eyes, that I had to confess to reading the paper in order to find out more about it.

> Adelaide has got hold of the *Tatler*, unknown to me [said my mother] and read the heading 'Bride changes her Faith as well as her Name'. She immediately wanted to known whether she (Venetia) had given up being a Christian. I found it a little difficult to explain, as the thought evidently shocked her

---

*Conversation between author and Mrs Henley 22 November 1964.

very much, but I sheltered myself by saying that sometimes people adopted their husband's or wife's religion when they married. She said 'Well I think it is *horrible* and very hard on poor Christ.' Edward said 'I don't suppose He will mind much!' with comfortable philosophy, but Adelaide cannot get over it.

I remember feeling more intrigued than shocked, and at the same time critical of my aunt's performance in the role of 'The Bride'.

My mother's birthday fell on 27 August and was an important day in our lives because we all received, as well as gave, presents.

We got up very early and picked large quantities of the best flowers in the garden, including violets, freesias and roses. Old Dyer grumbled but couldn't say anything as it was for her ladyship's use. I had procured a large box which I filled with all our presents and buried them under the flowers. We presented this trophy to my mother in her bed before breakfast. In the afternoon Miss McBurney came to Government House and we gave a concert. We sang 'Great Tom is Cast', 'London's Burning' and 'A Boat, a Boat unto the Ferry' in rounds, and a German student round in Latin. I played a showy piano-piece by Scarlatti successfully, without faults. After tea, which we had chosen ourselves – bread-and-butter cut very thin and spread with hundreds-and-thousands, and birth-day cake – we played a game called 'Hidies'. This consisted of numerous presents labelled with our names which my mother hid about in the garden and which we had to hunt for. I liked 'Hidies' even better than Christmas Stockings.

Ever since the departure of Captain Gale and Captain Wilson to join up in the war, we had had no regular ADCs, which made old Hoodiwinks even more cantankerous than ever. He snarled and glared if he saw any of us children in his path and we took care to keep out of his way. Now, at last, a permanent ADC was on his way out from England, invalided home from France with a wounded leg. We looked forward to his arrival with speculative interest. His name was Captain Nigel Conant. He was tall and good-looking, with languishing blue eyes and an interesting limp. We put him through endurance tests such as making him apple-pie beds, dowsing him with water from the big fire hoses in the garden, and calling him derogatory names. We finally settled on the nickname of Guinea-pig, or G.P. (as he objected, reasonably enough, to being called 'Pig' by us) and which was shortened eventually into 'Geeps'. But such was the charm of his character and so genuine his ca-pacity for affection that although we sometimes laughed at him, he won us over and he became a much loved friend, as well as, to me, a discreet

1 Adelaide and Edward at Penrhos, 1911

2 January 1914. 'Mammie stood at the carriage window' – illustration from 'The Book' of the voyage to Australia

3 'Zellie getting fussed' – another illustration from 'The Book'

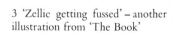

4 Arrival at Stonnington, State Government House, 1914. *Back row l. to r.* Captain of the Escort, Sir Arthur Stanley, the Hon. Victor Hood, Captain Gale ADC, Captain Wilson ADC. *Front row l. to r.* Edward, Pamela, Lady Stanley, Adelaide

5 Cartoon from Melbourne *Punch* of the Governor and Lady Stanley's arrival in Melbourne

6 Government Cottage, Macedon, in 1914

7 Sir Arthur Stanley in 1914

8 Lady Stanley in 1914

9

We had our photographs taken before we left for the ball. Edward is dressed as 'War', Pamela as 'Peace', and Adelaide as 'Plenty'

10

11

12 The Red Cross Committee in 1917, with Lady Helen Munro-Ferguson *(front left)* and Lady Stanley *(right)*

13 Mrs Henry Evans Gordon (Marmee) in 1915

14 Stonnington as it looked during Sir Arthur Stanley's term as Governor

15 *Left:* Lady Stanley with Edward, Adelaide, Victoria, Lyulph and Pamela in 1922 after their return to England.

16 *Below:* Maurice and Adelaide Lubbock after their marriage in 1926. *Back row l. to r.* Miss Sheila Grant Duff, Miss Kitty Henley, Miss Rosalind Henley, the Hon. Nancy Mitford, the Bridegroom, the Best Man, Mr Reginald Wendell, the Hon. Pamela Stanley, the Lady Mary Thynne. *Second row.* Miss Moyra Lubbock, the Hon. Victoria Stanley, the Bride. *Front.* Miss Susan Pelham, Master John Stanley.

and sympathetic confidant. Geeps would take Edward and me riding or
on exploring expeditions into the bush. He knew much about wild animals and birds and we started a collection of birds' eggs under his guidance. He showed us how to blow the eggs, and put them in cotton wool
nests in the special cabinet we were given, each egg properly labelled.
Our prize exhibit was an Indian bulbul's egg. This bird is now a pest
in many parts of Australia but in those days it was a rarity, at any rate
in a Melbourne garden, which is where we found the egg.

But my most absorbing pastime was writing 'The Book'. My mother
was diverted by my confidence in myself as an author. 'She is firmly decided about the headings of the chapters ... and without a pause starts
off in a very Arthur-like way. She has no sense of shame in recounting
her naughtinesses on the boat where she really made our life a burden,
but rightly says that if other children read her book they will like those
parts the best. She evidently knows her public.'

At the end of September my mother wrote a long and rather guilty
letter to Marmee announcing she was shortly expecting the baby. Her
excuse for not having revealed this news was that she was afraid Marmee
would think she was overdoing it and she had decided that she would
cause no additional anxiety 'in these trembling times'. 'Nobody at home
knew anything about it,' she said, but directly her pregnancy became
obvious she made it an excuse for giving up all public work. 'It is a
funny thing,' she remarked, 'that ever since it started, Pamela has talked
of nothing else and prays for a new baby every night.'

I had noticed the change in my mother's figure with some concern
and regret and I thought it must be a symptom of rapidly advancing
old age, but tactfully for once, I forbore to remark upon this to her.

My brother Lyulph was born on 22 October 1915. He was a strapping
baby, rosy and fat, with tawny-gold hair. From the day of his birth
my mother adored him and regarded him as the most remarkable, fascinating and intelligent of all her children. The morning after he was born
my father introduced us to him lying in my mother's arms and we were
solemnly elated at this addition to our number. 'The children are enchanted at having a Baby,' my mother wrote to Marmee.

> I do wish you could have seen their wonder and surprise when Arthur brought
> them in without telling me anything. They came over to my bedside and
> I told them I had a present for them and then revealed the Baby. Adelaide
> gave a piercing scream followed by a torrent of questions and gasps of ecstasy;
> while Edward clamoured to know *how* we could be certain it was ours, and
> Pamela ... folded her hands in an attitude of prayer over him and said sol-
> emnly 'Now my Prayer has been granted.' When I asked her if she was

surprised at having a brother she said 'Oh no. I was expecting a Baby but not before Christmas as I know it takes a long while for prayers to come true'. Adelaide, as you may imagine, was very sceptical of all Nannie's theories of 'the dear Baby coming from Heaven'. She asked me straight out whether Arthur and I hadn't expected it beforehand as he had turned out of his room and the Nurse turned in. Also she said 'I notice that babies always seem to be born in their mothers' room, and that the mother is always in bed.' So I told her that mothers do know when a baby is coming and that the excitement and joy makes them so tired that they have to stay quiet. She now says that whenever she feels tired she will expect to have a baby. How difficult it is to know how much to tell them!

Edward and I at this time were very interested in our anatomy and bodily functions, and perceiving that any mention of such matters was taboo, we were all the more intrigued by the subject. Nanny must have been eavesdropping on our private jokes and reported us to my mother, who said to Marmee:

> They are rather inclined to make little naughty jokes about Behinds with each other, so I put a stop to it and tried to show them that Behinds are not really ugly or 'rude', and of course was met at once by Adelaide saying 'Then why mayn't we show them?' I answered because it wasn't the custom to which she replied 'I see. It's like the custom of Eastern Ladies who veil their faces – we veil our behinds and it is the custom that makes you feel there is something rude under the veil.'

We went to Macedon for the Christmas holidays, travelling by train in the vice-regal official car. There was a crowd to see us off and to catch a glimpse of the new baby, dubbed 'The Young Governor' by the Press with their usual toe-twisting facetiousness. We processed along the platform headed by two policemen, followed by my mother escorted by the Station-Master; then Nanny and the Baby, then Geeps, Miss Barker, the new governess, and Grace, our nursery maid, coping with us three children, and the rear was brought up by Jukie and two footmen. It was an important moment and I enjoyed it to the full!

During the holidays Geeps took Edward out shooting and taught him semaphoring, but just then I was preoccupied with a new game called 'Borning Babies'. I was still mystified about the actual genesis of babies but, leaving this problem aside for the moment, I undressed my doll and put her in the fireplace before going to bed and dragged her out next morning as an act of birth.

Pamela would have liked to join in the game but I felt she was too young.

Pamela wishes to witness the birth of Adelaide's doll in the fireplace [said my mother]. Adelaide would not let her come anywhere near and I was appealed to. She declared that the child would die if gazed at by anyone but the mother, and that children of Pamela's age are never allowed to be present on such occasions. Poor little Pamela gave in and said resignedly 'Well Mammie, *you* help me to have Bulgie (the most cherished bald black doll) under the wash-stand and that will be much nicer than seeing Louise (Adelaide's doll) born in the fireplace for you can make it all just as it was the night the baby was born! ...

The new guv. is a nice creature and a success, so far. She is a little puzzled by Adelaide when she gives such unexpected replies as the following to a simple question. Miss Barker: 'Where are you going Adelaide dee-ur?' Adelaide: 'To the Tavern to drink!' Miss Barker: 'Adder-layde!!!' but A. has vanished with her demon mocking laugh before poor Miss Barker can get any further. However, they like her and she rides with them and is very simple and fond of out-of-door life and is companionable for A. who already is the better for being out of the nursery.

The baby was christened the week before Christmas. He was named Lyulph Henry Victor Owen, his godfathers being the Governor-General and Sir John Madden, and his godmother Sylvia Henley. My mother asked Lady Helen to stand proxy for Sylvia,

... and it is as well I did as the Governor-General (a Presbyterian) was quite vague and drawled out the responses at odd moments, or else after her, like a child repeating a lesson. Sir John Madden (a Roman Catholic) didn't attempt them at all. We were rather afraid that the parson might raise objections to performing the ceremony with such a pair of mongrel godfathers, but he didn't ... Sir John Madden is an old darling. He came without Lady M. to my great relief – not that I dislike her, but Mr. Hood has a chronic feud with her and *loathes* her, and she returns his feeling with quite as much intensity. Lady Helen, too, is very hostile towards her ... She is extraordinarily nice to me and has never shown the rude and disagreeable side I was led to expect ...

There was a heat wave over Christmas and New Year and my father invented a wonderful game to cool himself and Geeps after playing tennis. Along the gravelled path surrounding the house there were several out-size stand-pipes with huge fire-hoses attached and lying coiled up on the ground, ready for use in the case of a bushfire threatening the house. My father and Geeps changed into pyjamas and unrolling two of the hoses, turned the water upon each other on the terraced lawn below. Edward and I were allowed to join in and standing about fifteen paces apart we bombarded one another. The force of the jet was considerable

and whoever got knocked down first lost the battle. We became quite
wild with excitement and tore off all our clothes and rushed about naked.
My mother watched us from the nursery window.

> I was amused at the poor guv. who was also watching from another window
> and who kept going off like a minute gun; 'Adder-layde, what are you think-
> ing of? You can't go without your combinations! Put them on *at once*. Ayd-
> wawd, keep your trousers on, naughty boy!' As you can imagine, they were
> both quite deaf to any pleading or commands to be decent . . . Adelaide with
> her hair flying and pursued by Arthur in his pyjamas turning the full force
> of the hose on her – and Edward by Capt. Conant. Poor darling, he couldn't
> keep his balance against the force of it and kept tumbling about in the drollest
> way. You can't think how pretty it looked in the lovely summer evening
> light, with a back-ground of delphinium-coloured mountains and beautiful
> trees with the setting sun streaming on their trunks, and then the tangle
> of a great herbaceous border. Dear Nannie, who entered into the spirit of
> it all, kept saying, 'Well, it's really *Arcadia* come to life.'

We were not allowed to play this game unless the temperature was
over 90 degrees in the shade at tea-time, and then only for a short while,
on account of wasting water. Once my father thought it would be a
good idea to cool the house down by directing the hose on to the
galvanised-iron roof. But he made a bad shot and instead discharged a
jet of water into my mother's bedroom through the window when she
was changing for dinner. She didn't find the game so delightful after this
mishap.

7

Trouble and Strife

The year 1916 opened with sombre prospects on all the Allied Fronts. The ill-fated attack on the Dardanelles had been abandoned and the troops were evacuated from Gallipoli by the first week in January. On New Year's Day the Russians renewed their offensive against Southern Galicia in Poland which, although initially successful, eventually ran into difficulties owing to lack of ammunition. On 10 January, Austria defeated Montenegro and the Balkans were in turmoil. On the Western Front the armies were deadlocked in the Flanders mud awaiting the approaching holocaust. And in England the Zeppelins stepped up their raids and dropped their bombs on the civilian population with impunity. My mother, naturally, worked herself into a state of frenzied anxiety over the danger to Marmee from the Zeppelin raids, but Marmee replied calmly, 'Don't *fidget* about the Zeppelins ... they really do not come our way and certainly would not waste bombs on Ightham'.

The Germans had planned to wage unrestricted warfare against enemy and neutral shipping from the beginning of April but for the time-being they were deterred by the fear of the United States entering the war against them.* Nevertheless, the U-boat menace was increasingly effective and Allied merchant shipping suffered serious losses. My mother felt despondent that her line of escape was becoming so tenuous but she still talked of 'dashing home next year' – no doubt to keep up her spirits.

She turned for consolation to the baby Lyulph and her letters are full of adoring accounts of his beauty and precocity.

*Opinion in America had been outraged by the sinking of the *Lusitania* the previous May in which many Americans had lost their lives.

Pamela had lately taken a craze for music. She would waylay all and sundry to act as audience for her concert performances. We had been taught the Russian National Anthem by a Russian lady at the Melbourne University who was a friend of Miss McBurney's. This was Pamela's star turn and she would roll out the sonorous Russian syllables with solemn fervour.

The Governor-General, who was staying with us at Macedon, was button-holed by her and given a recital which, in addition to the Russian National Anthem, included the *Marseillaise* sung in French, an Italian song and, as a finale, a piano piece entitled 'The Huntsman and the Cuckoo'. 'I could sing you a German song too', said Pamela, 'but I don't think you would like me to sing you anything so nasty.' The Governor-General told my mother that he was much struck by this performance!

Edward got into terrible trouble before the holidays were over. Mr Hood caught him stealing Geeps's cartridges and cutting them open for the gunpowder ('for some nefarious purpose' said my mother) and was given a thrashing. 'He is very brave', she continued, 'and is just like a dog that races round with delirious delight when his hiding is over, but it *kills* me when I know he is going in for it.'

Fortunately, neither Hoodiwinks nor my mother discovered Edward's purpose for stealing the cartridges. He was going to put the gunpowder on Hoodiwinks' fire to blow him up! I was not involved in this iniquity but I also was causing my usual trouble and strife amongst the grown-ups.

> She is ... so impulsive and lightning-quick, and so imperious and ferocious with anyone who happens to irritate her, and yet so darling and devoted to those she is fond of. I heard hideous squawks issuing from her room tonight, and found her lying stark naked on her bed and refusing to be decently covered by Miss Barker, putting herself into the wildest attitudes and declaring that she had a feeling that something magic and wonderful was going to happen and that the spell would be broken if she were not allowed to be naked. And then she added 'Besides, I like to shock the flies'.

Poor Miss Barker's reign lasted barely three months. She was found wanting and given the sack by my mother before we returned to Melbourne after the holidays.

> I have now got (in despair!) a funny old identity called Miss Birch who has been eight years with the Strickland children* in N.S.W. She told me that she couldn't stick Sir Gerald a moment longer – the last straw being that

*The daughters of Sir Gerald Strickland, Governor of New South Wales, and Lady Edeline, his wife.

she had given the children a copy of Lamb's *Tales from Shakespeare* which so shocked him and Lady Edeline that they said she was not fit to be trusted to supervise their reading!

In April, Miss Florence Birch arrived, and I saw at once that she would not do. My mother, on the other hand, was delighted with her 'because she is like a person giving a life-like sketch of a little old guvvy who has been in the family for years' and her theatrical sense was tickled.

Miss Birch was a stumpy, fussy old woman with frowsy grey hair, pince-nez and a fat red face. She had a quacking nasal voice and she never stopped talking. After she had been in the house for a few days my father asked her if we were behaving tolerably well, but I answered before she could get a word in, 'I daresay we shall have some disagreements', which silenced her.

With the arrival of Miss Birch came an administrative re-organisation of the Nursery and the Schoolroom. Pamela remained under Nanny's command, except for a few hours of lessons a week with Miss Birch, while Edward and I were removed from the nursery and put entirely under the authority of Miss Birch. A schoolroom-maid was engaged to wait on us. Jessie was a self-assured young Aussie, described by my mother as the

... pertest young 'Baby-Cock' you ever saw. She outraged Nannie her very first night by going to bed at 8 o'clock. On being asked if she were ill she replied 'No, but I shall be if I have to go upstairs so many times a day'. There is one little flight from the kitchen to the schoolroom and she has to take breakfast and supper up!

As my mother was used to London houses where the kitchen was in the basement and the nursery on the top floor up five flights of stairs, she was naturally annoyed by Jessie's complaint. On the other hand, Jessie had never been inside anything but a one-storey cottage and so she was equally put out by having to perform this unaccustomed exercise. My mother pursued her criticisms indignantly:

She also retires to the verandah and rocks in the rocking-chair with a novel, just when she is most wanted to get on with her work. The children *hate* her and Adelaide is outrageously naughty with her. She came to me the other day to complain about Edward and finished by saying 'I must say the children are very spoilt, your ladyship'. I rounded on her and told her she was a saucy baggage (not in those words, exactly) and that her manner and demeanour were such that I could only suppose she was ignorant and had not lived among civilised or polite people. I was quite surprised that she knuckled under and is quite humble in her manner now ... The *aggressiveness* of a certain class of Australian is most exasperating: I wish you could hear Adelaide imitating her!

As the writing of 'The Book' was finally completed, memories of the voyage fired me anew with a desire to see the world. Fairy stories were replaced by books on travel and adventure in mysterious, remote places – India, the South Sea Islands and the United States. On one occasion Miss Birch overheard a conversation between Edward and me which she reported rather disapprovingly to my mother. It seems that we were both lying on our stomachs in front of the fire, roasting chestnuts. I said, 'I have quite made up my mind not to marry before I am twenty-three or four because I *must* travel first and see all over the world.' Edward said, 'I don't see why you can't do this even after you are married.' 'Oh no,' I replied, 'it would be so tiresome to have to be obedient to your husband while you were travelling – because I believe wives really do have to do what their husbands want. And I should *most certainly not* wish to have a whole family of children to drag around the world.' 'But you know, Adelaide,' said Edward, 'I don't believe you would ever obey your husband. I should think he and I might go off together, and if I were married you might take my wife with you.'

My mother laughed at our ideas and told Marmee 'This so illustrates Edward's attitude towards A. He has a great admiration for her lawlessness and contempt of consequences, and always relies on her to get him out of tight places. I am sure he *would* plant his wife on her to manage for him!'

I had decided to call a truce with Miss Birch. She had added 'Arts and Crafts' to my curriculum and I delighted in painting sprays of autumn leaves 'artistically' pinned on to a sheet of cartridge paper by Miss Birch, or copying 'Old Masters' from a book called *How to Study Painting* which was one of Miss Birch's prize possessions. She encouraged my efforts at knitting and with her help I actually finished a pair of socks knitted out of thick grey wool, which I took proudly to the Red Cross Comforts Depot at Federal Government House with my name pinned on them and a message of goodwill to the eventual recipient. I also learnt to do embroidery – satin-stitch, chain-stitch, cross-stitch and petit-point – and to crochet 'Irish Lace', which was called 'croshering' in Australian. 'I believe Miss Birch is going to be my salvation!' my mother exclaimed, but she spoke too soon. Already by the end of the month Miss Birch was showing signs of wilting and she confessed to my mother that she found it a great strain to be with the children all day. 'Adelaide informed her, the first day she arrived, that I always allowed her to act naked in the hall with a little gold tinsel round her tummy. Fortunately she is more amused than anything else by A's vagaries – which is a better way of taking them than the Nannie mode of treating them as criminal offences!'

So I held my fire for the time being as I really enjoyed the painting and drawing lessons, but otherwise I couldn't stand Miss Birch. She was a malicious and snobbish old cat, full of genteel, intellectual pretentions, over-bearing in her manner towards the servants, and particularly offensive to Nanny, of whom she was vindictively jealous. She was forever on the look-out for the Nursery to trespass on the Schoolroom sphere of command. I took advantage of this struggle for power and played one off against the other to gain my own ends. The feud between Miss Birch and Nanny was obvious to all except my mother, who continued to indulge in wishful thinking, reporting to Marmee that 'the children are so fond of Miss Birch who is still being successful in her methods with Adelaide'. She was predisposed to take her part as she felt that the Stricklands had dismissed her unreasonably.

In April my mother and father accompanied the Governor-General and Lady Helen on a state visit to New South Wales.

> The G.G. and she are at terrible loggerheads with the Governor, Sir Gerald Strickland, who is a cranky and difficult man, tho' Lady Helen's suspicions of the depths of his wickedness I should think are exaggerated ... Of course his being a R.C. prejudices the Presbyterian minds of the G.G. and Lady H. against him. I sometimes feel very uncomfortable when Arthur is appealed to by Sir Gerald to advise him on some squabble between himself and the G.G. There is supposed to be a sort of unwritten law for State Governors to stand by one another on questions arising between State and Commonwealth, and it is disagreeable for A. to be dragged into any matter between these two.

As the European spring advanced into summer, the Allies' situation on the Western Front became crucial. The German attack on the Verdun Salient bled France white although it failed to break through their lines. The Allies' counter-offensive on the Somme from July to November gained a few miles but at a horrific cost. The long, closely printed columns of casualty lists spread like a dark stain across more and more pages of the newspapers. And now came the news of the Dublin Easter Rising and the Irish Rebellion.

> Oh dear! how terrible and humiliating all this Irish business is, coming at a time when one was really hoping for some good news. However, the grand resistance at Verdun is cheering and I only hope the German losses are as great as they say they are. I always feel what a pitch of deterioration one has arrived at when one finds oneself wishing that a few hundred Germans

killed were a few *thousands*. I *never* can help thinking of all the poor things' homes and children and wives and mothers. Sometimes I feel I don't want to go on living. One can only hope that something better and greater will come out of it all – not only for us but for the whole world. I can't think why I go on writing about the war; I always try not to let it creep into my letters but it is so much part of one's thoughts now that one can hardly help it ... I see that some of our Australians have been engaged in France. I hope they realise that there are a few other soldiers there too.

With the Australian autumn there came an outbreak of cerebro-spinal meningitis in some of the Army camps which terrified my mother, as she said the authorities seemed to be too incompetent and ignorant to cope adequately with it. 'However, I try not to be a fusspot ... visualising some horrible accident or illness. I constantly find myself practising my demeanour when the news is broken to me of the violent deaths suffered by various members of my family!'

Even though my mother's morbid fears caused her genuine distress, she still could not resist dramatising herself in imagined situations of horror and grief. Indeed, as time went on she increasingly gave way to neurotic dreads and premonitions of disaster which, although they may have satisfied her sense of drama, ruined her peace of mind, and worked on my easily over-wrought temperament to such an extent that I began to suffer the same agonies of nervous apprehension – a tendency which has remained to plague me to this day.

A splendid opportunity occurred about this time for my mother to indulge in her propensity for play-acting.

Yesterday I performed the ceremony of laying a foundation stone of a church. The Archbishop and I solemnly walked at the head of a procession for about a quarter of a mile. There was a Guard of Honour to receive me which I had to inspect and which was all wrong but nobody minds that out here. I *laid* the stone ... but I'm sure you will be amused when I tell you that I snatched the Archbishop's lines from him and read the prayer over the stone which *he* ought to have done. Captain Conant says he was panting and blowing with agitation and I vaguely felt that something was wrong but I didn't care. I couldn't help feeling it was rather fun as I tried to read it so much better than the Archbishop! It has always been my ambition to read the Service and here was a real chance.

Having successfully up-staged the Archbishop, in her opinion, my mother now felt she should take a hand in the religious instruction of her children. She disapproved of the local clergyman at St George's, Malvern and stopped us going to his services. Instead, she instituted Sunday morning Bible lessons at her bedside for Edward and me. 'It consists mostly of singing favourite hymns, a chapter out of the New Testament and one from the Old. And they can choose any story or parable they like,' she told Marmee.

The favourites are Ananias and Sapphira (A's choice) and Shadrach, Meshach and Abednego in the Fiery Furnace (E's choice). Adelaide always moans that I did not christen her Sapphira – 'it's such a beautiful name and people would *not* think me a liar because I don't think that God would strike *me* dead, even if I did tell a few fibs!' ... Edward takes his Scripture just as keenly but with less criticism. It always touches me when he looks up and says 'Is it quite *quite* true?' How can one answer? I don't allow them to think the Old Testament is true, but there are things in the New Testament which I don't feel I can vouch for...

In the course of her vice-regal duties my mother went to open a college for young ladies 'at a place called Bendigo' – as she put it in a letter to Marmee. It was her second visit and she stayed with the rich widow of a gold magnate, reaping a fortune in comic experience, this time, instead of gold nuggets.

I must tell you about the *wonderful* house we stayed at for the night. Our hostess was a cosy, soft old pussycat whose late husband made mints of money in a gold mine which is still at work ... I was first taken into my bedroom, the chief feature of which were the windows which she showed me with great pride saying 'I seem to get so tired of *straight* windows so I thought it would be a nice change to have horse-shoes' – and each one was an enormous *horse-shoe* draped with terrible pink bows and they were kaleidoscopic *stained glass*! We then went down to dinner where the most enormous meal was provided of which one had to eat a portion of each course to avoid apologies and agitations that the food was not 'what I was accustomed to'. After dinner I was conveyed into the Billiard-room, most of which was papered in bright peacock-blue and yellow with imitation wood panelling and terrible Indian and Moorish things about. We had to listen to two gramophone [records] which I *detest*, and then my hostess said 'Perhaps Your Excellency would like a little change now and will come and sit in one of the other drawing-rooms?' So we got up and went through corridors and passages all filled with statues and busts ... and came to an even more wonderful room than the Billiard-room. It was almost dark, except for several brilliantly lighted niches in which were groups of statuary. Here we solemnly sat for about ten minutes, and then the dear old pudding rose and said 'Will you come and sit in one of the other saloons now?' I counted *seven* rooms, the last of which was the most glorious of all! Every sofa and chair was upholstered in sky-blue satin and gold. Most of the furniture consisted of Buhl tables and cabinets of the worst kind, and glass-doored cabinets stood all around, brilliantly lit inside to show the extraordinary collections displayed in them. You never saw such a jumble ... Beside a marble group of nude figures stood a life-size French doll in red velvet who, when wound up, powdered her face with one hand and held a looking-glass up with the other ... Capt. Conant at last said he thought I should go to bed, whereupon our hostess nodded solemnly and said 'Yes, Supper is just being served.' But I was firm and said I couldn't eat any more and insisted on going to my room – but not to bed, however. I was shown where the electric light turned on and off, which tap in the bathroom would give me a spray, shower or plunge and then she rushed at some unseen mechanism and the wardrobe doors rolled back displaying a most luxurious bath of beautiful marble! Having expressed my sleepy wonder and admiration, I hoped now for bed but just as I began to murmur for the hundredth time 'Well, goodnight and thank you so much', again she rushed to some other hidden spring and slowly a large tray swung out of a recess with 'refreshments' of every description on it – cakes, sandwiches, fruit, cider-cup, tea and coffee!

Back in Melbourne my mother continued her round of bazaars and Red Cross Committees, and predictably, the brief honeymoon between her and Lady Madden came abruptly to an end. 'You will be amused to hear that Lady Madden is on the war-path,' she told Marmee. A stupendous row blew up between Lady Madden and Lady Helen over precedence on the Central Red Cross Committee in which my mother was unwillingly involved, and which culminated in Lady Madden refusing to serve on any Red Cross Committee whatsoever. She railed and stormed at what she called Lady Helen's 'airs and pride and deceit' and berated my mother for allowing herself to be trampled upon, but my mother replied that she preferred to forgo all her prerogatives in order to avoid a degrading squabble. My father, on the other hand, said he was sorry not to see a pull-hair fight between these two old battle-axes. 'I would back Lady Helen to get the best of it,' my mother observed. Both my parents tried in vain to calm Lady Madden. 'So we left her at last, like Alice when she quietly left the Ugly Duchess, raving and roaring "Off with her head".*

Just after this episode my mother and Lady Helen went off on one of their Bush Nursing trips which my mother always looked forward to, even in the company of Lady Helen.

She has manoeuvred it so that Arthur should not accompany us, [she told Marmee]. 'I couldn't think why, but Arthur says he is quite certain that it is because she cannot bear to play second fiddle – as of course when he goes she has to take a back seat and she doesn't like it ... It makes us laugh, for the whole thing is really such a little tin-popo show that one cannot

---

* My mother misquotes: this exclamation was made by the Queen of Hearts.

really mind stepping second out of the motor car or getting out of the train last.

My mother was contemptuous of ceremony and etiquette on the whole, as she genuinely wanted to be friendly and charming to everybody, 'and I cannot see that there is any loss of dignity in behaving like human beings'. She tried as far as possible to reduce what she considered to be superfluous formalities and, in spite of Mr Hood, she succeeded in turning all but the most official functions into less stiff occasions.

Madame Melba came to stay at Government House and gave me a book for my tenth birthday. It was the story of *Undine* with Arthur Rackham illustrations. Melba said the pictures of Undine looked like me and I was duly flattered. She also gave us a grey Persian kitten which we christened 'Mimi'. Edward and I didn't much like the poor little thing, but Pamela adored it. My mother thought Melba's visit went off quite well.

Arthur was very good and not severe with her ... There is nothing *small* about her. Everything – her failings as well – are on a good, bold scale – and she is frank and straightforward to a fault. If she had been less so I daresay she would have made fewer enemies – she is full of wild enthusiasm and vitality and as impetuous and uncontrolled as a child – but all the same, she is a loyal friend to those she really cares for. I have *never* heard her say an unfair or unkind thing about other artists, but she does not spare her criticisms which are generally pretty good. Her kindness and generosity in supporting poor little struggling ones and their whole families is unbounded. She is very excited just now over a class of poor students she has got together and she slaves for a whole day once a week teaching them for nothing.* I am always glad when a really big artist, as she certainly is, is not the odious and petty character that some people paint them – but I can clearly see the sides of her that would arouse dislike and fury.

And now came the announcement of a wonderful birthday treat for me! I was to be allowed to accompany my father and mother at the Presentation of the Colours ceremony to the newly formed Pioneer Battalion. Not even Edward was to share in my glory. I went through agonies beforehand over the suitability of my clothes as I didn't consider that brown shoes and stockings went well with my new grey alpaca coat and black velvet and pleated silk bonnet. However, I was given a little silk handbag (the first in my life) to compensate for the offending stockings, and when the time came I was so transported by emotion and excitement that all else was forgotten.

* At the Albert Street Conservatorium.

The ceremony took place on the Melbourne cricket ground. I walked between my father and mother to the saluting base where she was to present the Colours. We were escorted by Geeps, and followed by various high-ranking Army officers, clergymen and an assortment of civic dignitaries. The Guard of Honour presented arms, and the band played the National Anthem. Two officers then knelt in front of my mother who presented each one with a banner. After the ceremony there was a March-past with the Colours, my father taking the salute and the band playing. I was carried away by the military thrill of the occasion. Later, I was taken to see a news-reel of the presentation and was mortified to see myself wriggling and jumping about like an eel. My mother said: 'Adelaide nearly had hysterics at seeing herself suddenly give one of her leg-flying capers of ecstasy, followed by a hug round my legs and a kiss planted on my muff.' She added rather complacently, 'Melba was with us and said she would like to make every actress or dancer in Melbourne come and take a lesson from me in movement and deportment!'

Soon after this a Newsboys 'Mothers' Tea-party was given at Stonning-ton. 'About forty of them altogether, and their babies,' my mother told Marmee. ' . . . Adelaide was riveted on some of the poor mothers who were nursing their infants. You can imagine her interest and the number of questions I had to answer! One was "Now what sort of coloured milk do you think a *Maori* mother might have?" She was very much dashed when she learnt that Lyulph was not getting any more – "as I *really* should have asked you to let me taste a little".

On the second day of June, the news of the Battle of Jutland reached Australia. At first it was not clear what had happened except that the British Grand Fleet, the nation's pride and glory, had been in action against the German High Seas Fleet in the North Sea and had sustained disastrous losses, while the Germans, though outnumbered, had managed to escape the clutches of our Navy. Jutland was indeed a shattering blow to British morale, and there were some who questioned the Commander-in-Chief, Sir John Jellicoe, for his tactics of centralised command and accused him of unwillingness to engage the German Fleet for fear of torpedoes. 'I always had to remember that I could lose the war in an afternoon,' he is quoted as saying. Amongst his critics were Winston Churchill and Commodore (later Admiral) William Goodenough, both connected by marriage with my family. Uncle Bill Goodenough in H.M.S. *Southampton* was in command of the 2nd Light Cruiser Squadron under Admiral Beatty, and he was the first to sight the German Fleet on the fateful 31 May. He was acting as wireless liaison between Jellicoe and Beatty, whose forces were sixty miles apart. Signals between these two

commanders were either misunderstood or disregarded by both, and
Jellicoe refused to delegate authority, although in a battle of such magni-
tude and complexity it was impossible for him to know the whole picture.
Consequently the Germans were able, under cover of darkness on the
night of 31 May–1 June, to retire right through the British line of battle
and regain their home base at Wilhelmshaven. Bill Goodenough's view
that the battle of Jutland ought to have ended in a massive defeat for
the German High Seas Fleet was shared by Churchill and Beatty, who
considered that but for Jellicoe's lack of resolution and tactical errors,
the war would have been won on that day of encounter between the
British and German Fleets.

In the subsequent feud which arose between Jellicoe and Beatty, and
the ensuing historical scandals, partisans of both sides sought with bitter
and often intemperate fury to pin the blame for the disaster on one
another, and to the present time the argument has not been finally resolved.

My family, naturally, supported Beatty and my mother was quite carried away by the stout-hearted heroism of the officers and men under
his command.

> We were thrilled, when we saw in our papers that Bill Goodenough (*Southamp-*
> *ton*) had fought with such splendid dash and success against the *Seydlitz* and
> two cruisers. It simply chokes me to read the accounts of that terrific conflict
> – our men's reckless valour and joy in battle is beyond all words, and one
> can't help feeling glad that they have had an innings at last, even though
> they didn't pound the Germans as severely as they would have liked.

Five days after the Battle of Jutland a further disaster befell Britain.
Lord Kitchener, the Secretary of State for War and a national hero at
that period, was drowned on his way to Russia when the *Hampshire*
struck a mine off the Orkneys. I was taken to his Memorial Service at
St Paul's Cathedral, Melbourne, suitably dressed I considered, this time,
in black from head to foot. The solemnity of the occasion made a great
impression upon me. I walked up the aisle behind my parents with Geeps
and Hoodiwinks on either side of me, and with Hoodiwinks' fishy eye
upon me I refrained from cutting any unseemly capers.

'What a week of horrors this has been!' exclaimed my mother.

My mother's spirits were now reviving at the prospect of a state visit
to South Australia. The Governor, Sir Henry Galway, had a reputedly
German wife who was said to be a highly intellectual person, widely
read and well informed on many subjects. My mother was curious to
meet her and judge the lady's attainments for herself. She was not disappointed and wrote to Marmee that she greatly admired Lady Galway,

in spite of her being 'very German'. In fact, she stood rather in awe
of her, I suspect, and was perhaps a little envious of her brains.

> She is a *wonder* in the amount she knows! There is no political aspect of
> the modern history of Europe she cannot descant upon nor, I believe, *any*
> subject – religious, philosophical, political, artistic or scientific that she has not
> a grasp of and cannot talk admirably upon. Her Italian, French and Spanish
> are all spoken with a perfection of accent and an accuracy which is really
> astounding. Funnily enough her English is not free from a distinct foreign-
> – German in fact – intonation.

But to her father-in-law she confessed that she found Lady Galway
rather too much of a *femme instruite* and a blue-stocking for her taste.

During this visit my mother persuaded my father to buy a water-
colour landscape by Hans Heysen.

> We drove out about 30 miles into the Bush to find [Heysen], and there
> he has built a big studio and a little house* where he lives with a wife and
> eight children and paints from morning till night. I believe that his father
> was a German settler and it is rumoured that he is German in his sympathies.
> Anyhow, he is living there as a peaceful and law-abiding citizen and I think
> works of art should be put above the bitterness of the feeling of war.

When they got back, my parents had to confess guiltily to Mr Hood
that they had bought a picture. Governors' allowances from the Government rarely covered their entertainment expenses and they were expected
to make the deficit good out of their own pocket. Hoodiwinks was
annoyed to find that my parents had spent money on indulging their
personal whims. 'He makes a great grumble about trying to cut expenses
down,' my mother compained, 'although he loves things to be done in
splashing style and would far rather we spent money on an extra footman
as an ornament than on a picture.'[†]

Another source of guilt was the reluctance of my parents to attend
church, but now they 'binged themselves up, after a disgraceful lapse,
to go in order to keep up an appearance of Church and State sort of
thing'. Edward and I accompanied them one Sunday to our parish church.
It was decidedly an unsuccessful effort, judging from the description which
was sent to Marmee.

> There was a new clergyman officiating, and as the service went on his ritualistic
> 'follies' (as A. calls them) became more and more apparent and he (Tib)
> became more and more annoyed as the parson and a shaggy, whiskered fellow

---

* Hahndorf. Still lived in by Heysen's descendants at the time of writing.
† Later, Melba gave my mother another painting by Heysen, which I now possess.

who acted as his acolyte bobbed up and down and went through all sorts of things like 'Ladies' Chain' and 'Gentlemen to the Centre' on the Altar steps. The parson had muffled his neck up with a large sort of white towel which looked as though he was going to his bath. He preached a sermon in which he alluded to Our Lord continually as 'the debonair companion of the disciples' and then went on to describe the intimacy and simplicity of their friendship with Him 'when they discovered Him bending over the frying-pan cooking their breakfast'! We hear now that the Arch-Bish has had to haul him over the coals as his vestry and congregation dislike his fanciful innovations.

The following week we all attended church again, as the Archbishop was preaching and Marmee heard the sequel to our previous week's dose of religion.

I'm sure you will be amused to know, that ... he gave out from the pulpit the resignation of the poor little 'High Priest', who, out of deference I suppose to the Arch-Bish, considerably modified his 'rites'. It was very characteristic of Tibaldi to point out that everybody was doing something quite foolish in turning towards the East out here as of course they are turning their backs on Jerusalem or whatever it is we are supposed to turn to.

On 30 July there was an eclipse of the sun. We were all given pieces of glass smoked in a candle-flame through which to observe the phenomenon. Everybody gathered on the balcony and my father explained what was going to happen. At the appointed hour we saw a little bite appear on the edge of the sun. Gradually the black, crescent-shaped shadow of the moon crept across the sun's orb, which glared livid through the smoked glass, and an ominous darkness descended. The birds stopped singing and there was an eerie silence. In spite of my father's scientific explanations, I felt a panic fear that it was the end of the world. I was just about to start screaming when the little sliver of sun in the dark sky began to increase. Soon it was daylight again and the forthright Australian sun was shining down as usual. 'You can imagine the hopping excitement of the children over such an event,' said my mother. 'They succeeded in quite eclipsing their own faces with the amount of black that was transferred on to them from the smoked pieces of glass.'

Jessie, the schoolroom maid, had been replaced by one of the under housemaids known as 'Plottie' – a fat girl whose guileless good nature, said my mother, was constantly being imposed upon by Edward and me.

However, this evening she jibbed at believing that Adelaide, as Goddess of the Mountains, was allowed to leap from the top of the wardrobe on to the bed, douching Edward with water in her descent ... Adelaide amused me last night by going off to bed with great alacrity when Plottie came for her. It is generally a signal for much groaning and wailing. I said I was pleased to see her go so readily and she replied, 'I'm not going because I am *virtuous* but because I've discovered that Plottie is really quite a Shakespearean character and it amuses me to make her use odd, rough words while I go to bed.' It's quite true. Plottie is a real 'Audrey' - with a strange vocabulary!

How strange, she little knew. I learnt a lot of Australian slang and swear words from Plottie which Edward and I used enthusiastically in our conversation - well out of earshot of the grown-ups, although my mother probably would never have heard of such words, or even have understood their meaning, as the following incident reveals.

One day the Governor-General and Lady Helen, the Archbishop and other guests were having tea at Government House. When Pamela and I came down to the drawing-room someone said, 'But where is Edward?' 'Oh,' said my mother, 'He has been sent to bed as a punishment for calling his governess a mysterious thing called a Bugger.' The company was dumbfounded with horror and the Governor-General hastily changed the subject by asking Pamela to sing one of her songs.

Miss Birch was beginning to get on my mother's nerves. 'The little old guvvy' was now referred to as 'that tedious old woman' apt to bore my mother by constantly 'popping in to make arrangements for the children which she could quite well do herself. However, I mean to hang on to her as she is certainly the best I could get out here'. My mother still deluded herself that Miss Birch was 'an excellent influence' on me, but the breach between the Schoolroom and the Nursery could be ignored no longer, despite all wishful thinking, and soon her star was on the wane.

Sensing our advantage, Edward and I defied Miss Birch, lying like troopers when reported for disobedience and insolence, and my mother was in despair. We really were more wild and unmanageable than other children, she felt, but her one rock of consolation was her belief that she held complete sway over our affections and that we always confided freely in her.

Above all else, my mother craved the love and admiration of the world in general, and her family in particular, and these demands were usually met. But in my case I sometimes felt that too much was being asked of me and I refused to worship her uncritically or confide unreservedly my inmost thoughts to her. To tell the truth, my mother would have liked her children to retain what she called the 'innocence of babyhood' and never grow into beings capable of resisting her possessiveness.

8

A Turning Point

The Battle of the Somme was launched on 1 July and continued till the end of 1916. The fighting swayed back and forth with no decisive gains despite the use for the first time of tanks – the Allies' 'secret weapon'. The troops still crouched in the festering trenches and dug-outs in between engagements with the enemy which decimated their ranks.* The tone of the letters to Marmee became more despairing than ever, and my mother resorted to pathetic little devices to ease her longing for home and palliate the misery of her exile.

> I suppose we shall be still at it next spring and summer, but it is no use looking forward ... Arthur and I are continually making new landmarks to pass the time. He watches a certain young pine tree from his window when he shaves every morning, which has grown much taller since we have been here. We have a bet as to how far it will have got on the day we start for home ... What a shocking thought that we shall have accomplished only half our full term by the end of this month!

In spite of her many apprehensions of, usually, non-existent dangers, my mother was admirably courageous when it came to facing a real hazard. On one occasion she and my father visited the Military Flying School near Melbourne and for the first time in her life she was taken up in an aeroplane. They were the most rickety and unreliable machines in those days and it really was a brave act on her part, although she was spurred on by an admiring audience.

*According to Churchill, Lloyd George 'improvidently exposed' the first twenty tanks on 15 September 1916 which was too small a number to be effective. The immense advantage and novelty of surprise was thus squandered.' W. S. Churchill, *The World Crisis*.

I flew with my heart and every other organ in my inside in my mouth, high up till every object below became like a little pinpoint. Arthur had taken a flight first – which he loved – but I could hardly bear to look at him, a little speck among the clouds. When he came down I was dressed in the aviating cap, coat and goggles, and to the admiration of the spectators, stepped into the machine. I amused our friends by calling out 'Give my love to the children!' as we flew off. We climbed and climbed and then I was taken out right over the sea and I felt that if only I could feel confidence enough I should be enjoying it. It was a windy day which caused the machine to keep giving sudden drops which gave me ghastly qualms each time and left my heart bumping. The wind and noise is dizzying but through it all there is a wonderful feeling of exhilaration and, as I say, if the feeling of helplessness could be overcome, it would be delightful. The part I was told I should probably dislike most was vol-planing to earth, but I liked that best of all – partly perhaps because I knew I was nearing safety.

Fortunately, she seems to have been unaware of the danger of a crash-landing.

We celebrated my mother's birthday by spending the whole day with her in her bedroom, at her request. She had had an operation for varicose veins a few weeks previously and although now able to lie on the sofa she still had two nurses, as well as the attention of Jukie. In the evening we dressed up in my mother's motoring veils and opera cloaks and a 'Dark-Mysterious' play was enacted. This was a serial performance played on special occasions, devised by me and based on *Ivanhoe* and the romances of King Arthur and his Knights with language to match, known as 'Prithee and Quotha'. These scenes always entertained my mother with their unconscious humour.

Edward made the most Apache-like love to Adelaide (the Princess) which she repelled by saying 'Sir, your kisses are too *wet*'. There was a moment when a dose of poison was administered to poor Pamela whose little face was contorted with horror as she took it. I protested and asked what they were giving her, to which Edward replied, 'It's all right. It's only some of our chocolates pounded up with a little paint water and Scrubb's ammonia.' Pamela, always ready to defend Edward, immediately said, 'I'm not really crying because it is nasty, but I'm crying a little because my chocolates will be rather wasted!!' [Pamela] has kept the unselfconsciousness and innocence of her babyhood much longer than the others. Her lessons are a great woe to her, poor darling. She has no powers of concentration and the flimsiest of memories . . .

My father took her to task over her lack of application and asked her why she did not try harder to learn her lessons. She replied, 'Because Nanny says I must never dwell on unpleasant subjects.'

On Pamela's seventh birthday a crisis occurred which resulted in Miss Birch's departure. The old creature flew into a rage with Nanny for taking me down to the kitchen without first asking permission. She ordered me upstairs and I refused to obey, which triggered off a full-scale battle between Schoolroom and Nursery. They went at it hammer and tongs for a bit and then old Birch-rod went marching up to my mother's bedroom to get redress. My mother reported to Marmee,

> I heard her voice rising to a shrill treble then Nanny's, and above all, Adelaide's howling. I thought that Edward had certainly climbed over the gallery running round the hall and been dashed to pieces but my nurses, who heard the disturbance, came back to reassure me ... Arthur hurried out and read Miss B. a lecture on the injudiciousness of allowing the children to see her contempt and dislike for Nannie ... but it resulted in her handing in her demission.

Miss Birch's row with my father was something I shall never forget. She was turkeycock-red in the face and screaming, while Nanny stood by opening and shutting her mouth like a carp out of water. Finally my father cut short old Birch's hysterical babbling with a peremptory 'Be *quiet*, Miss Birch. You may go.' I could have cheered out loud! She clucked several times and then in a voice strangled with rage gave her notice and flustered off, while I returned with my father to my mother's room and recounted my version of the drama. My mother was 'not really regretful' that Miss Birch was going.

> She has undesirable faults and Edward said the other day 'Miss Birch is very disdainful of the servants'. She has a very good opinion of herself and what is most amusing is her wish to be thought 'artistic' and 'bohemian'. The latter quality has rather dwindled of late. Captain Conant says it is because she is so puzzled by my want of convention in joining the servants' First-Aid Class and having tea with the Policeman and his wife ...

Melba invited my mother to stay the week-end at Coombe Cottage, her country house, to convalesce after her varicose veins. Although it rained for the whole time my mother enjoyed the respite from official duties and domestic worries.

> One afternoon, when she and I were left together, Melba sang for nearly two hours, accompanying herself, and I have never heard her voice more *wonderful* or she herself sing with more feeling and go. Anything I asked for she 'obliged' me with – Mozart, Rossini, Meyerbeer, Gounod, etc. The lovely room, the marvellous voice and delightful music fed a very starved corner of my soul. And yet, while I loved it, and it refreshed me more than anything else could have done after the boringness and ugliness by which I am always surrounded, it made me very melancholy and I could have howled ...

I was very much touched by a thing she did. She came into my room one morning before I was up and said she would like to tell me about her early life and her marriage and what happened after it . . . She said she just wanted me to know everything there was to know because she valued my friendship and appreciated the atmosphere of our house so much that she couldn't bear to be in doubt as to whether it might make any difference . . . I wish I could tell you all she told me. You couldn't help admiring the way she tackled the crashing smashes she got into when she was only 19 or 20, and I am glad that the man she sacrificed everything for then is still as true to her as when they first met, and is the one rock in her life to which she clings with all the passion and intensity of their first love. You can imagine that I satisfied her that what she had told me could not possibly make any difference and that I should probably have done the same if I had been her.

Melba liked men and loved admiration but she never 'sacrificed everything' for any man – as far as is known – nor did she allow anything to come between her and her career or her financial interests. However, from my mother's account it seems that she did have one true and lasting love from her early youth throughout her life. One wishes that my mother had been more explicit in her reference to this attachment.

In October, it was announced to our excitement that Edward and I were to accompany our parents on a visit to New South Wales. My mother and the two of us, escorted by Jukie and Grace, were to go by sea to Sydney, where we would stay with the Stricklands at Government House, and then we were to spend a short holiday in the spectacular Blue Mountains.

The sea journey took two days and it was very rough. Edward, as usual, was sea-sick the whole way – so were the maids – and my mother kept to her cabin. There was nobody to prevent me doing as I pleased and I had a glorious time scrambling and slithering over the tilting decks, exhilarated by the crashing of the waves and drenched with spray.

Sir Gerald Strickland was a little dark man with a sly expression. His wife, Lady Edeline, was a disconcerting sight, poor thing. She suffered from creeping paralysis and appeared in a wheel chair, shaking with palsy and mouthing unintelligible sounds by way of speech.

'I had forgotten to prepare Adelaide and Edward', said my mother, 'and I was seized with panic that they would laugh and think she was speaking to them in a funny way. However, they acquitted themselves well. Edward never turned a hair and Adelaide quickly regained her self-possession after a moment or two of horrified curiosity.'

We arrived at Katoomba ('a beastly little colonial town', said my mother) in the Blue Mountains the following day and stayed at an hotel grandly named the Carrington: Telephone Number One, Katoomba! It was a two storey building, squalidly furnished and freezing cold. The food was utterly disgusting, consisting of slabs of mutton dowsed in ketchup and accompanied by pumpkin, followed by stodgy puddings and custard twice a day at 'midday dinner' and 'tea'. There was one concession to gracious living at the table d'hôte and that was a dish of black olives on the dining table. I had never seen such things before and I thought they must be some kind of sweet. I pestered and clamoured to be allowed to eat one until my father finally said 'Very well. Please yourself. But you must not spit it out if you don't like it.' I seized an olive and put it whole into my mouth. I bit into it confidently expecting it to taste like chocolate. My face must have been a study! Everybody burst out laughing at my mortification, as with crimson face and tear-filled eyes I chewed up the poisonous-tasting object, asking in a choked voice whether I had to swallow the stone as well!

My parents were highly amused by a conversation between Edward and myself at the table d'hôte. Sitting near us was a very scented and dyed-haired lady with an elderly male companion who were subjected to prolonged and unabashed stares from us both. Edward whispered to me in a loud *sotto-voce*, 'Should you think that lady is the *wife* of that gentleman?' And I answered promptly, 'No, silly! If he was her husband he wouldn't let her dye her hair like that. They are probably just friends staying here for a bit.' My mother said our waiter grinned like a Cheshire cat, at the nail having been so neatly hit on the head.

My mother complained about the lack of circumspection in the behaviour of her fellow guests. 'At night the noise of "horse" laughter in the passages is "somefink awful" – not to mention the whistling and singing and flinging of boots in noisy cascades from the doors.' My father had to return to his duties after a day or two but we stayed on, spending happy hours 'exploring' or 'bushranging' and going for expeditions. One memorable day we went on a picnic to the Wentworth Falls and here my mother had an adventure with a gallant gentleman. As we were stumbling painfully back up the hillside track, hot, sweaty and tired, a man appeared and offered to help my mother who was beginning to think she would never make it, although Jukie and Grace were supporting her steps.

'Did you ever hear of anything so good-natured!' she exclaimed.

The result was that for the rest of the way I was nearly lifted off my legs up the steps and over the difficult places at a terrific speed which nearly took all my breath. In the intervals of rest I found out that our kind friend was a double-bass in the Sydney Orchestra ... At last we came to the top and as we emerged (he handing me gallantly up the last steps!) we were confronted by a large coloured lady who he seemed a little taken aback to find there and who, after a moment of slight embarrassment, he introduced as his wife! I don't know why, but I felt foolishly embarrassed too – it was somehow such an unexpected and funny ending. Jukes amused me afterwards by saying 'Well! I'm not surprised to know he was one of the acting kind from the way he handed you up those steps as if he was dancing the *Mignonette!* But to think of him having that black wife! Well, you never know who you may pick up with and I'm sorry I didn't tell him who you were when I heard him keep calling you *Miss!*'

We spent a day visiting the Jenolan Caves which to me were mysterious and fairy-like, glistening rose, white and amber in the artificial lighting, but I think my mother was rather bored, perhaps because no amusing encounters came her way. The final thrill of our jaunt to New South Wales was our return by the night train from Sydney to Melbourne in the vice-regal car and sleeping carriages. It was very hot and I remember being allowed for the first time to drink black tea with lemon to quench my thirst. It was a more successful gastronomic adventure than the one with the olive.

> The return to ordinary life and lessons has caused a good deal of groaning and miserable faces [said my mother] and flingings in desperate attitudes into chairs. But the beastliness has been slightly palliated by the excitement of the new guv. – who I can see will be quite a failure and plasticine in their hands. She is a prim little thing and really is quite pretty ...

Miss Dillon was a fribbling fool with a simpering manner and genteel to her fingertips. She spoke mincingly and said she was descended from an Irish Chieftain named Dilhoun of Dilhoun. Once when Edward swore at her she cried 'Oh! whay don't you employ a more refained expression?' 'What sort of an expression?' he asked and she replied, 'How about Great Caesar's Ghost!?'

Miss Dillon also irritated my mother, who would bite her lip (a habit she had of showing disapproval) whenever Miss Dillon opened her mouth. Eventually, she was given notice for disrespectful familiarity when she exclaimed 'Oh you *poor* thing!' to my mother who was wittily recounting her experience in the aeroplane.

Plottie had followed Miss Birch into limbo and had been replaced by a new schoolroom-maid of riper years and experience. Hilda had flaming, frizzy red hair and remarkable eyes, one of which was blue and the other brown. She dressed most unsuitably for a servant (my mother thought), following the latest fashion with skirts above her ankles and shoes with 'Louis' heels. She drenched herself in 'Californian Poppy' scent and powdered her sharply pointed noise with *Papier Poudré*. The upper servants, all being English, disapproved of her, but I rather liked her and admired her sophistication and her 'I'm as good as you are' attitude. She became my confidante and revealed certain fascinating facts concerning the function of parts of my anatomy whilst giving me my bath. She also used to lend me her novels occasionally, written by such authors as Ethel M. Dell and Marie Corelli, which I read surreptitiously and with avid interest.

Every letter from home now brought news of some friend or relation fallen on the gruesome battlefield of the Western Front.

The Australian Federal Prime Minister, William Morris Hughes, had recently returned from England, where he had made a notable impression on the political leaders and had been successful in getting widespread publicity as the spokesman for his country. Early in 1916 the British Parliament had passed Conscription and National Service Bills and Billy Hughes was set on getting the same legislation through the Australian Federal Parliament. This was opposed vehemently by Monsignor Mannix, the Roman Catholic Archbishop of Melbourne. I remember my father saying in private that he supported Hughes's policy wholeheartedly and that he thought it very mischievous and improper for the Church to meddle in affairs of state. Naturally, he could not express such views publicly, but both my parents admired Hughes and disliked Mannix who they thought was a rabble-rouser and subverter of liberal principles. In October the Federal Government ordered a referendum on Conscription to be held, each State voting separately. The verdict was a majority against the measure, which disappointed my mother.

> The truth is that the effect of the war has been little felt here yet, and the distance from it all gives many people only a half realisation of what it all means. The best of the men have gone already, but I cannot understand how those left here who are young and strong, can stand back and not volunteer to relieve them. . . . Poor Mr Hughes will have a difficult time in front of him. He is a very remarkable little man – entirely self-educated – and his position at the moment is a wonderful one. Whether he will be big enough to remain the outstanding figure that he now is *after* the war, will be interesting to watch. . . . I think the manner in which he has been boomed at home has done him harm with his followers here. . . . No one knows quite what is going to happen: the general opinion is that Mr Hughes will find some way of carrying on the Government in spite of his policy having been rejected.

Lady Galway came to stay with us about this time. She and my mother saw eye-to-eye on the subject of Lady Helen. 'Lady Galway is not a person to allow herself to criticise other people very freely ... but she did let fly to me about Lady H. and said she wondered how on earth we had managed to steer clear of rows.'

Edward and I were rather overawed by Lady Helen's spiky and coldly disapproving attitude towards us and we gave her a wide berth whenever possible, but Pamela, as usual, managed to make her unbend and gained her wintry affection. Lady Galway, on the other hand, we found delightfully friendly and easy to get on with. She had long talks with us and she allowed Pamela and me to come into her bedroom when she was dressing for dinner. We used to watch her doing her hair herself as, unlike my mother, she had no lady's maid. As she lifted her arms to stick in the combs and hairpins, we saw that she had a positive thicket of black underarm hair which caused us to stare in slightly horrified fascination. Afterwards Pamela said solemnly to me, 'The reason why Lady Galway is so *furry* is that she is a GERMAN!'

On the last Saturday in November a Grand Fête was held at Stonnington in aid of 'The Mothers and Babies of France'.

Miss Jennie Brenan had devised a ballet to the music of Mendelssohn's *Midsummer Night's Dream*, with Edward taking the part of Oberon and myself as Titania. Madame Melba gave advice on the costumes. Mine was made of floating panels of 'rainbow' coloured tulle, with a beautiful pair of gauze dragon-fly wings. I wore a wreath of green leaves. Edward had a green tunic and leggings cross-gartered with gold ribbon, and golden wings and crown. The chorus of fairies, 'Titania's Court', were dressed in white tulle with silver gauze wings and wreaths of pink roses. The day before the fête, marquees and stalls were erected and festoons of fairy lights were strung amongst the trees. We had a dress rehearsal of the ballet on the lawn with Signor Di Gilio's orchestra. At one point Oberon was supposed to bow over Titania's hand and kiss it. Instead, Edward gave my hand a sharp bite and the rehearsal was held up by a furious fight between us.

The morning of the fête dawned clear and hot. It was opened 'with a graceful little speech' according to the newspaper report, by my mother. She then cut open an enormous cardboard pie about six feet across out of which flew real blackbirds to screams of surprise and delight from the onlookers.

All went well until the beginning of the ballet when without warning a storm burst out of the blue sky.

The blackest cloud you ever saw suddenly opened like a great umbrella and emptied rain in gallons on the crowd [said my mother] with the most terrific thunder and lightning as well. There was a regular *sauve-qui-peut* and the verandahs were packed with steaming-hot, wet human beings. All the little ballet children were dragged into the house dripping with tears as well as rain over their spoilt clothes and disappointment. . . . Adelaide was in a grinding rage with everything and everybody and boxed poor Edward's unoffending ears with annoyance. He was quite calm over it all. Darling Pamela, who as a large water lily hadn't even a chance of making her entrance or doing her dance, arrived at the house after about an hour, quite happy and declaring she was very lucky because she had been covered with a pile of sacks by Grace till the rain went over. In spite of this disaster, they made £1,000, but the whole show had to be closed as all the stalls were ruined and many of the goods. It was a pity as the gardens had been illuminated by electric light and a big crowd would have come in the evening, had it been fine.

The next day being Sunday, none of the sopping wrecks of stalls were cleared away and Edward and I had a happy time pillaging them for treasure. My chief find was a beautiful emerald-green glass bottle of eau-de-cologne with a stopper in the shape of a silver crown.

As the end of the year approached, Australia was hit by a mounting wave of industrial unrest. Since the war started there had been no less than 874 strikes, according to my mother, who remarked to Marmee that it was 'a pretty good record!' She thought that there was much less stability and common-sense among the Australian 'working classes' than at home and they seemed to her incapable of rising above their own rather materialistic ideals or recognising that if the Allies lost the war it would mean the end of Australia.

We are living in the midst of a furious coal strike, and it is having an appalling effect on all industry. We are always expecting some blaze-up of rioting to take place. ... I am quite prepared for a 'Flight to Varennes' (Macedon!) if there is an attempted onslaught on Governors or Government Houses! ... Sydney is worse than here, but there are a lot of 'rum-skum' all over Australia. When our Fête had to be put off on account of bad weather the rumour got about that Arthur had stopped it as a Bomb had been found in our grounds ready to blow up as soon as the fun began.

The only 'bombs' in the gardens at Stonnington were made by Edward and me, in the shape of mud pies, which we threw over the laurel hedge at our neighbour, old Mrs Bowes-Kelly, when we saw her walking along the gravelled paths of her shrubbery, accompanied by her little white dog. We felt sure she was a German agent, as once she had reported Edward and me when she spied us climbing on the roof of Government House – a crime which earned us both a spanking.

Hoodiwinks took himself off on a holiday to India for Christmas, much to my mother's relief.

> We are all feeling like the children when the governess has left and I have at once relapsed into luxurious unpunctuality. The children go rioting and singing past his sacred door. ... Adelaide is the only one who really rather likes him – Edward and Pamela are abjectly terrified.

Perhaps it was the sense of liberation caused by Hoodiwinks' absence which emboldened me one day to dress up in my mother's clothes and promenade about in the garden. 'You would have been amused,' my mother said to Marmee.

> ... a mincing elegant figure [came] towards us with high-heeled shoes and parasol and the most Parisian walk and air. Arthur said to me 'Who is this vision coming down the garden? Are you expecting anyone?' In a moment we recognised Adelaide dressed in my shoes, hat and gloves, and the most charmingly contrived fashionable gown. She looked the greatest duck, but terribly grown-up! She had done her hair beautifully, too. Arthur treated the escapade rather severely, but the sight of Pamela appearing round the corner looking like Mrs Groat, dressed up in the most comical way, upset our gravity. The contrast of Adelaide's chicness and darling Pamela's innocent appearance was very amusing. She had evidently been foisted off with the odds and ends that A. had no use for.

On 5 December Asquith resigned as Prime Minister and was succeeded by Lloyd George. Although Asquith was a great friend of the family, my mother felt that it was in the best interests of the country that he should go. My father, no doubt, felt the same way. Indeed, my mother nearly always derived her opinions on politics and economics from him, and I never remember her dissenting in any way from his views on such subjects.

> I am sorry for the downfall of our own dear old P.M., and especially for the ungenerous and undeserved abuse flung at him by the Harmsworth Press, but I do feel that a change will be for the good. The whole situation has long since gone beyond a jog-trot like the P.M's and I'm sure requires a man possessing Lloyd George's energy and fighting power and organising genius at the head of it. Altogether one feels a fresh impetus is being given to the effort of winning this horrible war as soon as possible. Things really look so hideously black at present that one cannot help feeling down. That wretched Greece triumphant, Roumania beaten, and the seas thick with submarines

all go to show that Germany is far from being crushed yet. ... I cannot see that Germany's canting Peace Talk* can lead anywhere. ... I cannot think that even the most craven-hearted will be satisfied to think of Peace at this juncture unless we can dictate our own terms. The only comfort to be got out of the present talk of it is that it is in the air and that perhaps Germany may be ready for it sooner than we are.

Edward and I had recently been allowed to join the servants' First Aid Classes to improve our education, 'which', my mother said, 'under the present little guv is of the tamest and dullest kind'. We could not sit for the official Red Cross examination as no one under sixteen was eligible, but one of the examining doctors said he would set us a private paper. Edward did better than I did in the practical and I got more marks for the theoretical. The doctor told my mother that he had set us exactly the same questions given to the ordinary classes and that we had got much above the average number of marks. 'It just shows that if they are interested they can learn anything,' my mother remarked, 'for they did not work at all hard for this.' I daresay the doctor bent over backwards to mark us indulgently for it would never have done for him to announce that the vice-regal children were morons.

Just before Christmas my father began to be troubled with what my mother called 'gout in the tum'. In reality it was a duodenal ulcer brought on by overwork. 'I'm sure it is because he sits all day long writing and writing and doesn't work off the gouty poison. He is very good and never grizzles at the pain and discomfort...'

We went, as usual, up to Macedon for the holidays and started our Christmas preparations – collecting and labelling our presents and helping to make decorations for the Tree. Owing to the war there were no brightly coloured glass and tinsel ornaments to be had, as these were imported from Germany. So on Christmas Eve, my mother sat us all round the table in the drawing-room painting and gilding fir-cones in their stead.

We had a party for the Christmas Tree to which my mother 'democratically' invited the families of the outdoor staff employed at Government Cottage –

> about 40 children and a good many dear perspiring Lizzies in the form of our gardeners' wives and daughters. We generally get some children who have never seen a Christmas Tree and it is nice to watch their faces of wonder and pleasure. ... People kept coming up and saying 'Oh, Lady Stanley, *don't* leave us *next year*. We hope that you and the Governor will stay on and

*In reply to President Woodrow Wilson's Peace Note published 20 December 1916.

be our next Governor-General and Lady – we want to keep you *always* with us' ... It made my heart leap within me! (No darling, *not* the Babe within my w--- *this* time!)

In this last remark my mother was guilty of telling a downright fib. She was again pregnant, but as before, not a word is said about it in her letters home. I think her reticence was only partly due to excessive prudery, but it was also because she attributed to others her own apprehensions of calamity and pictured in her mind Marmee being torn with anxiety over the health of 'her little Mag'. She need not have worried as my grandmother was not one to meet trouble half way.

My mother ends her last letter of the year with the passionate hope that we should all be home for the following Christmas.

> I don't think I could bear it if I thought we should be here for another, and although the present Peace Talk leads one to hope that the first streak of its dawning may be getting nearer at last, it cannot mean (and I hope it doesn't) that we shall not fight to a finish and give Germany the smashing she needs so badly. ...
>
> America's attitude seems quite incomprehensible, and it looks as though German intrigue and influence had prevailed with Wilson. ... It would look pretty bad if America joined in against us – I can hardly believe, though, that they would want to fight us – but equally they cannot want to go against Germany, and it is very difficult to know what Wilson means by saying they are 'on the verge of war'. What will 1917 bring, I wonder?

The end of 1916 marked the nadir of the War, both politically and on the battlefront, for Britain. It was a black hour but, as my mother sensed, it was also a turning point in the fortunes of the Allies.

9

Enter Cor

The German submarine and mine warfare was slowly throttling the Allies at sea, in spite of the daring counter efforts of the British Navy's decoy ships or Q-boats. In November 1916 my mother had referred to this fearsome danger for the first time, expressing alarm for the safety of many Australian women who were leaving for England to be near their husbands, sons or fiancés at the Front, or wounded in hospital. Now, on 1 February 1917, the German High Command decided to give the *coup-de-grâce* – as they hoped – to the Allies and fulfil their previous threat of waging unrestricted warfare on the high seas.

Letters from overseas dwindled to an erratic trickle and sometimes two months would elapse with no mail from home. Owing to the increased peril to all shipping, information on sailing dates was withheld till the last moment – a belated security measure, my mother felt. 'I have often wondered that the departure of transports laden with valuable cargo (*advertised*) has been allowed to be published, as it is quite possible for the information to be transmitted to the German submarines who then lie in wait for the fat prizes,' she wrote from Macedon at Christmas time. Regulations were also issued preventing women and children from travelling overseas, except on duty. Again, my mother approved. It was quite ridiculous, she remarked, the number of girls who were going home just because they found life in Australia very dull.

There is a sort of feeling here among the worldly that all the marrying chances are to be had in England now, and so many Australians have become engaged lately at home. In spite of the new regulations being right, they give me

115

the horrible *helpless* feeling that I *can't* get home now, however much I may wish it. . . . Arthur is so immediately troubled and easily affected if my mercury goes a little low – I have never seen anyone react so quickly to whatever mood I am in and, unconsciously, this puts him in possession of a great lever over me. . . . I dare not appear down or depressed or he begins gloomily to pull tufts of his hair out and to look so miserable as to make me nearly cry. . . .

Country life didn't really suit my mother. Occasionally she would play a game of pat-ball tennis if it were not too hot or she felt in good enough health, but she never rode or walked, or took part in any sport or game. She did not even do any gardening. After a week or two at Macedon time would begin to hang on her hands and she was hard put to it to find fresh news for Marmee, let alone an occupation to interest her and fill her days.

One day is so like another here. I tried rather a successful experiment last week of painting some lace. I got so dizzy with boredom at knitting a Balaclava Helmet that I had to have a change. Jukes wanted something to make sleeves for a tea-gown so I found some old lace and gilded the edges on it and then painted the big flowers in colours like the brilliant pinks and purple ranunculas – you can't think how rich and effective it is – and how economical!

Edward and I had discovered a new and delightful pastime. We collected bull-frogs from the dam and lizards from the garden which we wrapped up alive in parcels and gave to unsuspecting grown-ups as presents. We had to be careful of lizards to make sure they weren't a small and deadly species of snake – the whip snake – which resembled a lizard, but if you could see their legs it was all right. We used to pick the lizards up by the tail and dangle them till after a bit the body would fall off and scurry away leaving the twitching tail stump between our fingers. This phenomenon held the greatest fascination for us. I hoped it didn't hurt the lizards but we were assured by Tom Quaife, the under-gardener, that they couldn't feel pain as they were cold-blooded like worms, and eventually they would grow another tail.

Although I was brave enough with frogs and lizards, I was terrified of snakes and of the hair-raising tales I had heard of people being bitten and dying within minutes. I hardly ever ventured into the garden or the surrounding bush without my legs being swathed in puttees and strong boots as ordered by my mother. However, there was a heat wave in the New Year and one day I ran out barefooted into the long grass beneath the gum trees which grew on the hill-side behind the house. A crooked stick, blackened by some past bushfire, lay partly concealed

in the grass and my heart jumped into my mouth as I thought at first
it was a Black Snake. As I was trembling from this fright I suddenly
felt a sharp little stab on my knee. I looked down and there I saw two
distinct red pin pricks. Without doubt, I thought, the fatal fang-marks
of a snake as described in the instructions of the anti-snake bite first-aid
box always kept at hand. That stick had been a snake after all, and I
had been bitten! I ran shrieking hysterically into the house where I was
picked up and carried into the schoolroom. My mother, hearing the com-
motion, came running from the drawing-room.

> I heard penetrating screams from Adelaide – I knew at once they were neither
> the shrieks of temper or acting, but real panic. I flew to the rescue and found
> her supported by the schoolroom-maid and the 2nd footman who said she
> had been bitten by a snake! I lost no time in applying the anti-snake bite
> cure,* but when I saw the place I felt reassured as it was a very tiny pin
> prick and no swelling visible. As soon as I could calm her enough to speak
> at all, I felt sure it was nothing and the shock and fright were the only
> things I had to cope with – but it did give me the deadliest of turns! ...
> [She] didn't recover for some time but lay absolutely white and quivering
> for hours afterwards. It is past history now, but it just shows the terrible
> sensitiveness of her nerves and one is not surprised at the difficulty of her
> nature when one realizes of what electrical stuff she is made.

Although it was only imagination, this experience was truly alarming
and I still have two faint little scars on my left knee as a memento of
my 'snake bite'!

Benjamin, the footman who had supported me during the 'snake' scare,
was a namby-pamby youth of about sixteen, with girlish features and
floppy hair. One day he was persuaded to go out riding but as he had
never sat on a horse before, he fell off on his head and got concussion.
My mother incautiously invited his mother to come and nurse him 'and
by now she has become so attached to the family that we can't get rid
of her!' Finally, the boy was sent off to a convalescent home, accompanied
by his mum, 'after the most affecting and cordial goodbyes' – and sighs
of relief from my mother at seeing the last of them. To everyone's astonishment, a few days later Mrs Benjamin suddenly reappeared at a Red
Cross garden party at Government Cottage dressed up in a silk gown
and silk stockings and a white feather boa –

> ... the greatest swell you ever saw! She greeted us with effusion and sat down
> to tea at our table quite as one of the house party. I happened to ask her
> if she was Australian born or an English woman. She replied with a wave

* A tourniquet, lancet, and a phial of permanganate of potash crystals.

of her parasol: 'Conceived in Woolwich, born in Ballarat – a bit of both'. Arthur says the time has come when we must be firm with her, especially as we now hear that the son has bolted from the home. I know she will come and weep on my shoulder!

In the end Benjamin and his mum disappeared from our ken whilst Hoodiwinks made caustic comments on my mother's tendency to encourage familiarity in the lower classes. Miss Dillon was got rid of at the same time as Mrs Benjamin. 'Our pestilent little prude of a guv has departed to everyone's relief,' said my mother. 'The new one arrives tomorrow. I suppose with luck she might remain three or four months . . .'

Miss Betty Curwen came into our lives on 6 February 1917. Edward, Pamela and I were assembled in the drawing-room and were introduced to her. I saw a tall and personable young woman with clear-cut features, dark hair and deep-set, vivid blue eyes. She had a calm and forthright manner, a pleasant, rather high-pitched Australian voice and a good hearty laugh. She was utterly genuine and without 'side'. Here was someone at last, I reflected, who might be a match for me. She was! 'Cor', as we came to call her, had many a tussle with me over the years to come, but eventually her integrity, her selflessness, loyalty and tact were to soften the asperities of my nature and help me to control my headstrong disposition. She remained the greatly loved and loving friend of four generations of our family till her death in 1976.

My father had come to the decision that Edward, now aged nine, must be sent to school. He started the year as a day boy at Melbourne Grammar School. I clamoured to be allowed to go to school too, but my mother said that it was out of the question. It was different for boys, she said, as they were always sent to a preparatory or 'private' school at an early age in England. She may have protested at the notion of an Australian school for Edward but if so she gives no inkling in her letters to Marmee. She merely wonders how he will like it when the novelty wears off, and remarks that she hopes he will be as happy as he thinks he will. 'Did I tell you of darling Edward's innocence in his pride of possessing his new school cap with the colours and motto of the school upon it? He was found sleeping in it every night.'

Edward soon became insufferable after he went to Melbourne Grammar – boastful, arrogant and contemptuous of girls. He was growing fast and the day finally came when I could no longer quell him physically as I had done in all our past battles. I had to devise other means of overlordship.

In the Bullycrub Room I had discovered a large royal-blue velvet tablecloth embroidered all over with gold thread, coloured beads and glass jewels. I didn't tell Edward about this treasure but picked all the rubies, emeralds .and pearls off when he was at school and hid them in a white painted doll's wardrobe which for some reason I called 'The Ship'. I kept this hidden from Edward, but if I wanted to get anything out of him I would bribe him from my secret store of jewels. Presently he found out they were not real and, discovering where I kept them, he threw them all down the lavatory. The only hold remaining to me now was the invention of swear words which I said were so terrible that even some grown-ups had never heard them! One I remember was 'Goth', and another was 'strunt'. In the sanctum of the Bullycrub Room I used to barter these invented oaths for schoolboy smut acquired by Edward at Melbourne Grammar, and 'Sherbet Suckers' or 'Aniseed Balls' imported from the school tuck shop.

An event now occurred which put me 'in high feather'.- as my mother announced to Marmee. Sir Baldwin Spencer, the distinguished anthropo-logist, asked me to open a Children's Room in the Melbourne Museum. 'It will be rather amusing to see her do it,' said my mother, 'but I think she will be overcome with shyness at the last moment.' Far from it! I was delighted to be the centre of the stage and spent hours beforehand composing and rehearsing my speech! The papers published front-page photographs of the ceremony with me standing on the steps of the Mu-seum, holding the Ceremonial silver Key, before a gathering of Bigwigs including my mother and father and Sir Baldwin. The *Australasian* reported the occasion as follows:

> Miss Adelaide Stanley, elder daughter of the Governor, formally opened a Children's Room at the Melbourne Museum. The room contains many exhibits of animals, birds, butterflies, flowers and shells. . . . Sir Baldwin Spencer . . . presented a golden key to Miss Stanley, who said in a clear unfaltering voice: 'Ladies and Gentlemen, I think it is a delightful idea to have a museum for children as well as for grown-ups, and I take great pleasure in declaring this museum open.'

The key was inscribed with my name and the date of the opening and lay in a black leather box lined with dark blue satin. It was my most treasured possession and I kept it for many years until it was finally stolen with the rest of my valuables in 1947.

On 16 March 1917 the Russian Empire fell and at the beginning of April the United States declared war on Germany, after trembling on the brink since the end of the previous year. 'So America has really taken the plunge at last,' wrote my mother on Easter Monday.

... one's only thought is how much will it help to shorten the war? ... If they can help to make good the shipping losses, that will mean a good deal....

Adelaide had a terrible 'frampold' fit for over a week – or as Nannie delightfully puts it – 'one of her ring-twisty phrases'.... Her changes of mood are the despair of her teachers who all say that the lessons are so very tiring with such a changeable child. She spent the afternoon with me the other day, which is always a great pleasure to her. I asked her whether she would like me to read to her or play games, to which she replied 'What I should *really* like would be for you to recount the time of your engagement to Dar. I have always felt curious to know what Dar said to you as your lover. I cannot think he was a *romantic youth* like Quentin Durward. I daresay he just *burst* a proposal to you without any sentimentalities beforehand.' I'm sure this will make you laugh, as it did me.... She has a great faculty of hitting the nail on the head in her observation of people and things, and both she and Edward have very good powers of expression.

Darling little dunce Pamela is only *just* beginning to read and is immensely proud of herself. The other two are very naughty and laugh at her unmercifully. She came to me the other day and said 'If you *promise* not to tell A. or E. I'll tell you something funny about my reading. Well! sometimes I forget which way I have to read and then I call GOD a DOG – and then, of course, I know God doesn't jump or bark and that makes me know the right way again.' Everything she says is with the utmost gravity.

I suppose that nowadays a mild case of dyslexia would be diagnosed in the difficulties Pamela had with reading and writing. She was an adorable little child with her funny, solemn ways and expressive gestures, her enormous blue eyes and flaxen, page-boy style hair. She was worshipped for her loving disposition by everyone from the Governor-General to the pantry boy at Stonnington. I was regrettably jealous of her popularity and bullied her in revenge.

The endless vice-regal functions and fund-raising activities continued unabated and my mother became increasingly bored and unwilling to make the effort required of her. Probably her pregnancy made her more easily tired and irritable than usual; nevertheless, she tried to do her duty, always feeling that she was on a stage, acting a part, and determined that 'the show must go on'.

Arthur and I stood and 'received' over 500 people for one hour. I often think how you would laugh at seeing us in our 'official' capacity ... and to hear me give my best official greeting and smile 500 times over. You've no idea what a strain it is and how my arm and shoulder ache afterwards. Australians are, I think, particularly hearty in shaking hands. I always know at a distance which the crushers are going to be from their appearance. I notice that vigorous handshaking *never* goes with *pince-nez* and when I see 'pinch-noses' among the never-ending line I know I may count on them for more gentle treatment.

Hoodiwinks also was getting thoroughly on her nerves.

In addition to an unusually prolonged and an unusually loose cold, he has been very grumpy and very obstructive and unhelpful about lists for dinners. He *hates* Arthur or myself to have any word in who shall be invited, and would just go on asking the same dreary old stagers over and over again, for no other reason than that they are on the Government House List. . . . He is, of course, *admirable* at his job and one need never have a fear of a detail going wrong in anything he undertakes. . . . The curious thing is that the moment there is anything afoot in the way of a function and he can don his top hat, frock coat and immaculate gloves, and there is a little strip of red carpet somewhere, he is a different being – genial, brisk and splendid at looking after one's guests. It is the 'petite intimité' with us he can't stand, partly because we do not keep up pomp and ceremony when we are alone. I *cannot* understand how people can regret any of the accessories of this sort of life. The only thing I may miss a little is having an ADC to write tedious letters and do all my telephoning – and also the habit of never taking any money out with me to pay for anything! I wonder if for a time after we get home Arthur and I will rush into dinner first! I'm quite sure that it will take us some time to get used to doing without 'God Save' to galvanise us into action in any public place.

Only two of my mother's letters survive for the months of May and June. In them she bewails the fact that the intervals between getting home mail are getting longer and longer, 'owing, I suppose, to the horrible success of the submarines'. There were rumours now of Australian waters being mined, and every night the long fingers of searchlights swept to and fro across the starry sky above Melbourne. The newspapers were full of accounts of food shortages in England despite the rationing of some commodities, which had been introduced early in the year. My mother wrote distractedly to Marmee on 1 May giving some not very practical suggestions as to how starvation could be avoided:

I do wonder how much you feel the new food regulations? I feel such a pig at every meal thinking that people are short while we are suffering *no* inconvenience of any kind, except, of course, a rise in prices – but it would really be impossible to tell that we were at war . . . Darling, *Darling,* I do hope that the pinch of food is not really felt, and anyhow you can grow potatoes and cocks and hens and a little wheat crop. . . .

My mother was so anxious that we should realise the deprivations being suffered at home that she issued a decree that we were to have no butter at luncheon! I indignantly pointed out that as we couldn't give the butter to our starving relations we might as well eat it ourselves-for which remark I was given a long lecture on the evils of self-indulgence and the desirability of thought for others.

Butter or no butter, we realised that we were luckier than the unfortunate Governor of New South Wales, who was being sent home in disfavour to England and its privations.*

> Yesterday, the poor Strickland family, who have been banished from their kingdom and recalled home, were passing through Melbourne so we had to have them up here from early morning to spend the day. Poor Lady Edeline however ... remained on board. But I had to go down and see her later in the day and her terror of the journey was painful. She was sitting alone in the most spacious and luxurious private cabin, huddled up in a corner, a helpless, inert mass. Her maid could not face the dangers of the voyage and the nurse ... will only venture as far as Fremantle, but this has not been broken to her yet. ... If the ship is submarined I think it is *certain* to kill poor Lady E., even if they were all rescued. They are frightfully sore at having to go at such a time, and I must say I think it is very hard after so many years of service. ... The whole business has been very humiliating and both he and she are very bitter against the Governor-General and Lady H. whom they suspect of having been instrumental in getting them removed. Oh! my little Marmee, how ugly and petty all the little ins-and-outs of official life can be!

On 6 June my mother covered three large pages of writing paper in pencil to Marmee, commenting on the gloomy war news, the Irish situation, Australian political and social affairs, before coming to the vital point of her letter. It must have cost her much uneasy thought, after months of deception, as to how best she could break the news of her imminent confinement. She resorted to a rather facetious, joking style.

> What shall I tell you now? Oh! perhaps I might as well break to you that *numero cinque-cento* will soon be appearing in the flesh. ... I could not make up my mind to tell you before, for fear of perhaps giving you little occasional

* Strickland, as Governor of the senior colony, held a dormant commission to act in the Governor-General's absence, but so bad had his relations with the 'Mun-Fugs' become that he was recalled on the advice of Sir Ronald (no doubt prompted by Lady Helen) who reported to the Colonial Office that in his official view, it would be dangerous in wartime if Strickland were to act in his place. It was his opinion, the Governor-General concluded, that Strickland was vain, ambitious and not altogether stable, and therefore he recommended that in the event of his demise, the Governor of Victoria, Sir Arthur Stanley, should be sworn in as acting Governor-General. (Gavin Souter, *Lion and Kangaroo*, 1976.)

twinges of anxiety. . . . It is silly however, to think there should be any reason for you to feel fussed, but being the Queen of Fuss-pots myself I'm apt to credit everyone with a like amount. . . . I am really very pleased at having another young 'gorilla' – if it is half as darling as Pupkin-pie; and I am especially glad for him, as he ought to have a companion. He is so much younger than any of the others that he is apt to be spoilt in having everything his own way . . .

Lyulph was certainly growing into a very headstrong little boy – 'A real young Turk' my mother calls him in another letter – 'and he will need very firm handling'. But she was powerless to 'handle' him. His masterful ways combined with a highly original turn of mind and an endearing sense of mischief completely bewitched her and she continued to spoil and indulge him in spite of my father's occasional remonstrances and efforts to enforce a measure of discipline.

We older children were equally amused and fascinated by Lyulph. He had all sorts of play of his own invention. Quite suddenly, in the middle of a game or a song he would say, 'I must just go and fetch my little girl now. Will you wait for me?' And off he would go and have conversation with his invisible playmate. When he came back we would say, 'Have you brought your little girl?' and he would usually reply, 'No, she's asleep so please talk in a "visper".'

There was a little gate in the garden at Melbourne which led into a paddock. He always wanted to go through this gate to visit 'my friends – Lady Markanette in the blue dress and the Cold Man of Glass'. Again he would have long conversations with these imaginary characters, taking their parts in turn and imitating their voices and gestures.

He would get into terrible rages if he was teased or thwarted in the slightest degree, and my mother always took his part and gave into him. 'I can't bear to see him cry or be distressed,' she said to Marmee, 'for it is always the most poignant and desperate grief.' But more often it was plain temper.

Although my mother's thoughts were centred almost entirely on Lyulph and the coming baby, she still kept up the daily hour after tea in the drawing-room for the rest of us. In addition to the reading aloud and singing, we now acted scenes from Shakespeare which my mother coached us in, and marvellously good she was at it.

Infinitely patient and encouraging, she never became irritable or sarcastic when we couldn't do what she wanted. Every voice inflection, every facial expression, every gesture and every move was repeated over and over again until we got it right. Timing of phrase and action was equally meticulously rehearsed. We achieved results mostly by copying her performance as exactly as we could, but sometimes Edward or I would argue with her about her interpretation of a role and she would always listen to our ideas. We all became stage-struck in varying degrees and enjoyed acting more than any other of our amusements. Pamela unmistakably showed 'star quality', even at that early age; Edward, none, although he had a fine stage presence and an uninhibited style in declamatory passages; I was considered too uncontrolled in voice and movement but possessing an admirable sense of drama. Lady Macbeth was my favourite role! I decided to become a great actress as well as a famous singer, not at all discouraged by the cold water thrown on my ambitions by my father. 'Adelaide has already approached Arthur on the subject of going on the stage and was much less dashed by his disapproval than I was when I made the same request at an even earlier age,' said my mother.

> She is of the opinion that women must have a profession. The other day I heard Edward say, 'Well, I know Dar won't allow you to be an actress, Adelaide, and I don't think he will want you to be a hospital nurse much, so what else can you be?' After a pause Adelaide said 'Oh well, I expect I'll be a delightful kind of virgin and always look beautiful and always be very kind to people'. To which Edward replied, 'Yes, but that isn't a profession exactly. You wouldn't be paid any money for doing just that'. The peaceful Pamela pursues her way untroubled, as yet, by these problems. The quiet strength of determination with which she resists every effort to be taught anything shows she has a certain amount of will-power in her otherwise yielding disposition. She told Arthur without a blush that she tried to *forget* her lessons instead of *learning* them!

10

Five of Us

Victoria Venetia, the youngest member of our family, was born on 29 June 1917. Having given Marmee a detailed and dramatic account of her confinement, my mother described the new baby's appearance which she found enchanting.

> She is like a little wren with the tiniest face and the most pointed little chin you ever saw . . . She is very delicately and neatly made, and has a pretty shaped head covered with thick, silky, light brown hair, and the prettiest slender little hands with long tapering fingers.
>
> Adelaide observed that it was a pity that I had to be ill whenever I had a baby. She added she wouldn't mind, however, being ill herself if she could have one and what sort of 'germ' must you get? I told her that she couldn't have babies till she was grown up and married. She said 'And how about if I am a widow? I have an idea that widows manage to have children when their husbands are dead, and I would prefer having children without a husband to fuss over as well'.

I had a pretty good notion by this time as to how babies were conceived and born from information extracted from Edward during our Bullycrub Room sessions. I remember wondering whether he was telling the truth (I knew what a little liar he was!) and therefore I decided to sound out my mother to see if she would confirm his story. But she hedged, and evaded my cross-questioning so I had to go to Hilda who was more explicit but said tartly that I shouldn't talk about 'rude' subjects to boys – even my own brother.

Again my mother lay in a darkened bedroom for four or five weeks after her confinement, although the doctor assured her that there was nothing to worry about 'and carried me himself and deposited me on the sofa where I spent the afternoon. . . . I am feeling stronger the last two days [and] I shall be glad to be done with feeding-cups and nurses . . .' At the end of August she told Marmee, 'I *was* very seedy till about a week ago but I have taken a turn now and am much more sprightly. If *only* the war would end and we were coming home, how gloriously well I should feel!'

My father had recently bought a car – a Buick – which he took to driving about himself. He was one of the worst drivers I have ever known in my life, and although my mother tried loyally not to criticise, his lack of expertise filled her with terror.

> I have been for several drives in our new car with Arthur as chauffeur. He is a dashing driver, but is really very skilful and better than either of our two chauffeurs. The only perturbing thing is that he never appears to look out for anything and very seldom slacks his speed. (Once he did change the gear and I thought we were going to roll down the hill backwards – a perpetual nightmare of mine – but he put on the brakes all right and we only stuck for a short while). He is really wonderful among the traffic in the most crowded streets, but I know one more agony has been added to my life, for whenever he goes out without me I shall always dread that some hideous accident has happened.

The industrial unrest in Australia, fomented by Communist and other left-wing elements, was going from bad to worse. The Conscription Referendum of October 1916 had split the Labor Party but nevertheless, in the following November, Billy Hughes had managed to form a coalition government with the Liberals and in March 1917 the new National Party, headed by Hughes, went to the country and was returned with a strong majority. It was hoped that this administration would achieve some sort of compromise between the employers and the Unions, but the divisions within the Labor Party had provided the militants with the opportunity of capturing the Unions, and my mother thought it was inevitable that there would be 'an almighty Stramash' one day. During August a rail strike in New South Wales was paralysing communications between that State and Victoria and disrupting the overseas mail service, but my mother managed to get off a letter to Marmee.

> We have just had word that a mail leaves here tomorrow . . . an American one . . . and it is quite possible that when the mail train reaches the N.S. Wales Border there will be no connection to take the letters on.* . . . All

---

* All American ships sailed from Sydney.

is quiet in our State at present, but there is an uncomfortable feeling that a sort of revolutionary outburst of the red raggedy Labor people is not unlikely. What soldiery there is left in Australia to deal with such a situation would not, I should think, be of very much use, and as likely as not would join the rioters. I suppose the feeling here is only what is going on in every other country of the world – and which has been seething and bubbling for so long without ever actually boiling over. Now that Russia has taken the lid off I suspect that others will follow her example and a good deal of steam will have to be blown off before things settle down. Will they ever do so, I wonder?

One of my mother's pet charities was the Melbourne City Newsboys' Club. It had been founded and was run by a remarkable Australian woman. Miss Edith Onians was what used to be called a charity-worker but she was no ordinary 'Do-Gooder'. She dedicated her life to the under-privileged out of compassionate love for humanity and gave help to the distressed and unfortunate with no thought of public recognition or financial reward. She never condemned or passed judgement on the failings of mankind, but there was no sentimental nonsense about her, and she was never shocked. Her serene calm was imperturbable. She carried out her schemes for the rehabilitation and welfare of prisoners, prostitutes and other outcasts of society with gentle but unremitting perseverance and an unshakable conviction in her humanitarian principles.

The Melbourne newsboys at this time were recruited from the poorest homes, or from orphanages and hostels for the homeless and down-and-outs. They roamed the streets barefooted and in rags, and were all too often sucked down into the criminal underworld. Miss Onians wished to right the wrong done to these children through no fault of their own. She raised money to rent a hall for them and provide newspapers and games, and a canteen. She also gave them clothes and books. She was determined now to build them a recreation centre of their own where they could bring their friends and families. This she managed to do, in spite of other more pressing calls on the public for donations to support the war charities, and eventually the City Newsboys' Club and Recreation Centre was opened by my mother in Little Collins Street, where it flourished for many years.*

Miss Onians adored my mother and so did the newsboys and their families. In turn my mother greatly admired Miss Onians as an example of a right-thinking person, and her soft heart was touched by the band of little ragged boys who swarmed round her whenever she visited Miss Onians at her centre.

* Now at 409 St Kilda Road.

I, too, was very fond of Miss Onians, who never seemed to expect me to behave badly and always treated me with kindly affection. She used to invite me sometimes to spend the day with her at her weekend cottage near Melbourne. There would be nobody else there – just dear Miss Onians and me – and I recall with unmixed pleasure the relaxed and happy times I spent with her. She would tell me stories about rogues and crooks who were her friends and who were always having the bad luck of getting put back into prison. One I remember, was Squizzy Taylor – and she would always end up by saying in her Australian drawl, 'Ah, he had a bee-ewtiful nyeture'.

When my parents revisited Australia in 1923, Miss Onians introduced my mother to Squizzy, then at large between gaol sentences for robbery and fraud. They met at Menzies Hotel, of all unlikely places, and each vied with the other as to which could exert the greatest charm. My mother, now in her late forties, was still a very graceful and pretty woman. Squizzy, from his photographs at this time, was probably about the same age – a dapper little cock sparrow of a man wearing a natty suit, and billycock hat, and carrying a cane. One would have given a great deal to have been present at that meeting! When my mother left Australia Squizzy gave her a silver box inscribed '*To Lady Stanley from one misunderstood to one who understands! Leslie Taylor*'. My mother was touched by this compliment and replied thanking him for bestowing on her 'the most precious gift of understanding'. She treasured the box until her death and never referred to Squizzy's bad end a few years after their meeting, despite her hopes that she had converted him to honest ways. He was murdered in 1927 in a gun duel with a rival gangster who was also shot dead. It was suspected that yet another crook was involved in the fight, as three revolvers were found on the scene, but the identity of this mysterious third man was never discovered. Squizzy Taylor's box is still in the possession of my family.

On occasions the newsboys and their families were invited to Stonnington, where they would play in the gardens and sit down to an enormous tea, with presents and crackers provided by my mother. After one such bean-feast, the baby Victoria's christening party to which the newsboys and their mothers were invited, it was discovered that Pamela and I had caught ringworm from contact with these poor little ragamuffins. Irregular circles of weeping, red sores with scaly centres spread over our necks and chests, and Pamela got it in her head and had to have her hair shaved off. My mother burst into tears at the sight of her shorn lamb and had her put into a white cap with a frill round the edge. My long, thick hair was washed night and morning by Hilda with carbolic soap, which made it shine beautifully and turned it into a becoming red-gold colour. 'Adelaide is divided in her desire to be as interesting as Pamela and her vanity over her hair,' said my mother. 'She has wheedled Miss Curwen into making her a cap, too.' My mother couldn't bring herself to believe that we had caught anything so plebeian as ringworm, so she told Marmee that it was a disease the soldiers had brought back with them from Egypt. 'It is not as bad as ring-worm, but the same kind of thing. My hospital nurse, to console me, assured me that it is rampant among the "first families" of Melbourne.' We had the disease for months and months, but I never got it in my hair; nor did anyone else catch it from us.

At the end of August Pamela and I were sent with Cor to a sea-side boarding-house to convalesce from our ringworm. Within ten days we were back, covered with renewed sores, and Pamela had to have her head shaved again.

Edward, who had escaped the plague, was invited to stay on a sheep station in the Western District, and Cor accompanied him. I wept miserably from envy and loneliness. My mother was entirely wrapped up in the babies, and in any case Pamela and I were 'untouchable' and not allowed to go near either the nursery or the drawing-room. We spent our days in the schoolroom, which was protected by a carbolic-soaked sheet hung across the door; and we were looked after by Hilda. When it was fine we played in a part of the garden well isolated from the rest of the community. Most of the time I climbed trees, which, as I have said, was forbidden but there was nobody around to prevent me. I used to pinch cigarettes from my father's silver box and fill my pinafore pockets with lumps of sugar which I took to an eyrie on top of a particularly thick pepper tree. Here I could not be observed and I settled down to enjoy my illicit pleasures while dreaming of the day when I would be grown up and my own mistress.

Once I set fire to my dress and had to confess to 'playing with matches'. I would never have dared tell about stealing and smoking cigarettes! On another occasion I fell out of the tree and although rather bruised and frightened I didn't complain, for fear of retribution. The next morning when I woke I found my sheets and nightgown stained with blood. On further investigation I felt sure I had sustained some fatal internal injury from my fall out of the tree and I was being punished by God for my sins.

I called for Hilda and in floods of tears I confessed my crime and fears. To my astonishment she took it all with the utmost calm! Presently my mother came in and I steeled myself to the worst in the way of

lectures and punishments. But again, there was a most unexpected reaction. She put her arms around me and said there was no need to be
frightened. My trouble had nothing to do with internal injuries but was
due to what she called 'the course of Nature'.

I couldn't really understand what my mother was trying to explain,
as she talked in an obscure and euphemistic way of God and the marvel
of creation. I was only thankful I was not going to die and, for some
inscrutable reason, was not even in disgrace. Afterwards, I wondered how
I had come to miss such an important piece of biological information
in my investigations into the mysteries of life, and I stored it up as a
valuable bargaining counter in my transactions with Edward. But when
I finally produced this revelation he sneered and said he'd known it long
ago, as his friend 'Breezy' Gale had told him during his first term at
Melbourne Grammar.

A state of armed neutrality now existed between Edward and myself.
There were fewer opportunities for fisticuffs and our interests began to
diverge. Edward's talk was all of football and sport and of scoring off
the masters, varied by the repetition of his school friends' sniggering witti-
cisms. I was beginning to take a real interest in music and I practised
assiduously at the piano and singing. In the evening there was homework
to be done and therefore we saw less of drawing-room life, which became
devoted more or less entirely to the babies.

Poor little Pamela was the odd man out and was treated with contempt
by me when she tried to join in my pursuits. I still had the vicious habit
of pinching her when I was overcome by an excess of irritation against
her. Afterwards I always felt ashamed at my cruelty and resigned to the
punishment which inevitably followed.

I was not spanked now but given improving pieces to learn by heart
such as Shakespeare's sonnets or excerpts from St Thomas à Kempis. But
the punishment I hated most was 'writing out lines'. 'I must not pinch
Pamela' – a hundred times. 'I must not be rude to Miss Curwen (or Hilda
etc)' – another hundred. And most heinous crime of all – 'I must not
answer Mammie back'. Sometimes I was sent down to my father to be
lectured when my mother could make no impression on what she called
my 'little heart of stone'. I didn't mind this particularly as he always
let me have my say before demolishing my arguments with a legal
adroitness which I could not help admiring.

Hilda was still my confidante in many things, but I had recently discovered a new bond with Geeps – the subject of being in love! I took
to visiting him in the ADCs' office when Hoodiwinks was out of the
way, and, sitting on the end of his sofa, I would discourse with him

about 'affairs'. Evidently he had great experience in such matters and I would listen spellbound to accounts of the beauty and fascination of his various girl friends, while I myself cast my eye around for a suitable swain of my own age. There were some older boys at Melbourne Grammar whom I had seen when we attended 'Sports Day', but I could only appraise them from afar, as they stood aloof from little girls, and on the whole I concluded that they didn't measure up to the heroes in Hilda's novels, or the interesting war-wounded soldiers in 'hospital-blue' who were often entertained at outings given by the Red Cross for them at Federal Government House and Stonnington.

My mother was beginning to feel that a family of five were more than she could cope with. 'I intend to give up, as much as I can, all public engagements to be more with them all ...' she told Marmee. 'Adelaide and Edward, especially, are at an age when they need to be supervised out of lesson hours.' In spite of her professed lack of class-consciousness and her love of 'the poor – the *real* people', her egalitarian principles were not profound.

> I notice little things that are picked up by them when they are left with the schoolroom-maid, or when Edward hobnobs with the groom and chauffeurs or plays football with the footmen. .... Everyone is so fond of the children that I cannot forbid them to go into the back premises. The only thing is to provide myself as a counter-attraction.

To this end she decided to wean Victoria in order to leave herself more time for the rest of us. Anyway, she said that feeding the baby was too much of a 'drag' on her, but she added 'It is always a pang to finally put them away from one and I howled all the morning when she didn't come to me – braved it out for two days and then tried to take her back when it was too late, and very troublesome.'

Sad to say, her efforts to take her elder children back were also 'very troublesome'. She demanded too much of Edward and me, and even Pamela, with all her sweetness of disposition, passively resisted my mother's efforts at complete domination.

Throughout September and October the industrial situation in Australia continued to deteriorate. 'Our strikes are spreading as merrily as the ring-worm,' said my mother.

> ... thousands of volunteers are being employed by the Government of N.S.W. and Victoria to replace wharf-workers, railwaymen and many others. It is very monstrous of these men, striking at this time on the flimsiest excuses, for there is no complaint of low wages or overwork or bad conditions of

any kind – but as long as these terrible I.W.W.* people are at work there will be unrest and revolutionary outbursts. The Arbitration Courts are an abject failure, for the Unions only abide by their decisions when they favour their claims, and just strike when their demands are not conceded.

By the end of October the strikes were settled, more or less on the employers' terms, which my mother feared would undoubtedly lead to renewed industrial trouble before very long. 'At times one feels *appalled* at the discontent and violent hatred ... raging in every corner of the world, and the dreadful thought forces itself upon one that after we have done fighting with Germany there may be fighting even more terrible than in this war before us.'

While Australia was being torn apart by bitter sectarian and political strife, the Bolshevik Revolutionaries had stormed the Winter Palace, captured the Tsar and his family, and formally announced that Russia was out of the war after the signing of the Brest-Litovsk Peace Treaty on 9 February 1918. On 24 October the Italians had been defeated by the Austrians and Germans at Caporetto and had fled in panic and disorder. Allenby and the British and Anzac forces were fighting almost alone against Turkey, and in Mesopotamia and Salonika the campaigns were being hampered by lack of reinforcements and munitions.

The collapse of Russia had released an enormous number of German and Austrian troops, as well as huge quantities of war materiel which were diverted to the Western Front. According to Churchill, 'our fighting units had been decimated fivefold in the last six months of 1917', and our peril was so great that at last a Supreme Commander had been appointed over all the Allied Forces in the person of Field-Marshal Foch. The outlook on all sides was grim.

As usual, my mother turned from the dark prospects of the outside world to the solace and cosy comforts of the nursery.

The darling little new Baby has become much more of a personality.... and is developing fast into a plump little partridge. She is growing quite pretty if it were not, as Adelaide puts it, for her 'calamitous nose'. It is not ugly but at present is rather large for her tiny little face. She is the greatest contrast to what Lyulph was. He is my darling little companion just now, when the other children have to keep aloof on account of their horrid little disease. Even when I am dropping with tiredness I cannot let him go. ... He always talks of himself as 'Little Lyboo' now and gets funnier and more engaging every day. ... He is not pretty really, but has a lovely skin and the most radiant smile, and cheeks like peaches. You will think me a drivelling mother – and so I am! I must tell you of a saying of Lyulph's. A little

* International Workers of the World.

quelquechose de naturelle was heard and I said 'What was that noise?' to which
he replied 'This was only little Lyboo barking in his trousers'. He loves making
a sensation and harrowing my feelings by saying in a breathless tone with
wide-open eyes, 'I-I-I made this noise *again* – I *did*!' I say, 'What noise?' and
then he bends down and tries to reach his fat arms around his darling behind
and purple with the effort says 'This noise round here in my other front'.
The children lie about in heaps with laughter when he goes through his performance ... Oh, how I do wish you could see him. ... I am beginning to
feel that even the danger will not deter me from plunging home if the war
is still raging by the time our term is up. ... It will be a real trial of nerve
to face the horrors of submarines and mines with five small children. ...
Adelaide and Edward of course desire nothing so ardently as the adventure
of being submarined. Pamela tries to follow in their valiant train but says,
'Of course, I should *love it* – but I think it would be nice if we could all
keep together in the water.' Shrieks of insulting laughter from the other two,
followed by a smart rap each with a ruler from me and prompt silence.

In the spring a weedy little clergyman arrived from Hong Kong, where
he was a missionary, bringing letters of introduction to my father. He
was some distant connection of the Stanleys.

I am sure he is very poor for MacKenzie washed his few poor little things
in order that he might have enough to go on with. Arthur has been very
good on the whole and has not pounced on any 'follies', but I noticed a
slight wearing off of this benign attitude last night when the poor little thing
exclaimed in the most throaty and wrapt voice 'But you know, Bishops are
sort of *Kings*.' Arthur replied with breezy promptness 'Oh Bosh! They are
merely Civil Servants'.

Cousin Eustace, as we were told to call him, had a wrinkled yellow
face like a Chinaman with squinty eyes behind owl-like spectacles. He
was very kind to us and offered to take Edward and me to the circus.
'He arrived back exhausted,' said my mother, 'A. and E. having dragged
him, as far as I can make out, into most of the lions' and tigers' dens.'
We had never seen a circus before and I remember being wildly excited
at the noise and smell, and the spangles glittering under the bright lights,
and being fascinated by all the turns, with the exception of the clowns,
whom I found hideously embarrassing and unfunny. Cousin Eustace gave
us each a bag of sweets and spent most of the evening peering earnestly
at us instead of the circus, to see if we were enjoying it.
While Cousin Eustace was staying at Government House a dinner party
was given for the visiting theatrical stars, Cyril Maude and Marie Tempest. In the teeth of Hoodiwinks' disapproval my mother also invited
Marie Tempest's lover Graham Browne, whom she found congenial.

Cousin Eustace questioned Geeps closely about the relationship between Marie Tempest and Browne, and declared that he would address her as 'Mrs Browne'. Geeps told him that she was always called 'Miss Tempest'.

> Our poor little friend then asked him straight out if they were living in sin. Rather awkward! [said my mother]. He also asked if *I* knew, and I have been expecting him to cross-question me. I know I should lose my head and say I hadn't seen them in bed so I couldn't tell – or something of the sort. However, the dinner party went off quite well. . . . Marie Tempest has grown very raddled but she was very chirpy. . . .

Naturally, I was much intrigued by all this gossip, relayed to me by Geeps, but found it hard to believe that two such ancient creatures as Marie Tempest and Graham Browne could conceivably be 'in love'!

One high summer's day with scorching sun and 'dragon's breath' North wind blowing, yet another garden party was given at Stonnington with unlimited strawberries and cream, much appreciated by all of us and none more than Pamela, who spent most of the afternoon in the tea tent. There was a brass band which riveted Lyulph's attention. He stood in front of them clapping and shouting 'Bravo!' 'Now some more Band!' The man with the big horn asked him whether he would like to be put inside it, to which he replied '*You* must get in and pick the notes out for Lyboo, H'm?' He always ended his sentence with 'H'm'.

Edward and I stood behind my mother and father while they 'received'.

> There was a good deal of giggling and whispering, and occasional explosions when Captain Conant and Mr Hood read out certain names of the guests which sounded like 'Miss Mud' and 'Mr Pump'! Mr Hood had to turn round and reprove Adelaide, whereupon she began to make a series of appalling grimaces at his back. I had to administer a cleverly timed back-handed rap on her legs with my parasol between gracious 'How d'you dos' to my guests.

Five days before Christmas another Referendum on Conscription was held. The country voted solidly against the measure, contrary to the forecasts of the Press and general opinion. 'Its rejection will cause a good deal of political complication and I should think that Hughes' star has set . . .' said my mother.

However, Billy Hughes was far from finished. He resigned, but there was no one else who could govern. The Labor Party had 'blown its brains out', according to the Melbourne *Argus,* in the split following the previous Conscription Referendum, and the Nationalist Party was now the only acceptable choice for the country. Early in the New Year the Governor-

General asked Hughes to form a government and he went back with the same Cabinet as before.

Edward and I started to play tennis during the Christmas holidays at Macedon. We were coached by my father and Geeps. We were taught to serve underhand, and to stand well back from the net. I would have liked to volley returns instead of playing pat-ball. 'Edward has a very good notion', said my mother, 'but Adelaide is a regular "Quangle-Wangle" and is generally up in the air somewhere with the ball.' It was considered inelegant by my mother to rush about the court or jump in the air. She herself played what she called a 'leg-and-shriek' game, dressed in a white shirt and bell-shaped skirt, white tennis shoes and her hat tied on her head with a white veil.

This Christmas, present-giving had assumed such enormous proportions that it was a real work, my mother said, to get the right thing for everybody and not cause any heart-burnings or jealousies. Besides giving to the household, which included the orderlies, police at the gates, chauffeurs, grooms and gardeners and all their wives and children, my mother provided each of us children with presents to give to the staff. This mass of presents was stacked in my mother's sitting-room and we spent hours helping to wrap them up and label them under Cor's supervision. 'Miss Curwen is a really nice creature and is a great help to me,' said my mother. 'She has that most blessed of qualities, *tact*, and is a *real* lady. ... She gets on so well with Nannie, too. I only wish naughty little Adelaide would be easier with her ... She is the sort of child that no governess would ever really get on well with ... she *will* not be submissive enough.'

I think that my mother was determined not to admit or concede for a moment that anybody else was capable of controlling me, as she herself could not.

Edward and I got into serious strife during the present-wrapping. We crept along to the sitting-room one night after everyone had gone to bed, abstracted a large box of chocolates destined for Tom Quaife, the under-gardener's family, and gobbled them up. When this misdeed was discovered, a fulminating lecture was given to us on the wickedness not only of stealing, but of depriving poor, underprivileged little children of one of the few pleasures in their lives by our greed. Edward shrugged the whole thing off with schoolboy bravado, but I remember the feelings of abject shame and self-disgust induced by my mother's biting words, and my enjoyment of Christmas that year was somewhat clouded by my sense of guilt.

11

Doctor's Orders

The combined effects of child-bearing and homesickness were beginning seriously to undermine my mother's health. She was nearly forty-two when the last baby was born, and although the doctors could find nothing wrong with her physically, her mental state was causing some concern and there were fears of a 'nervous breakdown'. Her anxiety and depression increased and she became convinced that she was suffering from heart disease. In January 1918 she wrote to Marmee from the nursing home in Melbourne to which she had gone for a 'rest cure'.

> Up at Macedon my heart took to doing unexpected things, so I came up to see Doctor Davenport who at once popped me in here. Yesterday he called in a heart and nerve specialist ... and his verdict was that I must give up most of my public work and any other occupation entailing strain or *fuss* or nervous apprehension for the next few months. . . . I am going to give myself up to getting strong and well now. The children need me so much that it would be dreadful if I couldn't be with them to direct their turbulent spirits.

She was referring, of course, to Edward and me, as Pamela never stood up to her and she idolised the two babies. She went on: 'Arthur wrote to say that they had been very good since I left except that Edward had had a lapse and had taken Pamela's beautiful Christmas-present paint-box and had painted Dingo, the fox-terrier, bright green.'

I, also, had had a go with Pamela's 'Reeves Water-colour' paint-box and had patriotically painted our two guinea-pigs with red, white and blue stripes. We thought painting the animals a jolly joke but Edward was given a whacking for his misplaced sense of humour. Nothing happened to me, although I wondered why my father thought it was wrong to paint Dingo but permissible to daub the guinea-pigs. I came to the conclusion that it was because a dog was more intelligent and therefore more liable to feel ridicule. Or perhaps it was because my motives were considered loyal and therefore the act was pardonable. I wrote to my mother in the nursing home but refrained from mentioning this episode.

> Yesterday Cor and I and Edward and Nanny and Sparkums went to the top of The Mount. We started about 7 o'clock and it was lovely and cool after the hot day. When we got up there it was the most beautiful sight I have ever seen. All around by the right there was nothing but heavy white smoke from the bushfires showing up against the dark sky. And then half-way round the sky it was flaming orange-red, looming even redder as it got lower down. Round by the Camel's Hump we saw the bushfire and we heard an occasional tree crack. It was a wonderful sight to see trees looking as if they were made of fire. There were lots of bats and possums and other queer animals [fleeing from the fire] ...

My father wrote every day he was away from my mother – rather dull letters telling her all he had been doing in a brisk, factual style, and begging his 'own Titania Queen' to do everything the doctors ordered, 'don't overtire yourself, either by doing too much or by conjecturing mishaps which have not yet happened'.

My mother was enjoying the sensation she was causing in the nursing home. 'It is funny how to certain people it is a real excitement to have "Vice-Regality" round them,' said she. 'The first day or two ... a number of nurses who had nothing to do with me kept coming in and out, ostensibly to make kind enquiries as to how I felt, but really I think to carry back to their patients a description of my *saut-de-lit** and the ribbons in my cap.' She then told Marmee a story about some little newsboys who visited her – an incident which both gratified and touched her.

> A message was brought up to me that some flowers had come for me but that the messenger seemed very unwilling to give them up. I sent down to ask who they were from and found they were from my friend, Miss Onians, and that three little boys had brought them. I knew at once that they must be some of her newsboys. I sent down again to ask them whether they would like to come up and deliver the flowers themselves to me. That was evidently what they wanted for they didn't wait to be shown up but tumbled over one another on the stairs, I'm afraid breaking the Sabbath afternoon slumber

* Bed-jacket.

of all the old lady patients. When they got to the landing, however, they didn't know which my room was and a man whose door was open was amused to hear the discussion as to the mode of procedure. One said "'ere 'Arry, you're eldest. You pop round quick sharp into the rooms and see if Lady Stanley is in any of 'em.' Another said 'Stupid! Y'ave ter knock in these-'ere plices. Blowed if I know 'ow yer goin' ter do the job without yer 'oller outside the doors and foind aht oo's on the other soide.' At last the Sister caught up with them and ushered them in. They were three of the darlingest, dirtiest little villains I ever saw. After a few minutes of petrified shyness and nudging and digging at each other, the biggest of them said, 'These-'ere is some flowers what Miss Onians told us to leave yer but we didn't loike to give 'em up to anyone else.' After suitable thanks I made them undo them for me and in arranging them and pouring out water and incidentally breaking the soap-dish, they lost all *gêne* and we had the jolliest of afternoons. One of them was looking at Arthur's photograph and I asked him if he knew who it was. He was silent so I gave them each a guess and the littlest of them squeaked out 'Why it's Arthur Stanley!' Whereupon the big boy turned on him and said '*The Governor*, you mean, my son. Where's yer bloomin' manners gorn?' I found at last that I should have to be the one to make them depart, but I had to promise to wave to them out of the window. If only some reporters had been round the corner they would have had the unique sight of the Governor's wife in her night-gown and cap making wild demonstrations at three prancing little urchins in the middle of the road – and who were shouting messages and adieus at the tops of their voices.

Unfortunately for my mother's *penchant* for being the centre of an effective scene, no report appeared in the Press of this whimsical incident. The only allusion to my mother's illness was made by the *Bulletin* some time later, who remarked in its gossip column 'Excellency Stanley's Lady is holiday-making. Don't ask me what was her malady because I don't know. So little has been happening socially of late that Sassiety, for the most part, was not aware that her Ladyship was ill until it was announced that she was well'.

By the middle of February my mother's nerves were considered strong enough for her to recuperate by the sea. Doctor Davenport lent her his villa at Sorrento, and thither she went accompanied by Nurse Mangan, Jukie, us three eldest children marshalled by Cor, and a houseful of servants.

In spite of my *enragement* at this place being called 'Sorrento' it is really rather lovely. Our little house is right on the sea. . . . There is a pretty little piece of garden that just divides us from it, and we have our own pier and bathing place. It is a pity one cannot have the run of the sea but sharks abound on these shores. . . . Adelaide and Pamela can swim quite well now, and Edward not far behind. . . . Adelaide considers herself an exquisite creature in the water and swims many different strokes. She looks like some water-sprite, especially when her long hair flows out behind her in the breeze. Pamela looks like a Dicky Doyle* and it is pretty to see her riding on top of the waves. They are absolutely happy here and live in a bathing-gown nearly all the time. At other times they go fishing in a little sailing boat. . . . Pamela, the little savage, likes cutting up the bait and yesterday was caught surreptitiously tasting it. It is only quite fresh clean white fish (dead) but she was very much ashamed at being caught.

Sorrento was indeed a magical place to us. The house looked over the sheltered blue waters of Port Phillip Bay, but on the other side a short walk across the sandy spit of the Head brought one to the southern coast of Australia upon which the great rollers thundered along the empty miles of shore. Sixty years ago it was quite deserted as far as eye could see, but nowadays the surfers in hundreds ride the breakers, their cars in regimented ranks in the nearby carpark under the supervision of an attendant, and sealed bitumen roads have replaced the sandy tracks of my youth.

I used to creep out of the house at dawn and go down to the end of the wooden jetty to watch the sunrise. The air smelt of salt and seaweed and the honeyed scent of the flowering shrubs and trees in the garden behind me. Now and again I would slip into the cool sea and swim up and down the bathing enclosure practising my 'many different strokes', quite safe, supposedly, from sharks until a large gap in the wooden pales was discovered under the water at the deep end through which a gummy shark had made its way and was caught by Charles the footman. He cut its throat and laid it on the jetty where it was instantly acrawl with blowflies and was finally removed by Matt the boatman.

Matt was a Norwegian with pale blue eyes under a battered hat and a straggling yellowish moustache. Our fishing expeditions in his boat were my greatest delight. We used to go out into the Bay and anchor. The fishing lines had several hooks attached and a lead sinker. You threw the baited hooks over the side and watched them sink to the bottom. The water was so clear that you could see the fish come swimming towards their doom and you felt the thrill of the tug on the line as you saw them gobbling up the bait and struggling on the hooks. Sometimes you would get a fish on every hook – mostly schnapper, gurnard or flounder. Once I had a fine schnapper on my line but as I was hauling

---

* Nineteenth-century illustrator who designed the original cover of *Punch*.

it in a shark took it and I was left with only the head, looking like the decapitated Louis the Sixteenth.

My father came down to stay for week-ends, bringing with him on one occasion an enormously tall and god-like young man named Geoffrey Luttrell who was on the Governor-General's staff. I instantly fell in love with him and would hang about the jetty when he and my father were setting out on a fishing expedition, hoping that I would be asked to join them. Once, to my joy, my father said casually, 'Do you want to come with us?' and I spent the day in a romantic dream, fishing by the side of my hero.

We stayed at Sorrento for more than a month and my mother spent nearly the whole time in bed, waited on by Nurse Mangan and Jukie. She said she had *une bronchite.* 'Antiphlogistine' (a sticky grey paste smelling of wintergreen) was warmed and spread on her back and chest by Nurse Mangan, and 'Friar's Balsam' was prepared by Jukie in a jug of hot water for her to inhale every four hours with a towel over her head. She was very irritable with all of us and we were in constant bad odour. She took to giving us tasks in the house such as helping the servants to dust and wash up, and we were ordered to tidy our own rooms. 'I am trying to make that minx Adelaide make her own bed, and Edward too. They *hate* doing it and I am not strong enough to battle with them over a comparatively trivial matter. If I tell them every time, they do it – but unless I do they have naturally dashed out to bathe before my eyes are open.'

We were getting too independent in the glorious free air of Sorrento, so she tried to prevent us doing things on our own and escaping from her fretful and disapproving eye. As I was the chief recipient of her annoyance, our relations became more strained than ever.

Edward was due back at school at the end of the month and my mother decided that she must go back to Melbourne in order to supervise him.

> I don't like leaving him alone in the house with Mackenzie as I know he would never do his preparation and would be all over the place. I won't let him board at the school – even for a few weeks – as I believe boys can learn all sorts of vague little piggery notions from each other, and he is a nice clean little fellow now.

Although my mother was so set against sending Edward to boarding school, she changed her mind shortly after we came back to Melbourne. I think she reluctantly began to face the fact that he was not quite the 'clean little fellow' she had supposed. Cor had tried tactfully to enlighten her, and my father had put his foot down and said that Edward must be sent away to school in order to get the discipline which was lacking at home. Finally she was persuaded that he should be removed from Melbourne Grammar School and sent as a boarder to Geelong Grammar School.

> It is a regular public school [she told Marmee] and is very well run in every way, besides being in the healthiest of places. He will get splendid sun-bathing and cricket and football. The boys are very carefully chosen, whom they admit. The school he goes to now is not having a very good effect on him – rather slack discipline and not a good tone. Miss Curwen reported Edward to me when we were at Sorrento for using unsuitable language so I have made him sit down and write a list of all the bad and nasty words he had learnt at school. I sent him back several times and each time a few 'worser and worser' were added – but not a very bad list after all, the most offensive out of 20 words being good old Shakespearean or Biblical ones. I made him read the whole list out to me which caused him a good deal of shame, and then we solemnly burnt the paper. I don't feel very sure of myself coping with boys but I take immense trouble to try and teach E. to be fastidious rather than coarse – and I'm sure that all little boys go through a *dirty* little phase, and I cling to the hope that with a clean home and parents whom he loves (and is a little afraid of) he will come out all right. But beyond impressing E. to wash *everywhere* I find it difficult to get any farther.

It is typical of my mother's attitude to 'coarse talk' that she was prepared to condone 'unsuitable language' if she thought the words could be found in Shakespeare or the Bible. Edward, of course, gave me a blow-by-blow account of the rumpus, laced with all twenty expletives in his repertoire and many scornful boasts of how he would pay her out for humiliating him. He was counting the days till his departure for Geelong and disappointed my mother by showing unconcealed delight at his coming emancipation.

> He was very cheerful till the last, but his little face looked very white and small as it disappeared with the train and it was a struggle not to let the tears come. I took Adelaide and Pamela with me so I didn't have to turn away alone. It is a *horrible* moment, but I'm glad it is over for it had been hanging over me for weeks. One feels so worried, too, for fear one may not have done all that is possible to equip them for their new life. I was very doubtful in my mind as to what I should tell him. I know there are 'Horrid Mysteries' (*Northanger Abbey*, isn't it?) – little talks that mothers are supposed to have with their boys before they go to school – but I really never quite know what it is all about and I never like to ask! I believe there is too great a tendency to instruct children on subjects they cannot understand

and which only excite their morbid curiosity and wonder. If they are properly looked after at school I don't believe there is any necessity to tell them things when they are so young.

My father realised sensibly that Edward was in no need of enlightenment from my poor mother with her woolly-minded attitude to 'Horrid Mysteries' into which she dared not enquire, her euphemistic detours round any 'dirtsy' word or subject and her terrified shirking of all responsibility for imparting biological facts.

At the end of March the Germans had launched their Spring Offensive on the Western Front, which was intended to bring the Allies finally to their knees. To my mother it seemed that the terrible prospect of defeat must be faced and the crucial point was approaching as to whether the Allies would stand or fall.

> If we go down – and it is simply stupid not to admit the possibility – I think it will be like the death of Samson and we shall all say 'Let us die with the Philistines' ... but who can tell what is going to happen? ... If only we can hold on till [Germany] has exhausted herself, all will be well – but can we go on standing the terrific shocks and overwhelming weight against us for an indefinite time, I wonder? Oh my darling, who could have thought of such terrible times happening while we were out here! ... I don't think things have ever been so terribly anxious as they are now – not even in those dreadful days of 1914 during the retreat. ...

And now a further anxiety arose. This time there was a very real cause for apprehension, although my mother does not seem to have fully realised it at first, pre-occupied as she was with her own health.

> I have nothing interesting to write about [she told Marmee] I am sitting in my poor Tibaldi's room where he is in bed. He has not been well for some time and it is at last decided that he has what is called a 'Duodenum Ulcer.' ... Just lately the attacks of pain have been very severe and he has looked so ill that I have been horribly anxious. I am happier now he is in bed and on a diet. *Months* ago I told Captain Conant I was sure it was ulceration and I feel so vexed that I did not force my opinion on the doctors and compel them to treat him long before this. ... If he does not get better I shall call in a surgeon to consult as I believe more in operating than trusting to medicines which I don't believe ever effect a permanent cure.

After some weeks my father recovered enough to be allowed up in his bedroom but he was still on a rigorous diet of slops and milk.

I fear it is a thing which is liable to return if he is not very careful and that is an impossibility with him. ... He wouldn't hear of a nurse and treated the thing much too lightly. Fortunately I love nursing so much that it was no difficulty to me to do for him and I have become quite adept at preparing invalid foods. Jukes and I had a regular little kitchen off his room and felt quite professional in the way we carried out the doctor's orders.

My mother, in fact, rather enjoyed playing the part of Trained Nurse and she even put on an apron and cap borrowed from Agnes the housemaid when she stirred the boiled milk and supervised Jukie making the egg-flip. But my father resisted firmly being turned into a permanent invalid and escaped her watchful eye on his diet as often as he could.

He is such a villain about seizing upon something to eat which might bring the whole thing back again. I do hope and trust that he will go on getting better and will keep so till we get safely home. I can stand being ill myself but it is just beyond me when he gets ill – or the children. . . . Don't worry about me, darling, I am much better than I was. . . . I am still under the Doctor's eye and when this month of Red Cross Appeal is over, I shall be able to take things more easily again.

The Red Cross Appeal helped to distract her thoughts. Melba again raised a large sum towards the total by giving concerts, the proceeds of which she enclosed in the following letter, written in her big sprawling hand:

Darling Lady,
I would like to see you today, but alas, the time flew and I had to give up all idea of getting to you. I enclose a cheque for £3,000 – I think there will be a little more which Mr George Allan will send you in a few days. I have given £50 for two beds for the soldiers – I hope you don't mind?
My love to you – Nellie M.

My mother's appeal eventually made over a quarter of a million pounds and she could not help crowing a little in private at this enormous sum which was presented by the Victorian Red Cross to the National Fund of Australia; but she was thankful when the whole thing was over and, as she put it, she had managed to 'sail through without a *ponk*' with Lady Helen.

Some time before his illness my father had written to the Colonial Office to remind them that his term of office was up in January 1919 and that he did not intend to stay on. Months passed but no answer was forthcoming.

[Arthur] has had no word from the C.O. about the appointment of a successor. It is very flattering, by the way, to find how many regrets are being expressed at the end of our term drawing near. Arthur has been privately sounded as to whether he would consider extending his term, but unless it is quite impossible to get home he will not think of doing so. If only, only, *only* we could feel that the war would be over and that we should be able to sail safely for Home! The waiting for the next great onslaught is almost the worst time to go through. . . . The raids on Zeebrugge and Ostend read like the splendid exploits of a past age with all the same romance and dash about them.*

But by June the Allies had lost all they had gained since 1915 on the Western Front, and the Germans once more reached the Marne. The crucial last months of the war were at hand.

* The attack by the 'Dover Patrol' under the command of Roger Keyes (later Admiral) on the German submarine bases on the Flanders coast had taken place on 23 April, St George's Day, and on 10 May. The canal entrances were blocked and the U-boats trapped within the bases, and all had been sunk.

12

Everything Went Wrong

Geeps was a very handsome young man. He was referred to by the irrepressible *Bulletin* as 'The Aide with the Killarney-blue eyes' and, as they would have put it, the belles of Melbourne 'Sassiety' vied with each other for a languid glance in their direction from the orbs of the gallant Captain! Many of his lady friends were on the stage, dancers in cabaret and revues, and they told him that with his appearance he would easily get £50 a week as a movie actor in America.

Fired by these flattering words, Geeps conceived the brilliant notion of writing and acting in a film in aid of the Victorian Red Cross. It was a spy drama entitled *His Last Chance*. He took the part of the villain, and the rest of the cast were drawn from the 'Toorak Push' and the social Upper Crust of Melbourne Society. He asked my mother for her advice on acting and production and at his request she attended a rehearsal at the Auditorium Theatre to coach the rest of the cast. But alas, she couldn't do much to help, she said, as the performers were so put out and bewildered if stopped that they found it impossible to take up their words again.

She added in the rather theatrical manner she was inclined to assume when on the subject of her own experiences on the amateur stage, 'I longed to be treading the Boards once more myself and felt much more in my proper sphere in the *coulisses* of the dingy theatre than in the vice-regal limelight'.

My father had been very dry about the whole affair and I suspect disapproved of the project. On the other hand, I admired Geeps's talent as an author and actor uncritically and was enthralled by his accounts of the rehearsals and backstage gossip. On occasions he would ask me to 'hear his lines' and I wished I had been old enough to have taken part as a 'movie actress' in this glamorous adventure.

The great day came at last for the first performance. My father did not attend as he was away on business. Neither did Lady Helen, who certainly would have frozen the whole theatre with glacial displeasure at such unsuitable 'goings-on' in vice-regal circles. But the Governor-General benignly put in an appearance and my mother allowed me to accompany her. We were escorted by Geeps 'in civvies, nursing his shining top hat and looking modestly self-conscious,' according to the *Bulletin*'s reporter. 'Lady Stanley came in her gorgeous blue cloak with a little nasturtium dress underneath it.' A gentleman in the audience was unconventionally dressed for those days. 'He had frills on his linen boiled shirt, and perky little frills outlining his boiled waistcoat ... his dress clothes seemed to be painted on him.'

I sat next to the Governor-General in his box and enjoyed the performance hugely. It was entertaining to see Geeps on the screen acting the villain and to recognise many familiar faces disguised unconvincingly as policemen, crooks, cabaret dancers and foreign diplomats.

The Press notices were not very complimentary and the *Bulletin*, as usual, poked sarcastic fun at both audience and players.

> The *Auditorium* was like a hill of Sassiety Ants on Thursday night ... there to see themselves as others see them. In fact, half the house was occupied by intense people on the same mission. The amateurs had made an unintentional burlesque of their job. ... Still, the film provided the heartiest laugh some people have had since the outbreak of war, and as a money-making novelty for the benefit of the Red Cross, it was an inspiration.

In spite of the *Bulletin*'s rather snide and disparaging notice, Geeps's 'amateur movie' netted £800 in one showing and he was a 'much gratified Aide', according to the less waspish notice in *Table Talk*.

Geeps now seriously considered the thought of going on the stage professionally. My mother scouted the very idea of him becoming a 'movie actor'. 'When he came to me full of his project to ask my advice I was horrified! He was all for going to America as soon as possible but I begged him to wait and make more enquiries about the profession and conditions before he plunged off. Without being too brutal I told him that I doubted whether his 'Film Personality', as he was pleased to call it, would entirely make up for his want of dramatic talent.'

Geeps was thoroughly cast down by this advice and promised meekly he wouldn't do anything more about it without consulting her. She remarked to Marmee that his mother ought to be grateful to her for her efforts to restrain him from his folly and added that she looked upon it as good practice for dealing with Edward when he reached manhood!

Soon after this episode poor Geeps fell ill and came to my mother to say that his doctor had ordered him to go to hospital for a week and after that to take two months rest in the country. It seemed that he had not fully recovered from his wounds, but no doubt a contributing factor to his ill-health was frustrated theatrical ambition, combined with Hoodiwinks' bullying. He confessed to my mother that 'he could not stand old Hood's *odious* and cantankerous behaviour any longer'.

> He is a mean old thing – always sleuth-hounding about to find out things about Capt. Conant – not with a view to giving him a helping hand but in order to catch him out and report him. . . . However, we are in the highest spirits today as old Hoodiwinks has asked for six months leave of absence. When Arthur came to tell me I threw myself into his arms and hugged him for joy . . . his removal will be a relief to us all. He wants to go home I fancy, as his job with us is nearing its end, and poke about to ascertain who the next Governor or G.G. is likely to be, and sign on [with one of them]. It is rather a triumph to have suffered longer from him than any other Governor and yet not to have had a row with him. . . . I don't know a bit if he likes A. or me which, after living with us for nearly five years, is rather odd. . . . I don't think he is ever really at ease with Arthur, but he is afraid of him as [he] has put him properly in his place on one or two occasions. Poor old fellow! I am sorry for him, and he has his good points. He is a gent, and always gives the children the most expensive presents on their birthdays . . .

By the middle of the year the war was entering its final phase. The rumble of the battle on the other side of the English Channel could be clearly heard at Prestons. In June, Marmee wrote describing the garden:

> I wish you could see the Horse-shoe Border – the thick purple-blue of catmint, in front [of] sheaves of mauve campanulas, and at the back tall blue larkspurs. I work hard at all sorts of jobs to the accompaniment of the guns which will not let one forget for one moment the horrors that are going on. . . . The other night when I went to the front door, the air was literally shaking with the bombardment from the Belgian Coast and all day long there is incessant booming of guns.

By mid-July the curtain went up on the final act of the war on the Western Front when the Germans launched their long-awaited offensive at Rheims. But in the preceding days an ominous calm had brooded over the battlefield and my mother voiced her disquiet to Marmee.

> Still no news of the expected German onslaught and we are anxiously waiting, hardly daring to open the papers in the morning and dreading to read the cables that come in.... How the men can stand the waiting, never knowing when the attack is going to be launched, I can't imagine. I do hope that we shall be able to muster large reinforcements quickly. The Americans seem to be hustling and I daresay the Germans are not entirely happy at the prospect of her increasing armies joining the fight.

In a postscript to her letter of 15 July – the very day the German offensive was launched – she is still anxiously wondering when the blow will fall.

> What horrible thing does this prolonged inactivity portend on the Western Front? ... and the developments on the Murman coast?* The cables are very brief and give no information about this last move ... I have given up trying to understand anything about Russia and the hotch-potch of Bolsheviks, Soviets, Czecho-Slavs, etc.

The prolonged strain of the war years, and now the suspense of waiting for the end, severely tried my mother's already jangled nerves. She became increasingly disenchanted with the land of her long exile, and our life at home suffered from her constant fault-finding and criticism. Now that Edward was away at school, Pamela and I bore the brunt of her displeasure. Pamela endured the lectures and punishments more philosophically than I did and took the course of least resistance, but I provoked a searing row on every occasion, which would sometimes be prolonged over several days if I refused to offer the most abject apologies and confessions of guilt. My mother would bite her lip and maintain a huffy silence when I was present and I took to spending long, solitary hours in some concealed and inaccessible hide-out in the garden during these periods of disgrace.

Edward came home for his first *exeat* from Geelong more boastful and swaggering than ever, defying all attempts to put him in his place. 'He tells me that he still is liking his school very much,' said my mother to Marmee, 'only partially pleased,' she admitted, that he showed no signs of missing his home life. In order to lure him back under her wing she gave him what she considered to be the greatest treat she could devise,

---

* On 13 July the British had landed at Murmansk and the Japanese were about to land with an Allied Force at Vladivostok in an abortive attempt to scotch the Bolshevik Revolution and save the Imperial Family. On 16 July and following days, the Tsar and his family were murdered at Ekaterinburg.

that of sleeping in her room. 'The darling – but it is a treat that cost me a night's rest for he is a hideous fidget.' Edward, needless to say, did not appreciate this bid for his affection and was relieved when my mother found he disturbed her sleep and returned him to his own bed.

Before long she was again at odds with us all.

I have been having a stormy time with the children who have been very insubordinate and tiresome ... Adelaide rebellious and insolent; Edward *filthy* and impervious to any instructions about washing himself, besides laying about him if Adelaide and Pamela cross him; poor Pamela involved in a tissue of lies to shield Edward from his villainies being discovered and, incidentally, herself from being found out bagging the grapes from the lunch table.

Lyulph, too, was beginning to get out of hand and refuse to do her bidding. On one occasion he went outside the back gates of Government House into the paddocks beyond and paid no attention to the frantic calls to come back at once. When at last he rolled up my mother scolded him roundly and asked what he was doing in the paddocks. He disarmed her by replying 'Mammie dear, I was just listening to Mrs Provis's cat purring on the violets'. It was such an unexpected answer that she had to laugh, 'but it was an untrue one', she complained, 'for he had been tooting the horn of the Orderly's motor bicycle which was left standing by the gate'.

Sometimes when I was in favour, my mother would allow me to take Lyulph to play in the garden. One day he escaped from me and ran through a gap in the fence into Mrs Bowes-Kelly's garden where there was a smart tennis party in progress. I was in my usual grubby state with tangled hair and dirty hands and face and was embarrassed at having to go in after Lyulph to retrieve him. He, however, was perfectly at his ease and had just taken a plunge into the goldfish pool to try and catch one of them. I persuaded him to leave at last and he went round graciously shaking hands with everyone in true vice-regal style. When he came to Mrs Bowes-Kelly he said, 'Thank you very much for letting me wet myself in your pond'.

Edward went back to school after his weekend without a sign of regret. His account to me of school life was revealing. He had fought with every boy in his class and was constantly being punished for his insubordination, although he boasted that as he was the Governor's son he got off more lightly than the other boys. When he went too far he was summoned to the Headmaster's study for a beating, which he described jauntily to me. 'The Beak' would say mincingly, 'Bend ovah, Boy' and give him several swishing cuts with a cane. But as Edward had learnt to pad his

trousers seat with exercise paper he felt the minimum of pain. I was
rather envious of his emancipation from home rule, but he was no longer
my companion-in-arms against shared misfortunes, and on the whole
I was not too sorry to see him depart.

At long last the war news was encouraging and the great Allied
counter-offensive on the Western Front seemed to be succeeding. Even
my mother's spirits began to rise cautiously, and the future looked less
drear.

> The news has all been so cheering and good the last weeks that one begins
> to dare to hope that the end is dawning, tho' it cannot be for some time
> yet. I shall look back and wonder how I have struggled through the dire
> home-sickness of all these years ... Melba has returned* – a Dame – and is
> to be invested with due pomp! [She laughed slyly at this title and made
> jokes about Pantomimes behind Melba's back.] She is lunching here tomorrow.
> I always feel a little nervous after not seeing her for some time as she is
> inclined to be skittish at first, and it makes Tibaldi such a dry-pots, and
> old Hoodiwinks can't bear her. Lady Helen rather hates her too, and I know
> is made nervous of what she *may* be going to say.

On occasions my mother went on what she called 'one of my rounds
with my dear "St Onians", visiting the families of the newsboys'. Having
never had any experience of 'slumming' or any contact with the sub-
merged and sometimes criminal life of the urban poor, these expeditions
held a morbid fascination for her and at the same time she was moved
with intense longing to help and befriend these unfortunate outcasts.

> We penetrated into some very miserable and sad little homes. In one we
> found the husband very drunk. The poor man kept holding my hand and
> patting me on the back saying 'Guv's LUVVERLY *Lady*'. It was embarrassing
> and I found some difficulty in extricating myself, but I hear it gave them
> great pleasure that I went, in spite of this slight contretemps. Another poor
> little household was in dire grief over a son who had been arrested for stealing.
> Such a dear woman, the mother, with a beautiful face, and a poor deaf old
> father who sells flowers at street corners, and whose tears rained down his
> face all through the visit. At the end he rushed out of the back door and
> returned with his arms full of his precious flowers which he pressed into my
> arms – and the tears rained down my face, too. The tongues that wag about
> the discontent and selfishness of the working classes neither know them nor,
> I believe, try to get to know them. I sometimes think that if I were reduced
> to their means I would far sooner go and live among them and be one of
> them, for they *are* good to each other and fine in so many of the things
> in which the rich and better educated are small.

* From the United States.

My mother's admiration for the sterling worth of the 'Deserving Poor' rings a somewhat falsely sentimental note in our ears today, but she was quite sincere in her emotions. She had a genuine sympathy with the underdog and her compassionate heart went out to them. However, had she been forced into any close or prolonged contact with the degradation, squalor and violence of their lives, her esteem (though not her pity) would soon have been quenched, I fear.

The malignant Spanish Influenza had been spreading rapidly in Europe since it first manifested itself in 1917. It was eventually to add millions of deaths to the already astronomical casualties of the war. It appeared in Australia during the winter months of 1918 and my mother shuddered at this new peril. I fell ill and she feared the worst – 'What is called 'Spanish Flue' is going about a good deal and the Doc. thinks it is a touch of it' – but it turned out to be a false scare and after a few days I recovered.

'Adelaide asked if I thought it likely we should all die of Spanish Influenza,' my mother remarked. 'Pamela said contentedly, "Well, anyhow if we do, we shan't have to do any lessons".'

A new addition was now made to the list of accomplishments my mother thought desirable for us to acquire. On certain days we were escorted by Cor to the Ice Rink, or 'Glaciarium'. There were little boxes all round the rink where you could have refreshments, and Signor Di Gilio's band played from a gallery.

I liked skating even better than swimming and, guided by the instructors, I soon learnt to do 'inside' and 'outside edges' and later on figure skating, waltzing and an exhilarating dance called 'the Ten-Step'. Some of the boys from Melbourne Grammar used to go, and when I got more proficient I would sometimes be asked to partner one of them for a 'number'. We would link hands across our bodies and away we would swoop round and round the rink till the music stopped and I was politely returned to my chaperone in one of the little boxes. It was heavenly! One of these boys was specially attentive. He had a charming, smiling face with high cheek-bones and a large mouth, and crinkly, dark hair. Of course I fell in love with him and confided to Geeps's sympathetic ear my state of bliss.

August came and went and my father was still waiting for an answer from the Colonial Office, much to my mother's vexation and anxiety, 'and no good is done by bombarding them. Sir Henry Galway has tried those methods with no results. I shall strive to come home at the *earliest moment* – I only hope the journey won't be too anxious – I dread it with the children. . . .'

My mother had almost got to the pitch when she was prepared to leave my father, ill as he was, in order to end her own misery and get back home. The war news continued to encourage her hopes of release. The British attack at Amiens on 8 August had driven the Germans back to the Hindenburg Line* and by the end of September they had broken through this defence.

> How wonderful it is to be writing with a heart lighter than one has known for nearly five years! [she exclaimed] The marvellous recovery we have made since those weeks in March, April and May, when irreparable disaster seemed possible, makes hopes of Victory a substantial thing now. We shall soon have reached the Hindenburg Line which, though encouraging, is still a long way from beating the brutes back to their own country. Directly they are down and under I know I shall feel sorry for them but until then I feel as blood-thirsty as a Jaguar and *pray* for the day when a fleet of British and American aircraft will *rain* bombs on Berlin and demolish a good part of it. I should hate for any children to be killed but I really should not mind a *dicke Frau* or two!

My parents and Marmee had been reading simultaneously the autobiography of Benjamin Haydon, the once popular historical painter. They had wondered at the time what had become of all his pictures in the 'Grand Style'. My mother now announced:

> I have discovered by the merest accident that they are *here in Melbourne* in a squalid little gallery adjoining a still more squalid aquarium. . . . I somehow feel it is a suitable fate for them to have been bought by wealthy and crude Australians who probably valued them for their size than anything else. The one he speaks of so much, and which apparently did have a measure of success with the British public, 'Christ entering Jerusalem'† is among those here. I am told that in the same gallery there are several 'Rembrandts' and 'Titians'!

Melba had taken to inviting herself to Government House rather more frequently than my mother liked, as she found her an exacting guest although she was flattered by her friendship. At times, my mother said, Melba made her shudder at her vulgarity. 'She gets so "beady-eyed" the

---

* The Germans had made a tactical withdrawal between Arras and Noyon in February 1917 and formed the Hindenburg Line 50 miles eastward in order to consolidate their forces for the final assault on the Western Front in the Spring of 1918.

† It is doubtful whether my mother saw this particular picture as experts say it never came to Australia. The aquarium and gallery referred to were in the Exhibition Buildings. Two huge historical paintings by Haydon are still stored in the basement with other forgotten pictures in a state of disrepair, stacked face to the wall behind various bits of junk. Until a thorough search can be made of the vaults of the Exhibition Buildings, it is not possible to say definitely that my mother did not see 'Christ Entering Jerusalem' (or a copy) hanging in the gallery.

moment a man appears, and makes the mistake of thinking "noise" makes a thing go. However, I forgive her for she sang the whole of Sunday morning ... her voice is as lovely as ever and the finish and quality of her singing always strikes one anew ...'

Melba always allowed me to listen when she was singing at Government House. She was particularly kind and affectionate towards me and I think perhaps I was her favourite amongst us children. M. Francis de Bourgignon, the Belgian pianist who now acted as her *répétiteur,* was treated with much more respect than his poor little predecessor as he was an accomplished artist in his own right.

At last, in September, the Colonial Office replied to my father's letter asking to be released with a request that he should extend his term for another year. He decided he could not refuse on merely personal grounds in spite of the sulks and lamentations from my mother. With a heavy heart she broke the news to Marmee.

> I won't try to tell you what the prospect of extra months of waiting is, or the extent of my depression. I feel I hate everything and everybody and for the rest of the time I shall do everything in a *'cattiva maniera'* [with bad grace]. ... I still think we shall get back by the summer [the English summer of 1919] unless the war ends much quicker than we expect. Anyhow, I shall resort to a breakdown in health for which there will be *no cure* but the journey home!

One slight ray of light relieved the gloom. Old Hoodiwinks had at last departed the scene for six months after many false starts and procrastinations. She said she felt as if she had got off a very tight pair of stays and she could let herself go and see whom she liked without a feeling of sneaking guilt and consciousness of his disapproval. But the organisation of the vice-regal routine immediately fell apart, as she ruefully exclaimed.

> The day he left, *everything* went wrong! The car was not ordered and Arthur and I were late for our respective engagements. The officials who were by way of receiving me were not there and I had to get the office boy to hunt up some members of the Committee to take me to the Exhibition I was opening, and altogether *we felt his loss* – but didn't care a bit!

A new private Secretary was soon engaged who was 'overwhelmed by the honour and confidence shown him', said my mother; a temporary ADC, Colonel Knox, arrived whom Lyulph thought was called Curleylocks, and Geeps returned from his 'rest-cure' when he found that Hoodiwinks had really gone. 'So', my mother concluded with relief, 'we are settled, we hope, for the remainder of our time here.'

13

Peace – At Last

Towards the end of October 1918 a French Military Mission visited Australia, headed by a one-armed veteran, General Pau. My mother described him as 'a lovable old warrior of the 1870 War – we have all fallen victims to him – he is the greatest old darling'.

General Pau was stubby yet dignified in appearance, with a walrus moustache and a bemedalled breast. He had a mild almost childlike expression which reminded me of the White Knight in *Alice in Wonderland* and he spoke not one word of English.

A 'men-only' dinner was given by my mother and father for the General and his Mission – perhaps to overcome the difficulty of finding enough unattached, French-speaking ladies in Melbourne – and a grand reception was held afterwards.

Pamela and I were allowed to attend. My mother had had new dresses made for us which embarrassed me as they were 'fancy dress' copied from a Velasquez picture. They were made of stiff black satin with full skirts down to the ground, tight bodices, long sleeves with Venetian-point lace cuffs and wide 'bertha' collars of cream net edged with the same lace and decorated with a row of little bows in 'vieux-rose' taffeta down the front. How I longed for a flounced and embroidered organdie confection with a fringed sash such as Wilma Clarke or the Syme girls wore to parties!

I was introduced to the General, who bowed over my hand and kissed it. This took me by surprise as I was preparing to shake hands and nearly had the mortification of hitting him smartly on the nose. I had a

154

marvellous evening talking away to him and his staff in my best French, and felt myself quite a *femme du monde*. Many of the guests envied me my fluency, said the *Herald* newspaper – 'Adelaide, Lady Stanley's school-girl daughter who seemed to be thoroughly at ease conversing with General Pau in his native tongue', and the *Bulletin* reported:

Governor Stanley and his lady gave a dinner party and reception on Wednesday night. General Pau and his Missioners were guests of honour. His Ex. wore his most gorgeous uniform, a dream outfit with silver epaulettes. He spoke French with his visitors with half-amused half-nervous glances at his wife who is a fluent French scholar. Dad was also put in the shade by his small daughter who speaks French like a Parisian. The Stanley dame looked even better than usual in a trained gown which wound round her figure in brocaded velvet of rose and silver and billowy clouds of tulle rising like a floating mist above her shoulders up to her chin. This last was a wrap concession to a cold from which she was suffering. A diamond tiara flashed like an advertising sky-sign. The drawing-room, wide open to the terrace, was filled with roses and lilies-of-the-valley.

The General complimented my mother on her French, telling her that she not only spoke like a Frenchwoman, but in the stylish manner of the 'aristocratic families'. This flattered her greatly as she considered it 'common' to speak French in anything but the elegant tones of the *Faubourg* and the *Comédie Française*.

I may tell you that Adelaide and I mugged up a little before he came with the Head of the Berlitz School here, I really was very rusty and she was more fluent than me. We are going to have him once a week just to keep in practice for a bit. . . . Adelaide had quite a success at the reception and was surrounded by members of the Mission all the evening. Pamela was so terrified at the possibility of having to speak one word of French that she remained in the Gallery and directed the Orchestra. The Italian conductor is a great friend of hers [and she] was overheard telling him he was beautiful after he had said she danced like a little fairy.

As October drew to a close, events began to move inexorably to a climax against Germany. Her destruction seemed imminent. The Allied onslaught on the Western Front gathered momentum: the British reached and occupied the Belgian coast while the French troops advanced across the Aisne and the Americans down the Meuse: the Turks had been driven from Egypt and annihilated in Palestine by Allenby: Syria was overrun and the Turkish Army in Mesopotamia capitulated. On 30 October, Turkey surrendered unconditionally and the next day the Allies passed at long last through the Dardanelles.

'Hurrah!! for the splendid news that keeps coming through!' cried my mother in jubilation. 'I have not yet got accustomed, after four years of bad news, to opening the papers and seeing the dizzying headlines. If only it would come to an end before the Spring, we should be packing up pretty soon!'

She began there and then to look out trunks and boxes for the packing up of all our possessions. She still hoped that my father would get away by January 1919 and she resented the fact that he alone, among the State Governors, had been asked to extend his term of office. 'I think Arthur may have been asked to do so in order to tide over the Governor-Generalship if the G.G. is going home in April or May,' she said. 'But he would not take it on if it were offered to him, unless it were just for a few weeks if the C.O. were in a hole. It is generally rumoured and believed that he will be the next G.G.* – General Pau told Adelaide that he heard it said on every side. This must not be whispered in Gath!'

By the beginning of November there was an electric atmosphere of suspense and excitement throughout Australia. People went into the streets to get the latest news from the bulletins posted up outside public buildings and post offices. On the third of the month Austria surrendered and there were rumours of the Kaiser's abdication. My mother made haste to write to Marmee.

> We keep getting cables, first to say he has abdicated and then to say that he has put it off! I like to think of the fuss and 'Ach Gott! Was für ein abscheuliches Ponk' they have got themselves into! I expect if Wilhelm does not abdicate ... he will probably share the fate of the poor Tsar.

On 7 November there was a naval mutiny at Kiel and Communist forces seized the German navy. The revolution spread rapidly and soon the German 'Red Guards' were in control of all the major cities except Berlin.

Negotiations for an armistice had begun on 6 November and on the ninth the Kaiser fled to Holland with Hindenburg and the German General Staff. At the eleventh hour of the eleventh day of the eleventh month the Armistice was signed in a railway carriage in the Forest of Compiègne. The Great War was over.

My mother's first reaction to Peace was to send a 'secret' cable to Marmee saying she was coming home almost at once, followed by a long and incoherent letter of rejoicing.

*See footnote page 122.

I can hardly write, my heart is so full with all the wonder and excitement and bursting gratitude of the last wonderful week. My head has had two sentences ringing in it ever since we knew we were safe – England is saved! England is saved!! Soon I shall see them all – Soon I shall see them all. . . . I think somehow the next cable I send will be to say that we are packing up!

I have not said a word about the enthusiasm and joy with which the wonderful news was received here. Of course people insisted on rejoicing several days before it was official – but we happened to be at a function in town on the night that it was confirmed and saw all the great crowds who surged and roared through the streets bursting into songs and hymns and cheering at intervals. On the whole there was very little rowdiness, which was unexpected as there is always the larrikin element pretty strongly represented in any sort of demonstration or crowd. It was quite impossible for our car to get through the crowds to fetch us so we all piled in to Lady Helen's which had remained in a side street and we got through without much real trouble. We were afraid at first that the windows might be shivered as several enthusiasts boarded the step and battered the panes with joy. We held our coats up to avoid being cut in the face but the Police hauled them off.

For several days before the Armistice we had done hardly any lessons as Cor found it impossible to get us to fix our minds on anything but the coming event. I remember the almost unbearable tension of waiting over the weekend for confirmation of the signing – the rumours and contradictions, the premature flag-waving and celebrations, and the sense of flat disappointment when no official news came through, hour after hour.

Late on the night of Monday, 11 November, I was with the rest of the household on the balcony at Stonnington, watching and waiting. Suddenly there came a pulsating rumble which swelled into a tremendous burst of shouting and cheering. Car horns were honking and tram bells were clanging. We ran through the garden and out of the gates and saw a great tide of people milling past, waving flags, blowing whistles and banging on tin cans. The crowd was solid from side to side of the wide road with the trams and cars marooned in the midst of this torrent of rejoicing humanity.

Newsboys were running up and down the crowd shouting 'Special Edition! Armistice – Official!' I wriggled away from Cor and managed to get a copy. It is before me now – a single sheet of newsprint – the paper yellow and crumbling with age. Banner headlines across the front proclaim in thick black letters:

THE HERALD EXTRAORDINARY EDITION
Melbourne
Monday Evening
November 11 1918

GERMANY SURRENDERS TO THE ALLIES
SIGNING OF ARMISTICE FOLLOWS NEGOTIATIONS – RED
GUARDS IN BERLIN

Beneath is a blank space in the middle of which is printed:

(REUTER)
PARIS OFFICIAL MESSAGE
Vancouver, No. 10, Midnight

THE ARMISTICE HAS BEEN SIGNED.

'One day,' I said to myself, 'this paper will be a valuable memento of this historic occasion. I shall keep it as my most treasured possession to hand down to my descendants.'

And so it has survived through all the vicissitudes of the intervening years, not perhaps the priceless heirloom of my youthful imagination but a curiosity, the sight of which brings back to my mind with a sense of total recall that night on 11 November 1918.

To the sound of muffled drums and Beethoven's Funeral March, a Memorial Service to the Fallen was held a week later on the steps of Parliament House in Melbourne. The Governor-General and Lady Helen, and my parents accompanied by Pamela and me were escorted by a Guard of Honour of Returned Soldiers as we drove through the streets packed with people and lined with troops to take our places on the dais on top of the steps.

As we arrived, the National Anthem was played and the British and Australian flags were broken from a yard-arm erected on the dais. The two flags fluttered out in the brilliant sunshine above the heads of the silent crowds. The service was short and there were no addresses. Prayers were said, the murmuring throng following the words of the Lord's Prayer like the moaning of the wind. And then 'O God our Help in Ages Past' was struck up by the massed bands and the hymn swelled into a mighty chorus from the multitude below. The Last Post was sounded at the end of the Service, its clear notes piercing the silence with almost unbearable poignancy, and many people were weeping.

Now that the war was over, my mother was determined that nothing should stop her from taking the first boat home.

'I think I shall probably make up my mind to leave my poor Tibaldi,' she wrote to Marmee. Although she felt 'terribly torn at flying at the first opportunity to you', she persuaded herself that my father would follow within a month or two, in spite of not having received any answer from the Colonial Secretary confirming his recall. 'But we have got as far as making enquiries as to what ships are sailing and when. We are hoping that the fares will come down before we leave, for at present they are appalling – £126 for one single ticket and we shall be 13 people!'

I was in two minds about leaving Australia. On the one hand I felt unhappy that my father was to be left behind and thought it unfair of my mother to take us all back without him. On the other, there was the exciting prospect of our return journey and the reunion with our English relations: also the novelty of English life which from all accounts was so different from our luxurious Australian one, what with the food rationing and other shortages.

There was another reason which made me regret our departure. For some time I had been taking my singing and piano-playing very seriously and I was sad at the thought of leaving Miss McBurney to whom I was much devoted and who had taught me all the music I knew. Just before Christmas she gave one of her 'little evening parties', this time as a farewell to us, at which I sang 'Where the Bee Sucks' by Doctor Arne with apparent success.

'People who did not know who she was were charmed,' said my mother, who was more critical of my performance. 'She has a dear little voice and has a great sense of phrasing but otherwise her singing is very childish.'

Pamela and I were taken to one of Melba's many 'Farewell' concerts and Pamela went to sleep, despite surreptitious pokes and pinches from me.

Governor Stanley was aloft in the Balcony [the *Bulletin* reported] with her Ex. and a selection of their young family, including the eldest daughter with long streaming fair hair and young Pamela with her hair cropped. . . . 'PEACE' was written across the footlights in water-lily buds and hydrangeas were blooming on the stage.

I can't remember what Melba sang on this occasion, but at the end of the concert a flock of white doves was suddenly released which flew about the auditorium and woke Pamela up. 'It was rather pretty as well

as rather silly,' said my mother. 'One perched up on the ledge of the
big organ, just exactly over the bald, gleaming head of the fat tenor – and
I don't know, but I *think* I just saw a little plop and the tenor was
seen scrubbing his pate with his programme.'

For the last time we spent Christmas at Macedon. All over the house
there were packing-cases and wooden crates and steamer trunks being
filled with our household possessions, and piles of wood shavings and
tissue paper to wrap everything up. Everyone was too busy to put up
Christmas decorations, which disappointed poor Pamela dreadfully, but
we did have a belated Christmas Tree party in the second week of the
New Year. It was terrifically hot and the bushfires roared and crackled
on the forested slopes of the Mount Macedon Range. The pungent,
eucalyptus-scented smoke drifted down and hung in the stifling air.

I was in a state of constant irritation with everybody and everything,
torn between excitement at going back to England and unhappiness at
leaving Australia. I didn't feel English any more, and didn't want to!
I quarrelled with Edward and Pamela drove me frantic with her
dreamy, babyish ways. My mother was so immersed in her thoughts of
home and plans for the return voyage that she seldom had the time or
inclination to arbitrate in the schoolroom ructions, and left Cor to deal
with my tantrums and Edward's hooliganism. My mother admitted at
last that she couldn't manage us and decided that, notwithstanding the
extra expense, Cor must be taken back to England so that she should
not be burdened with the responsibility of her unruly elder children.

She felt that Marmee would have a good influence on me and proposed
that when we got home I should spend a lot of time with her alone
at Prestons, no doubt hoping that if I went there without the others
I would be less unmanageable. 'She is still a fireworky creature and goes
off like a squib with Edward and Pamela – especially poor Pamela!'

Before we left Macedon, Edward perpetrated the worst of all his many
iniquities.

Some time early in the new year, my parents had gone to Melbourne
to make arrangements with the Orient Shipping Company for our home-
ward journey. At Government Cottage all the boxes and cases were
strapped and corded, standing in the hall awaiting the removal men.

The morning of Edward's awful deed dawned fiercely hot and before
breakfast I had a fight with him over the plans for the day. He wanted
to play our game of 'Ned Kelly and the Siege of Glenrowan' up among
the tall gum trees and scrub on the steep slope behind the house, but
I said it was too hot. He went off in a rage and I saw him put a box
of matches surreptitiously in his pocket.

After some time he re-appeared, white-faced, and raised the alarm of a bushfire behind the house. He said he had been climbing up the big water tank and had seen the fire starting to burn down the trees on top of the ridge. Everyone rushed out and we could see the flames and hear the roar of the fire as it took hold of the trees and sent them crashing down in a blaze of sparks which set the rest alight all round. The wind was blowing the fire towards the house. There wasn't a moment to lose.

The big fire hoses were laid out in readiness but the fire was not yet within their reach. The men seized boughs and sacks and beat down the flames while a human chain was formed up the hillside to pass buckets of water to the fire fighters. The men tried to burn a break but it got away and the flames raged even more furiously and closer to the house.

Nanny and the babies went down to the tennis courts which were in a clearing cut out of the slope below the house. Some of the boxes were also carried down in an effort to save a few possessions. Our faces were blackened with smoke and running with sweat, and we gasped with the heat as we toiled for hours up the slope with the buckets of water and big enamel jugs of sweet tea for the men. I can't remember how long the fire lasted, but suddenly a miracle happened. When it was within a few yards of the house, the wind changed and blew the fire back over its charred and burnt-up course. We were saved.

All the time I had been suppressing the nagging fear that Edward had started the fire. In the evening my suspicions were confirmed. I went into the sleep-out on the verandah and found him face down on his bed sobbing distractedly. Finally, he admitted that he had been playing 'Ned Kelly' and had lighted the fire to re-enact the burning down of the Glenrowan Hotel. The flames took hold at once and in seconds they were out of control. The poor little boy had been terribly frightened and now his terror was redoubled at the prospect of having to confess his wicked act to my father, who had returned that evening. My heart was rent with anguish and pity for him, but all I could do was to hug him and sob in sympathy.

I don't know what happened at their subsequent interview, as Edward was too ashamed and shaken to speak to me about it, but he was not given the usual beating. No doubt his crime was considered to be beyond normal methods of punishment, and perhaps my father felt that he had suffered enough from fright and remorse. A lot of valuable land was burnt, but fortunately no homes or lives were lost. My father paid for the damage out of his own pocket.

On our return to Melbourne, preparations for the voyage home continued unabated. We were vaccinated against smallpox and inoculated against Spanish flu. Owing to the epidemic of this disease now raging, the quarantine regulations were very strict, and my mother lived in hourly apprehension that one of us would develop some infectious illness. I got a mild form of skin eruption and for a time it was thought that the dread ringworm had reappeared, which might have delayed our departure. My mother was beside herself and I could sense the waves of barely concealed irritation directed against me, but luckily my rash cleared up after a few days.

We visited various shops for new clothes suitable for the English climate and dressmakers came to the house for fittings of 'best dresses' for Pamela and me. To my relief, the black satin 'Velasquez' picture dresses were discarded.

It was the patriotic thing to do, both in England and Australia, to buy articles made by disabled soldiers. My mother bought a length of speckled black and white tweed, I remember, which she had made into a coat and skirt. She wrote to Marmee:

> I am most interested to hear you have plunged into the extravagance of a Blighty tweed, for I have done just the same – only mine is made by the returned Anzacs and is very thick and so durable that I am sure I shall go on hating it for years! *How much did yours cost?* My stuff was £17. 17s. 6d. – quite enough – and it is being made by the worst shop in Melbourne but the only one that has been really good and helpful to the returned men. So I have sacrificed myself on the Altar of Patriotism and am allowing them to exhibit in the window, labelled that it is made for me.

Meanwhile, nothing had been definitely settled about the date of our departure. Most of the mail steamers had not, as yet, been reconverted from troop-carrying to passenger ships. There were constant disappointments as no ship could be found with enough vacant berths to accommodate the large number of people accompanying my mother. Finally, the Orient Line office managed to find room in the *Osterley* – the same ship we had come out in – which was due to sail some time in March. My mother was asked if she could possibly reduce the size of her party as there were so many people trying to get back to England, 'but', she said, 'I don't see how we can very well – except that Agnes and Mrs Drabble and our hideous old butler could go by another boat . . .'

She remained adamant, and in the end she was accompanied by the entire staff of servants from Government House, leaving my father with only his valet and Mackenzie, the housekeeper to look after his personal needs, and Geeps to deal with the office work.

We left Melbourne on 21 March. The poor old *Osterley* looked shabby and battered by her war years as a troopship, but I remembered my way around her from stem to stern and Edward and I set off on a reminiscent tour the moment we got on board. My father came to see us off, but I don't recall saying goodbye to him. On the quay there were crowds waving and we stood, waving back, among the other passengers. The coloured paper streamers broke one by one as the ship slowly swung away from her moorings and we were on our way home.

Part III
1919–1926

14

Homecoming

On the day we left Australia, my childhood came to an end. I was nearly thirteen years old and I embarked on adolescence with the conviction that I was now perfectly grown up. I took to plaiting my hair in a 'door-knocker' and tying it with a large bow of black silk ribbon. I aped the affectations of various 'flappers' on board and made eyes at the ship's officers, in particular the purser with whom I indulged in badinage whenever the opportunity presented itself. 'Buttons', the messenger boy, fell in love with me and would waylay me to offer sticky ginger biscuits warm from his pocket. All was grist to my mill and I was full of romantic ideas, no doubt appearing supremely ridiculous to all except the poor little Buttons. My mother, of course, was thrown into a frenzy of irritation by my antics and put on her chilliest and most devastating act of disapproval whenever she caught sight of me on deck.

It took us nearly six weeks to reach England. We were met by my grandparents and various members of the family. Grandpapa was just as I remembered him. There he stood in his pot hat, ruddy-faced with twinkling eyes and bristling white beard. The only difference now was that he had an ear trumpet. Also, he was much crippled by arthritis and walked with two sticks which he waved at us and called his 'bastions'. I knew Muzzie and my Aunt Sylvia immediately and rushed up to greet them but for the moment they did not recognise me in my 'grown up' guise and the thrill of my home-coming fell a little flat. My mother went straight down to Prestons where she was reunited at last with her beloved Marmee. We were sent to an hotel for the night and then down to Alderley.

167

In May we got the news that my father had had a severe duodenal haemorrhage but that he was now out of danger and would be well enough to return to England in September. My mother was still at Prestons and it seems not to have occurred to her to go back to Australia to be with my father. No doubt, considerations of expense were involved but probably the real reason for her apparent lack of concern was that, at this time, she was on the verge of a nervous collapse and she opted out of all family obligations, apart from Marmee, for some months after our return.

We children, meanwhile, stayed on at Alderley under the not too sympathetic eye of Muzzie and the rather fitful and detached discipline of Grandpapa, trying to fit into our new English life. After the novelty had worn off I found it was not at all to my taste. Gone were the visions of grown up emancipation! No more gallant French officers, skating beaux or young sailors to bring glamour into my life. I was firmly back in the schoolroom in the company of Rosalind and Kitty Henley, my cousins, under the rather eccentric sway of Mademoiselle Marie-Leczinska Dombe who, in her day, had been French governess to both my mother's family and the Stanleys. At the outbreak of war she had been living in Paris, but being terrified of the German invasion, she returned to England and was given refuge at Alderley where she taught the Henley girls, evacuated there for the duration of the war.

Lessons with Dombe were an unpredictable adventure and her methods were highly original. There seemed to be no fixed routine and she would talk about whatever came into her head. We learnt French composition, literature and history with her, and on the last two subjects she held idiosyncratic views which she expounded with verve and conviction. She would assume that the French classical writers outshone even the Greeks and Romans; or that Shakespeare was a mere pygmy compared with Molière; or that the Battle of Waterloo had been won by Napoleon Bonaparte. Once, I remember, she was discoursing on the life of Madame de Pompadour and we were spellbound by her account of '*cette concubine*' and her influence over Louis XV. 'What is a *concubine*?' Kitty asked. '*Ma chère,*' replied Dombe, 'it means enjoying all the pleasures of marriage without the disadvantages.' We found her a stimulating and amusing teacher.

Music and arithematic were taught us by visiting tutors but of English grammar, literature or history we learnt not one word at this time. Pamela was given lessons by Cor; Lyulph and Victoria were under Nanny's wing in the nursery; Edward was sent to a crammer run by a local clergyman to prepare him for Eton. Here he got into bad company and was reported by the vicar for his misbehaviour. Cor tried to discipline him but in the end she went to Grandpapa and said she could no longer cope with him. He was threatened by Grandpapa and cajoled by Muzzie but he became progressively more unmanageable until he went to Eton at the beginning of 1920, where he was partially subdued.

As before the war, the summer holidays were spent at Penrhos with my grandparents, together with all the aunts and uncles and their, by this time, numerous offspring. And now it was that Edward and I fell well and truly foul of the grown-ups! We shocked and appalled our English relations by our uncouth 'colonial' manners and our defiant attitude towards authority, and were considered to be a very bad influence on our well-behaved and submissive cousins. We were complete misfits and, sensing this, we became all the more rebellious under the combined sanctions of the family. Edward, being Muzzie's favourite Stanley grandchild, evaded some of the censure, but I was exposed to its full blast. Certainly, I brought most of my troubles on my own intractable head and deserved what I got, but my life was out of gear and the more I was punished the worse I behaved. I was loathed by every one of my Stanley relations, it seemed, and in turn I paid them out by refusing to conform to their rules.

My father arrived back in England in September but he was clearly still suffering and almost at once my mother took him to London to see the specialists. He was operated on in October and for many weeks he was very ill. He and my mother were lent my grandparents' London house where they stayed for the following six months while he recuperated, but he never fully regained his health.

In October I was sent to live with Aunt Sylvia Henley in London where I shared a governess with Rosalind and Kitty, Dombe having returned to live in Paris. I kept up my piano lessons, given by an uninspiring teacher quite unlike dear Miss McBurney, and was expected to practice an hour every morning before breakfast on the schoolroom piano. It was icy-cold before the fire had been lit, and my fingers were often so numb I couldn't play. Singing lessons were replaced by art lessons, which I enjoyed.

I remember our first post-war Christmas at Alderley chiefly for two things. The first was the bitter cold of the house and the second was an access among the grown-ups of what we called 'Work-House Fever' which made them all believe that the war had ruined them. Frantic economies were put into effect, servants were dismissed, food, light and heating were cut down, the hunters were sold as well as some of the pictures and furniture, and Grandpapa said he would have to give up his London house as soon as my parents had found somewhere of their own that they could afford to live in.

In due course we rented a large corner house in Gloucester Square, Paddington – an unfashionable part of London in those days – and we moved in during the early months of 1920.

I hated London and was oppressed by the gloomy rows of tall houses with sunken basement areas surrounded by spiked iron railings instead of front gardens. The dun-coloured pavements reflected the overcast skies; the peasoup winter fogs and the reek of soot permeated everywhere, even on a summer's day. I longed for the sunlit space of Australia and the hot, dry air and aromatic scent of the Australian bush.

Cor had returned to Melbourne in the spring and Pamela and I were sent to Miss Faunce's day school. We were well taught and I began to catch up on subjects such as English grammar and mathematics. But it was too late to learn these subjects (or else I had no aptitude) and I never really mastered the mysteries of syntax or double fractions.

I had spent most of the Easter holidays at Prestons and, as usual, I was absolutely happy there, for I was given a sympathetic hearing by Marmee for all my aspirations. I confided many a secret longing to her and she never snubbed or derided me. The five years absence in Australia had not altered the affinity between us and when I was with her I felt I was understood and loved, in spite of my shortcomings. I used to go for long walks by myself and collect wild flowers which Marmee would look up in her book and name for me. Or I was taken 'district-visiting' by one of the aunts, which meant taking food and sometimes clothing to various poor families or old persons in the cottages. Nobody appeared to resent this as 'charity' and the people we visited seemed to me to be genuine friends of long standing, as interested in our news as we were in theirs.

Not many recreations were provided for us in London. Sometimes we would be taken to a museum or a church, or an occasional Sunday concert, but I remember often feeling at a loose end and longing to escape into the country and, most of all, to be within sight and sound of the sea.

I had very few friends of my own age. My mother did not allow me to invite my class-mates to the house as she knew none of their parents. But I did have one friend who was given approval. Kitty Kinloch was a year older than me, a lovely wax doll of a girl with dazzling pink-and-white colouring, blue eyes and golden curls, and a rather vacant expression, but she was always smiling and good-natured, and was idolised by her parents. I admired her, and envied not a little her self-assurance and poise.

The Kinlochs lived in Eaton Place, surrounded by elegant possessions, in a house usually full of people, particularly Kitty's friends. Her brother Alex, who was in the Grenadier Guards, often brought his fellow officers round for tea or dinner and these young guardees were a source of curiosity to me; but, on the whole, I thought they were complete nincompoops with their affected manners and vapid conversation.

At this period, the 'Troubles' – as the Anglo-Irish War of 1919 to 1921 was euphemistically known in Ireland – had supposedly been resolved by the Anglo-Irish Treaty signed in December 1921. This Treaty gave effect to the Government of Ireland Act of 1920, which provided for separate Parliaments for Southern and Northern Ireland. Thus was the State of Northern Ireland first brought into existence.

But almost immediately, bitter sectarian and political strife broke out between the Republican Army of the Irish Free State and Ulster Unionists of the new State of Northern Ireland. This Civil War was eventually ended in 1923 by the temporary defeat of those who had opposed the terms of the Treaty.

In 1922 Field Marshal Sir Henry Wilson, Chief of the Imperial General Staff, was assassinated by the IRA on the front steps of his house in Eaton Place, only a few doors away from the Kinlochs. The world was shocked at this outrage and people in London went in fear of being gunned down by the Irish terrorists. I felt important at knowing somebody living in the same street as the murdered General, and my mother was in a state of alarm and apprehension for some weeks afterwards, whenever any of us went out.

A short while after the murder of General Wilson, Edward came home for the weekend on long leave from Eton. He had taken to studying chemistry and his latest craze was for making stink-bombs. He would buy the ingredients (all perfectly harmless by themselves, it appeared) at the chemist over the way, and then he would throw the little bombs he had manufactured in the Square Garden where they would go off with a small bang and a puff of nasty-smelling smoke. It occurred to me that if we went to the top of the house and threw one of these bombs from an attic window there would be a much more satisfactory noise and smell. Accordingly, we went into one of the maids' bedrooms and hurled the bomb out. As I have said, our house stood on the corner of the square on the busy main route to Paddington Station. The bomb burst in our basement area with a shattering explosion, followed by clouds

of greenish-black stinking smoke which billowed up and across the street.
The traffic swerved and came to a halt. Passers-by screamed, policemen
converged on the house, surrounded the area and started hammering on
the front and back doors. Of course, everybody thought it was the IRA
who had struck again. Luckily, my father and mother were
both away and we heard Drabbety explaining to the policemen that it
was only an Eton schoolboy's prank. Nonetheless, Edward had to go
down and face the law. We were rather frightened at what we had done,
and I thought Edward would certainly be arrested. But nothing happened
to him, apart from a wigging from the police. Pamela, who was
eavesdropping on this interview, reported that the policemen merely asked
Edward whether he had not thought that his action might have frightened
any old ladies in the neighbourhood! No doubt the bobbies considered
the operations of the IRA terrorists 'top secret' and, being ultra-cautious,
decided to make no mention of the subject in front of a schoolboy and
the servants. Nothing was said to me for my share in the escapade.

Although I didn't get into trouble over the bomb, storm clouds, nevertheless, were gathering for me on the horizon. In the spring of 1922,
I had fallen in love with my cousin, Simon Baring.

His mother, a Stanley cousin who had been widowed in the war, often
came to Penrhos during the holidays with her family of five children
of whom Simon was the eldest. He was an attractive scamp with a bawdy
wit and a rollicking sense of fun. There was a kind of don't-care devilry
about him – a light-hearted charm which I found irresistible. We continued our idyll throughout the summer at Penrhos, and fell more deeply
in love than ever. No doubt our attachment would have been sneered
at as calf-love by the grown-ups, had they been aware of it at the time.
As it was, Edward was very disagreeable to both of us and threatened
to give us away. However, as he himself was involved in many a crime,
such as climbing on the roof, stealing the peaches and grapes from the
hot-house, or putting calomel pills in the grown-ups' breakfast coffee,
he didn't then dare to carry out his threats. But later it so happened
that I had written a letter to Simon and put it in the pantry for Boyles
to stamp. Edward saw it among the correspondence waiting to be posted
and took it to my father.

Presently, I was sent for by my mother to her bedroom where she
was resting on the sofa before dinner with a Tragedy Queen expression
on her face. My father was standing beside her, frowning with gloomy
severity and holding the fatal letter. Everything went black for an instant
as I waited for disaster to overwhelm me. My father now revealed
Edward's double-dyed disloyalty. In addition to taking my letter, he had

also confessed to every one of our recent misdeeds, implicating the Henleys and myself, and accusing Simon of being the ring-leader. We had gone too far this summer, he had said with an apparently genuine show of repentance and self-abasement: the only thing now was to make a clean breast of everything, he concluded, and turn over a new leaf.

I was aghast, and remained sullenly silent when asked if I had anything to say for myself. My father then ordered me to open the letter and read it out aloud. I refused, tried to snatch it from him, and in the ensuing tussle, the letter was torn. I burst into tears and fled from the room, out of the house and into the hayloft in the stable yard. Here I lay hidden all night and most of the next day till hunger drove me to give myself up. I crept up to Nanny in the nursery who gave me some hot milk and biscuits and said that the grown-ups had been mightily alarmed at my disappearance and had been sending out search parties. I was sent to my room to await developments with a quaking heart. After a while, my father came in to me and said briskly, 'Well, I propose that nothing more is said about this incident'. I flung my arms around him in an agony of contrition and relief, sobbing that I was sorry to have caused so much trouble and thanking him for his forgiveness.

My mother never alluded to the matter, no doubt at my father's insistance, but she treated me with cold and silent displeasure for a long time afterwards. Simon was given an objurgation by my father and made to write a letter of apology for his behaviour. We were forbidden to communicate, naturally, and my mother censored any letters I wrote or received. I was also debarred from seeing the Henleys. I felt that my heart was broken and that I never could forgive Edward for his treachery.

Things came to such a pass between my mother and me that it was decided that I must be sent away to boarding school in spite of the common, giggling manners my mother feared I would instantly acquire. Anything, she felt, was better than having me at home. As I was rising seventeen I begged to be sent to a 'Finishing School' abroad to study music and singing but I was told that I could not be trusted away from England and strict family surveillance, and I plumbed further depths of humiliation and resentful despair.

15

The Facts of Marriage

My father's business interests now took him back to Australia on a six months visit. My mother was going with him and therefore plans had to be made for looking after the family during their absence. Edward was at Eton and, it was hoped, under control; Pamela, Lyulph and Victoria were parked at Alderley with a Swiss governess under Muzzie's supervision; and I was packed off to boarding school in January, 1923.

Malvern Ladies' College was a vast Victorian building which had originally been the Railway Hotel at Great Malvern when it was the fashion to take the waters at the Wells during the latter part of the nineteenth century. Here I spent three terms and the experience was one I look back upon with revulsion. Far from being corrupted by schoolgirl mannerisms, I found my fellow students, almost without exception, to be silly and immature, with their 'crushes' on various mistresses or on one another, their passion for playing hockey and basket-ball, and their inane chatter about film stars, fashions and 'boy-friends'. The lack of any male leavening in this female pie of insipidity nearly choked me with boredom and frustration.

Although I still felt unwanted, there had been a reconciliation of sorts between my mother and me before my departure to school. She escorted me to Malvern and presented me to the headmistress with whom she had a 'little talk' about my wayward and recalcitrant nature. This was followed up with a letter:

174

You will find plenty ... to interest you in the new world in which you find yourself. Mind you are *discreet* in your talk and keep off criticising anyone – even those whom you select as your friends. ... Before I forget, do be sure not to write letters to *anybody* that could be picked up and read – I mean by this, asking how the 'Grown-ups' tempers are, or anything of that sort which is flippant and unfitting. ... Bless you my darling little child – great armfuls of love from your Mam.

Early in February my parents embarked for Australia. I looked forward eagerly to her letters which broke into the wilderness of my present banishment with a gleam of memories from the recent past. She wrote describing the voyage and her fellow passengers in her sharpest satirical vein, ending on a note which raised my spirits considerably. 'The purser came up to Dar the other day and asked how you were! He is the same who travelled back with us in the *Osterley*. I showed him your photograph and he remarked that you had grown up very much. He evidently had quite a soft spot for you!' she concluded quizzically.

On their arrival in Melbourne they stayed at Stonnington and my mother slept in her old bedroom.

I feel we are back again for good – or rather, that we have never been away. The garden is just the same and I went to look at all your old places – I looked into the Bullycrub Room and 'Dryniby Plice'. It is funny to hear the orderly going up the stairs every morning to hoist the flag and I always think of you and Edward! ...

I went to The Briars this afternoon, and as I walked up through the little garden I heard an exclamation from behind the window and dear little Miss McBurney ran out and flung herself into my arms saying, 'It must be a dream. I can't believe it's true!' I went into the little drawing-room where everything is just the same – all the ornaments you used to play with are still there. We talked of you and I told her everything I could think of. Then dear Mr McBurney came in with his little sister (Annie, isn't it?) and he very nearly kissed me! I feel certain more poems will be inspired in his breast before I leave. [Mr McBurney was given to writing odes as well as singing ballads] I had tea with them and then went and had a second tea with Gardiner (the policeman at our gate, you remember?). They are all so touchingly pleased to see me and are so interested to hear all I can tell them about you all. . . .

My parents returned from Australia in July and, finding me improved in my ways, my mother took me with her on a round of visits. At Longleat Lady Bath, she said, was much impressed by my good manners, and in the letter my mother wrote me on my return to Malvern, she commented:

I want to tell you that during those few days we had together you seemed to be the Adelaide I had always hoped you would become and visualised. All through the summer holidays I have noticed it and felt it ... You are growing and improving in many directions, my darling, and I want you to go on building your own character on sure and fine lines. Aim at *self-control* and *selflessness* as the foundation stones of your efforts...

In November my father was nominated Liberal candidate for Knutsford, much against my mother's wishes as she feared the strain would be too much for his always precarious health.

'He hasn't a dog's or a cat's chance of winning the seat, [she said] as there is a majority of over three thousand against him, I believe. But for personal reasons we shall not be sorry if he loses as he doesn't particularly want to be in the House of Commons again, tho' it would be a good thing if the seat could be won for Free Trade. ... 'Grampy' is on the rampage properly. Yesterday there was a picture of him at Winston's meeting in Manchester in the most characteristic attitude, his ear trumpet to his ear, a cascade of papers on his lap, sitting sideways and almost *upon* Mrs Shimwell [an Alderley neighbour], his bastions well in evidence.

A week later my father got mumps but he continued his campaign from his bed. A life-size photograph of him was carried round the constituency and placed on the platform at every meeting. 'I think it is a great pity', my mother said, 'that they don't have a gramophone at the same time with a few records of some of his speeches.' Surprisingly, he only lost the seat, after a recount, by 80 votes. No doubt he would have got in, had he been able to conduct his electioneering in person but although he was disappointed, my mother was much relieved at the result.

I left Malvern at Christmas and 'put up my hair' in preparation for my 'coming out' during the 1924 London Season. In January Pamela was sent to school in Switzerland to be out of the way of the approaching social whirl. My mother took her to Berne where she was deposited with a Swiss family, and I accompanied them. We went on to Paris to buy clothes for my début and I was allowed to choose the things I liked, almost without criticism and advice, which highly delighted me. I remember one evening dress, in particular, which I thought quite ravishing. It was turquoise-blue chiffon, embroidered all over with tiny crystal beads. The hem was up to my knees and it had a 'boat neck' and no waist line, as was then the fashion. A turquoise-blue chiffon scarf floated from one shoulder and concealed the mark on my arm. With this confection I wore flesh-pink silk stockings and satin court shoes dyed to match my dress.

I now looked forward to a life of emancipated gaiety but I soon found I was mistaken. I was never supposed to walk alone in the streets or go out without my gloves and hat. One day, in a fit of reckless daring, I made my first appointment with a hairdresser and had my long hair shingled and my nails manicured. This led to an angry scene and accusations of insubordination from my mother who declared that my cropped hair looked like the backside of an elk and I had ruined my appearance. I retorted that I would do my hair as I chose, now that I was grown up, and that it was none of her business. We had a furious row and I was sent up to my room and told to remain there till I apologised for my 'unfitting' attitude.

I was presented at Court in May. It was a balmy evening and there was a queue of chauffeur-driven limousines stretching right down the Mall, each with its occupants of uniformed men and the women with three small, white ostrich feathers stuck in their coiffure, and wearing décolleté evening dresses with trains. I had a white 'georgette' silk dress and a silver lace train and I had difficulty in keeping my feathers in place with a bandeau encircling my newly shingled head.

Sightseers lined the Mall to watch the scene and often came quite close and peered into the cars as they waited to move on, sometimes making uninhibited remarks about the appearance of the passengers which could be distinctly heard by the immobilised victims.

The débutantes and their sponsors were ushered into the Drawing-Room by Court officials who straightened out the ladies' trains and called out their names as they entered. King George and Queen Mary sat on a dais surrounded by other royalties and various courtiers. After curtseying to the King and Queen we went in to supper where a cold buffet was served on gold or silver plate and we drank champagne.

I went to dinner-parties and balls and an occasional *thé-dansant*. I was invited to the New College Commem. Ball at Oxford where I met Basil Murray*, who was studying law. He was full of radical ideas which, of course, appealed to me, and he was to play a significant part in my life.

I was rigorously chaperoned at all these social functions. I used to hate going to balls with my mother as she always managed to make some derogatory remark about my appearance just as we arrived. 'I hope you haven't got *make-up* on?' she would say, rubbing my lips with her handkerchief in the ladies' cloakroom. Or, 'What a pity you are looking so tired with such circles under your eyes'. If I sat out with any partner she would come round looking for me and when she ran me to earth

* The son of Professor Gilbert and Lady Mary Murray.

she would put up her *lorgnette* and say in a falsely sweet voice (which boded no good for me later on) 'Oh, *there* you are!' I think her anxiety that I should be a success made her hypercritical and often led her into saying things which rankled and pricked my perhaps over-sensitive feelings.

I was not allowed to invite friends to any meal without first asking my mother. I didn't know many girls of my own age and she often disapproved of my choice of acquaintances as she said they had 'no background'. Most of my co-débutantes I found silly and boring, and the young men who were on my mother's 'list' were either supercilious sprigs of the aristocracy or spotty youths 'in the City'. These last were dubbed 'Fluikins' by my mother.

I was not enjoying my first season and I longed all the more to take up singing seriously, but I pleaded in vain. 'Perhaps when you have been out one or two seasons,' my mother said, 'and if you have not married by then, we might possibly consider the idea.' It was thought to be the height of social success for a girl to announce her engagement before her second season. In spite of the disruption of the war, the habits and outlook of the older generation of the upper class in England had not changed in fifty years. However the seeds of dissolution were already planted in their way of life which, in less than a decade, was to be swept away on a tide of economic depression and finally, destroyed by World War II.

At the end of the Season, London society retired to their country seats for grouse, pheasant and partridge shooting. There were large house parties given where any incipient romance which had budded in the ballroom was given an opportunity to flower into an engagement.

I had made friends with Mary Thynne, the youngest daughter of Lord and Lady Bath, and I went again to stay at Longleat. I admired Mary's classical good looks unreservedly, but I had also been delighted to find that behind her Greek Goddess profile and marmoreal beauty there lurked a dry sense of fun and love of a good joke which she shared with her brother, Henry Weymouth. I laughed a lot with them and enjoyed their company.

Nancy Mitford, my scintillating cousin, also asked me to stay at Asthall, her family home in the Cotswolds, and this was the beginning of a long and affectionate friendship only ended by her death in 1973. Nancy's parents, David and Sydney Redesdale, were very eccentric, and Nancy later portrayed her father as 'Uncle Matthew' in her novel *The Pursuit of Love*. He struck me as being quite unbalanced, if not mad.

From the Redesdales, my mother and I went on to the Kinlochs at

Gilmerton for my first visit to Scotland. Alex Kinloch was there on leave and we used to ride together over the Lammermuir Hills and jump the hurdles set up in the park over which he schooled his steeple-chasers and his hunters. He mounted me on one of his horses, Bolderwood, a handsome, dark fellow with a star on his forehead and a splendid jumper. Later on, when Alex went abroad, he lent me Bolderwood and gave me his cocker spaniel, Duster, whom I adored. I think Alex was planning to ask me to marry him eventually, which was discreetly encouraged by both our parents, as my mother subsequently revealed to me. But I had no intention of falling in with this plan, although I was very fond of Alex as a companion.

My last visit before returning to Penrhos was to Sir Hugh and Lady Alice Shaw Stewart of Ardgowan in Renfrewshire. Edward came with me here and, for a wonder, we were unchaperoned. We did not make a good impression on our hosts who were old and very strait-laced. They led a life of Spartan discomfort and stultifying boredom based on rigid Scottish customs. No games or amusements were allowed on Sundays when everybody was expected to attend the kirk and go for a long walk in the afternoon. Edward and I refused to conform to this dreary programme and instead spent Sunday in my bedroom playing 'mumbly-peg' poker, a game I had learnt in London from a rather dubious American, for match sticks. We were discovered by a fellow guest and we departed for Penrhos under a cloud.

All the family was at home and the younger ones were flatteringly interested in my accounts of social gadding. Pamela was now fifteen, dreamy and detached as ever, and nursing a secret ambition to go on the stage, which she confided to me. She and I got along much better now, but my father would sometimes have to defend her against the combined bullying of the family and of my mother in particular, who was often irritable and impatient with poor Pamela's vagueness and self-protective reserve. Pamela achieved her ambition in the teeth of my mother's disapproval. She became the first actress to play Queen Victoria on the English stage and had a successful theatrical career till World War II when her war work and subsequent marriage caused her retirement.

Lyulph was as spoilt as ever and his odd and original personality was developing in rather a disturbing way. He was still highly imaginative with a brilliant gift for mimicry and intensely musical, demonstrative in his manner and fundamentally affectionate; yet there was a streak of malice in his make-up which came as a shock, even at this early age. He was now at a preparatory school which did not improve him and fostered traits in his already unstable character that, eventually, were to dominate his passionate and volatile nature throughout his comparatively short life. That my father noticed these danger signals is certain – he was perhaps more critical of Lyulph than of any of his other children – but his strictures were of no avail. My mother continued to champion her favourite against all aspersions and idolise him beyond reason. He could pull the wool over her eyes and make her believe any outrageous rigmarole he chose to invent to cover his tracks.

Little Victoria or 'Tordie' as she was always called, was, next to Lyulph, my mother's pet. She was enchantingly pretty, with beguiling ways, and 'bright as a button', as Nanny used to say. Her loving disposition and sense of fun made her Lyulph's willing slave, but if it came to an argument between them she could often outsmart him, in spite of his dexterous shifting of polemical ground.

Lyboo and Tordie had a happier childhood than the rest of us, perhaps because being the youngest, they were so indulged by my mother; but sometimes I was amazed at her gullibility in the face of Lyboo's truth-twisting and Tordie's blandishments and caresses whenever they wanted to get their way or conceal some misdeed!

During the autumn of 1924 Grandpapa's health began to fail. Up to this time, in spite of his deafness and arthritis, he had remained vigorously alert in both mind and body. Almost to the last, he kept up his 'mania for running about', as he called it, constantly journeying by train to London, Manchester or Liverpool to attend meetings and conferences. Occasionally, he even travelled abroad. 'Grampy bustled off to Geneva the day before yesterday with a beautiful speech in French which he has written,' my mother had told me at the end of the previous year. But now his splendid intellect suddenly gave way and he rapidly became senile. 'It has been very heartbreaking to see him fighting every inch of the way to Death with his unconquerable vitality,' said my mother. 'It will be a great relief when the end does come.'

He died at Alderley in March 1925 in his eighty-sixth year, and was succeeded by my father.

We were all plunged into ceremonial mourning for the next six months and wrote our letters on black-edged paper. This meant a release for me from the tedium of a second Season as we were not to be seen anywhere in public during this period. My mother arranged that I should visit various relations in the country to keep me out of circulation in London, while she and my father took over the reins at Alderley and Penrhos.

At the end of May I was invited to stay by Alice, Lady Avebury, a formidable cousin with the usual family propensity for quarrelling. I arrived on Friday 29 May, at High Elms, the Lubbock family home in Kent, to find a large party of Lubbock relations of all ages whom I had never seen before. That Saturday was my nineteenth birthday. My mother hoped that I would get on with Cousin Alice – '. . . she is so handsome and not a bit frightening really. She is a sad woman, having lost two sons in the war, and a son-in-law. I wonder how you will like Maurice Lubbock? He is rather amusing.'

Maurice, her youngest and only surviving son, worked in the city and I was prepared to disdain him before we met. That weekend he came down from London in an Alfa-Romeo racing car accompanied by a group of his friends from the Bachelors' Club. They drank sherry before dinner and discussed politics and world affairs among themselves, no one else in the house-party being interested in anything beyond family gossip and scandal. After dinner they went into the card-room and played bridge for high stakes until late at night. During the day they took themselves off to the golf course and played tennis or billiards between tea and dinner. Clearly, they were far removed from the 'Fluikin' breed, in spite of working in the city, and I observed them with interest. However, they took no notice of me, rather to my mortification, until an incident occurred which brought me to Maurice's attention.

I was sitting next to him at dinner and he was obviously bored at having to make small-talk to a young female relation with whom, apparently, he had nothing in common. I was equally out of my depth and the conversation languished. In desperation I seized upon the glass of wine in front of me, but in my usual impulsive way I knocked it flying and spilt it all over the white table-cloth.

'*Feelthy* little beast!' said Cousin Alice loudly. (This was her usual term of abuse, hurled indiscriminately at offenders whatever their age or sex.) She rang furiously on the silver bell placed in front of her on the dining table and summoned the footman to come and 'mop Miss Stanley up'.

'She seems to think I did it on purpose,' I muttered to Maurice, crimson in the face with indignation and embarrassment, 'and I jolly well wish I had.' Maurice burst out laughing and said, 'Huh! Take no notice. Come and have a game of bridge with the chaps after dinner.'

Thus I was admitted by my gaffe and Maurice's kind heart into his 'inner circle'. They laughed at my jokes and were indulgent when I made mistakes at bridge or held them up by losing my ball at golf. I was accepted as a companion in this exclusively male world and I delighted in the society of the 'genkas', as I used to call all men when I was a child.

From now on, I was invited down to High Elms by Maurice nearly every weekend that summer, and during the week he took me to dine with his Bachelors' Club 'chaps' at the Savoy Grill or the Ritz. He would take me for hair-raising drives in the 'Alf.'. Either he would remain completely silent on these occasions or he would launch into technical descriptions of the superiority of Alf over any other racing car. Never a word was said which led me to suspect that I was anything more than a captive audience. Although I was rather mystified by these attentions, I asked for nothing better than that we should continue on the same delightful footing of camaraderie. But one evening in June he suddenly proposed as he was driving me home. For once I was speechless! I thought perhaps I hadn't heard him aright, but he stopped the car in the Park and repeated, 'I want to marry you'. I refused him as kindly as I could, saying that I didn't want to marry anybody; but because I couldn't bear the thought of giving up all the fun and enjoyment of his world, I begged, as girls do when they want to have their cake and eat it, that we might still go on being friends even though I never could be in love with him. Maurice paid not the slightest attention to anything I said but continued to take me out and renew his offer of marriage with imperturbable persistence.

My mother took me to task for the way I was behaving. She said I was 'making myself cheap' by going out with Maurice if I didn't mean to accept him, and tried to forbid me seeing him. I was hauled up in front of my father so that he might add his veto to hers; but all he said was, 'Please yourself'. My mother was furious and it was the only time I ever saw her display open annoyance with my father.

I tried to take stock of my situation. I was not in love with Maurice in the way I had been with Simon, yet I was fascinated by his original personality. I respected him for his integrity of purpose, his good judgement and clear grasp of political and economic affairs, and admired him for his wonderfully sure and persuasive touch in all his dealings with people, whatever their walk in life. All that was lacking at that time was the spark of physical love, and I began to wonder whether it was worth rejecting so much that attracted me for just that one thing.

I was in a state of bewilderment and doubt about my future, and I turned for guidance to Marmee. When she had heard me out she advised me to accept Maurice but added characteristically, 'Of course, in the end you will have to make up your mind yourself. Nobody can take the final decision for you. Only remember this – even at the Altar Steps you can still say *no*!'

I wrote to my mother at Penrhos about the quandary I was in although I was still rather under a cloud for resisting her edict that I should stop seeing Maurice: but she replied with such concern for my happiness that I felt a surge of gratitude and a certainty that I could now discuss my problem with her more freely.

> It is difficult to *write* about you and Maurice, darling, but I am quite certain of one thing and this is, that it would be folly on your part to come to any decision while you have any misgivings, even if they are momentary or fleeting ones, or when you are in an 'agony of perplexity' . . . I understand and know that you are really torn in two, and that while Maurice fills one side of your capacity for love, he just doesn't the other. And tho' I think the love you have for him is of the kind to stand the wear and tear of a lifetime, yet if it is quite without the kind you felt for Simon, I would keep you from marrying him. . . . I cannot let you make up your mind for yourself in this matter, at present – perhaps that will make it easier for you. I want you to have much longer and wider opportunities than you have had yet of seeing other men besides Maurice before you think of settling down and marrying anybody.

This advice seemed to me less forthright and sensible than Marmee's, in that my mother still was convinced that she knew best and that I was too inexperienced to make my own decision about my future. However, I left Prestons with a lighter heart, knowing that I had so much understanding love from both of them in my soul-searching over Maurice. But I never saw Marmee again. She died peacefully and gently some weeks later.

So much had happened in my life during the past two years that the memory of Edward's betrayal had gradually faded. By this time I had forgiven him and the breach between us was healed. Now he was rather proud of me as his sister, and envied my grown-up status. He admired my men friends, especially Maurice, and as boys often will, he tried to emulate their example in word and deed; but although he had a first-class intellect, he still could not resist showing off in order to create an effect. Later, he developed a bitter tongue which cost him many a friend and he became a lonely and pathetic figure towards the end of his life. At this period, however, on the threshold of his manhood, he had the advantages of good looks, brains and breeding, and was indeed a brilliant and attractive personality.

On his eighteenth birthday I wrote to him at Eton and he replied:

> Thank you for your letter which came this morning. There is dam-all to say . . . God, it makes me furious that I have to stick here in this ultra and

super bloody hole. I have seen a certain number of good friends since I have
been back – John Goschen, Simon, Basil etc. – which relieves the tedium slightly. Write and let me know the following things:
a) when Maurice's birthday is that I may write to him;
b) if you have got my uke! ... Let me know about Maurice and all the
up-to-date news. ...

I have been amusing myself this half by pretending to be an aesthete which
is quite fun; also I have been preaching atheism to all the beaks which is
better fun. I wrote a poem about my religious creed for the benefit of one
beak which shocked him highly.

This is it for your edification!

That God created all the earth
The world has long found out
But tell me who created God?
The Theist, I've no doubt.

I feel now that in writing this I'm being like Basil so I won't write any
more. ... Ever your loving Edward.

I had come across my disreputable cousin Basil Murray now and again
since our first meeting at Oxford. He gambled and drank, had the morals
of an alley-cat and was always broke, but I found him a diverting companion and enjoyed sharpening my wits on the whetstone of his lively,
if unprincipled, mind.

I had somehow persuaded my parents to invite him to Penrhos that
summer. He arrived in the middle of August and although I thought
him as entertaining as ever, his effect on the rest of the family was disastrous. To begin with, he annoyed my mother by changing several times
the date of his arrival, and then coming by the most inconvenient train
of the day which arrived at 7.50 in the evening so that dinner had to
be kept waiting. During the meal he uttered subversive opinions and laid
down the law on every subject under discussion in a maddeningly superior
'Oxford' drawl which goaded the grown-ups to indignant fury. One and
all, they were outraged by the arrogance of this 'unspeakable young cub'
as they called him, but Edward and I egged him on and, to make matters
worse, I embarked on a shameless flirtation with him which was none
the less enjoyable for the lack of any serious feeling on either side. After
all, my mother had suggested that I should get to know more men before
finally settling down and here was an excellent chance of putting her
counsel into practice!

All the same, sometimes Basil's conceit irritated me and I was determined, if possible, to take him down a peg by extracting a proposal of
marriage and snubbing him by rejecting it. I cornered him one evening

when we were watching the sunset from the top of one of the turrets and inveigled him into saying reluctantly that, in the unlikely event of his ever having enough money, he might, some day, ask me to marry him. I didn't refuse him straight away as I could not resist the satisfaction of seeing him squirm with anxiety, but after a bit I took pity on him and let him off the hook. Whereupon he appeared slightly abashed but undeniably relieved!

Basil left Penrhos at the end of August to go back to London where he tried, unsuccessfully, to raise some cash. He had cadged an invitation early in September to stay with the Henleys who were with Muzzie at Alderley. He was conducting a flirtation with Rosalind simultaneously with me but this affair did not prosper and ended by Rosalind throwing a billiard ball at his head and twisting one of his fingers.

He wrote to me every few days after leaving Penrhos until events some weeks later put an end to our correspondence. Poor Basil! On re-reading his letters today I can still recall the exasperated affection I felt for him at the time. And perhaps he may have been more than a little in love with me. We remained on good terms and I continued to see him until his death from pneumonia during the Spanish Civil War.

In a curious way, my relationship with Basil acted as a catalyst on my feeling for Maurice. It seemed, till now, that my inclination had led me towards two unreliable, if engaging characters. Gradually, I began to realise that what I needed most in my life was a steadying influence and it was borne in on me at last that Maurice was going to be the answer to my future happiness.

I still hesitated for a time before making an irrevocable decision, but on 17 October, Maurice's twenty-fifth birthday, instead of going to Oxford to stay with Basil's parents as planned, I went down to High Elms, resolved to take the plunge.

Ironically, Maurice departed from his usual custom of proposing regularly every evening after dinner and I had, eventually, to take the initiative myself. I waited till Monday morning and, as he was driving me back to London, I said to myself, 'Now or never'. With a dry throat and thumping heart, I muttered as we were crossing Southwark Bridge, 'We can't go on like this – I think I had better marry you'. There was nearly an accident as Maurice took both his hands off the wheel and hugged me. That evening we returned to High Elms together to announce our engagement to Cousin Alice. 'Feelthy child!' she cried. 'Why couldn't you have accepted the pore darlin' on his birthday? If I had known before now that you were comin' back tonight I wouldn't have had the sheets on your bed changed.'

Maurice and I were married on 9 January 1926 at St George's Church, Hanover Square, and the wedding reception was held at Gloucester Square. Although it was the most important day of my life since, I suppose, my birth, I was too overwhelmed by excitement and trepidation at the great step I was taking to feel anything except a rather stunned sense of importance at being the central figure. I longed for the hurly-burly to be over and to be alone with Maurice.

As I was leaving the house for the honeymoon, my mother said, 'Darling, you do know all the Facts of Marriage, don't you?'

Bibliography

Unpublished correspondence

Letters from Margaret Stanley to	Mrs Henry Evans Gordon	1906–1919
,, ,, ,, ,,	,, Lord Sheffield	1914–1918
,, ,, ,, ,,	,, Lady Sheffield	1914–1918
,, ,, ,, ,,	,, Venetia Stanley	1914–1915
,, ,, ,, ,,	,, Adelaide Stanley	1914–1926

Letters to Margaret Stanley from	Mrs Henry Evans Gordon	1906–1919
,, ,, ,, ,,	,, Arthur Lyulph Stanley	1914–1919
,, ,, ,, ,,	,, Lord Sheffield	1914–1918
,, ,, ,, ,,	,, Adelaide Stanley	1914–1926

Letters to Adelaide Stanley from	Margaret Stanley	1914–1926
,, ,, ,, ,,	,, Arthur Stanley	1914–1919
,, ,, ,, ,,	,, Edward Stanley	1925
,, ,, ,, ,,	,, Basil Murray	1925

Books and Periodicals

Anderson, Hugh. *Larrikin Crook.* Jacaranda Press, 1971.

Barnard, Marjorie. *History of Australia.* Angus & Robertson, 1962.

Casey, Maie. *Melba Revisited.* 1975.

Clark, Manning. *Short History of Australia.* Mentor Books, USA, 1963.

Churchill, Winston Spencer. *The World Crisis 1911–1918.* Macmillan, 1941.

Hetherington, John. *Melba.* Faber, 1967.

Jenkins, Roy. *Asquith.* Collins, 1964.

Moorhead, Alan. *Gallipoli.* Hamish Hamilton, 1956.

——. *The Russian Revolution.* Collins & Hamish Hamilton, 1958.

Souter, Gavin. *Lion and Kangaroo.* Angus & Robertson, 1976.

Table Talk

Melbourne *Punch*

Various Melbourne and Sydney periodicals and newspapers from 1913 to 1919.

Lady Stanley's Family Tree

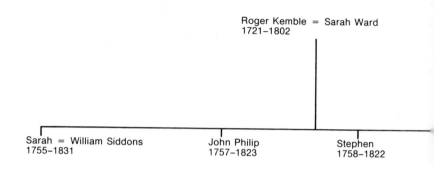

Roger Kemble = Sarah Ward
1721–1802

Sarah = William Siddons
1755–1831

John Philip
1757–1823

Stephen
1758–1822

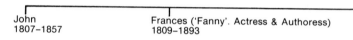

John
1807–1857

Frances ('Fanny'. Actress & Authoress)
1809–1893

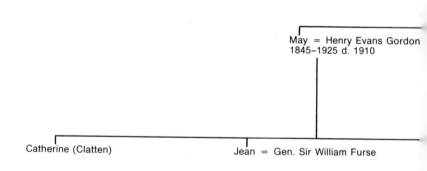

May = Henry Evans Gordon
1845–1925 d. 1910

Catherine (Clatten)

Jean = Gen. Sir William Furse

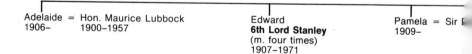

Adelaide = Hon. Maurice Lubbock
1906–   1900–1957

Edward
6th Lord Stanley
(m. four times)
1907–1971

Pamela = Sir
1909–

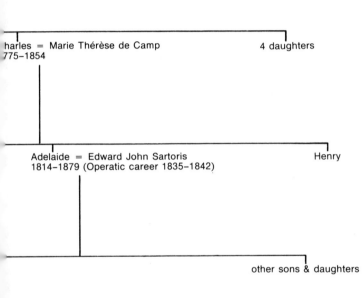

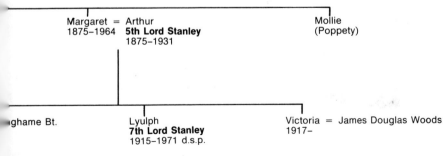

The Stanley Family Tree

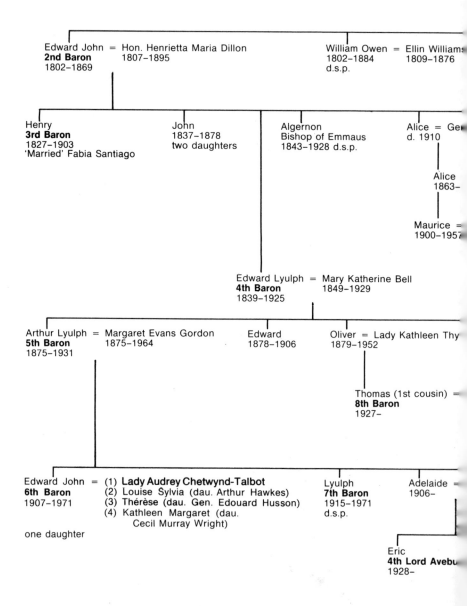

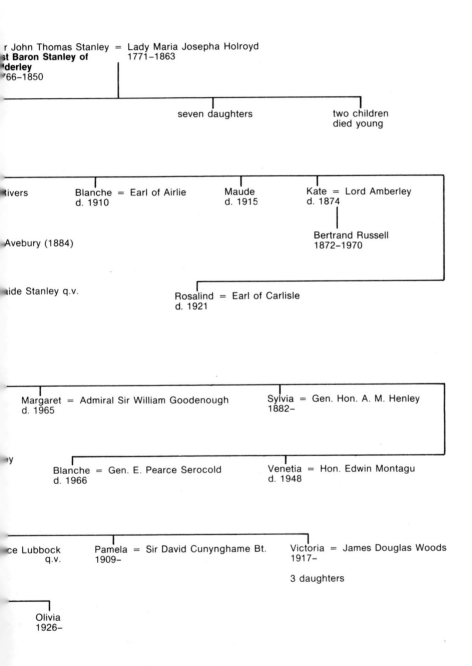

r John Thomas Stanley = Lady Maria Josepha Holroyd
st **Baron Stanley of**   1771–1863
'derley
'66–1850

seven daughters   two children
                                   died young

Rivers   Blanche = Earl of Airlie   Maude   Kate = Lord Amberley
                d. 1910   d. 1915   d. 1874

Avebury (1884)   Bertrand Russell
                                                             1872–1970

ide Stanley q.v.   Rosalind = Earl of Carlisle
                           d. 1921

Margaret = Admiral Sir William Goodenough   Sylvia = Gen. Hon. A. M. Henley
d. 1965   1882–

'y   Blanche = Gen. E. Pearce Serocold   Venetia = Hon. Edwin Montagu
            d. 1966   d. 1948

ce Lubbock   Pamela = Sir David Cunynghame Bt.   Victoria = James Douglas Woods
    q.v.   1909–   1917–

                                                 3 daughters

           Olivia
           1926–

Index